Critical Internet Literacies

An introductory critical internet studies text that builds upon media literacy and digital culture theory to offer a thorough examination of the intersection of online technology and culture.

We are now collectively at a hinge point in the evolution of the web where online influencers can sway national discourse, geopolitical events are remixed through memes, and online harms are misunderstood. This book argues that people are generally aware that online media has repercussions in off-platform spaces, but sometimes lack the language to properly critique online trends, memes, and internet-born media. How are citizens, activists, and marginalized groups able to use these tools effectively and safely in these times? Jamie Cohen explores aspects of internet culture in an approachable manner, building upon critical media literacy and applying a critical technocultural analysis as a methodology to reimagine how media literacy can operate in an online media environment. The book explores key topics such as accessibility, the creator economy, content moderation, tech bias, platform capitalism, internet culture, and safety.

Offering a new way of reading internet media and critiquing content and creators, this book is essential reading for students and scholars of digital culture, internet culture, media literacy, social media, and beyond.

Jamie Cohen is Assistant Professor of Media Studies at CUNY Queens College, USA. He is also the head of education for Digital Void, an internet literacies project, and a faculty fellow at the Salzburg Academy on Media and Global Change. Jamie's work is focused on internet culture, visual communication, and tech criticism and the topics of memes, AI literacies, and internet culture.

Critical Internet Literacies
Reconsidering Creativity, Content, and Safety Online

Jamie Cohen

NEW YORK AND LONDON

Designed cover image: AzmanL /© Getty Images

First published 2025
by Routledge
605 Third Avenue, New York, NY 10158

and by Routledge
4 Park Square, Milton Park, Abingdon, Oxon, OX14 4RN

Routledge is an imprint of the Taylor & Francis Group, an informa business

© 2025 Jamie Cohen

The right of Jamie Cohen to be identified as author of this work has been asserted in accordance with sections 77 and 78 of the Copyright, Designs and Patents Act 1988.

All rights reserved. No part of this book may be reprinted or reproduced or utilised in any form or by any electronic, mechanical, or other means, now known or hereafter invented, including photocopying and recording, or in any information storage or retrieval system, without permission in writing from the publishers.

Trademark notice: Product or corporate names may be trademarks or registered trademarks, and are used only for identification and explanation without intent to infringe.

ISBN: 978-1-032-77591-3 (hbk)
ISBN: 978-1-032-77514-2 (pbk)
ISBN: 978-1-003-48388-5 (ebk)

DOI: 10.4324/9781003483885

Typeset in Sabon
by codeMantra

For Nickie, the most amazing wife and loving mother I know, and to our children Vera and Hank, who will live in this changing world with us.

Contents

Acknowledgements		*ix*
Preface		*xi*
1	Introduction	1
2	Critical Perspectives on Digital Cultures	21
3	The Creator Economy and the Hyper-Niche	52
4	Memes and Visual Communication	96
5	The Online to Mainstream Media Pipeline	131
6	The "Social Dilemma" Dilemma: Critiquing Awareness Media	158
7	The Moderated Internet: Reconsidering Safety Online	180
8	Creating Content with Accessibility	204
9	Building Resilient Online Communities	224
	Index	*229*

Acknowledgements

It goes without saying that this book project is thanks to the support of my family, colleagues, and friends. This book is a product of a long-term passion of sharing internet literacy and my "ecosystems of support" helped guide the way to tell the story. First, the most amount of thanks goes to my wife Nickie and her understanding of the writing process – this isn't the first time, nor will it be the last. Nickie is also the illustrator of all the images contained in this book. I must also say that the constant support from my research partner and former student Josh Chapdelaine helped me through to the end; his podcast project is also one of the inspirations for later chapters. My colleagues, whom I trust with guiding me and helping me clarify my thoughts, are indispensable. Many thanks to Douglas Rush-koff, especially his Team Human philosophies and ongoing media theory, and to Mara Einstein for her mentorship and the huge support of Amy Herzog and Connie Lasher.

This book is also possible because of the incredible abundance of critical writing about internet culture, and I am especially honored to connected with many of these brilliant people. Thanks to Ryan Broderick, especially his cogent work in *Garbage Day*, and the works from André Brock Jr., Idil Galip, Kara Alaimo, Emily Gillcrist, Steffi Cao, and Taylor Lorenz. Also, a huge thank you to the collaborators and connections of Digital Void, especially Jenny Chang and Matt Klein, who share their passion for cultural theory, always aiming to make the esoteric accessible. The second half of this book would not be possible without the insights about trust and safety and moderation from Matt Soeth, a person who extends care and compassion in his work. Further, there are not enough thanks to give to Paul Mihailidis and Chris Harris, both of whom helped me rethink case studies and talk through my rough drafts. I also owe the students and incredible faculty of the Salzburg Academy on Media and Global Change many thanks for their feedback of my research in its first public iterations. The memory of Moses Shumow inspires this work as well; Moses was an incredible and passionate media and social justice activist, and his energy

x   *Acknowledgements*

continues to influence my hopes for optimism and persistence. I'd like to thank my students at CUNY Queens College, many of whom were patient with me as I put this book together, and my former students at Hofstra University, especially Arianna Collura, who helped me understand accessibility online. Finally, a special thanks to the small community at my coffee shop Tusk & Cup, especially Peter, Gabe, Bryn, Hope, and Ray, who heard my updates nearly every day while I bought more coffee to fuel my writing.

Preface

This book is a culmination of nearly two decades of critical internet studies, deployed primarily through pedagogy, scholarship, and public writing. This book is inspired by my experience as a former reality television producer who worked on television shows while YouTube was launching. Watching these media industries collide was eye-opening and I felt like a shift in popular media was about to emerge, especially in the case of populist media, leveraging the common person to stardom – with very few guardrails. With access to affordable cameras, easier editing tools, and video hosting, it seemed that the internet would be a space of unprecedented creativity. However, based on the libertarian ideological makeup of the internet, the inherent reactionary stance would soon embed itself into nearly all online content, slowly shifting culture at large. I began to study the new and digital media production environments, ones that claimed to uplift marginalized voices and resist the structural hegemony of traditional media industries, but what I found was that many of these creator spaces seemed to be reproducing systemic issues of legacy media models while simultaneously expressing a reactionary disgust with the "way things were."

In the aughts, I developed critical media courses on web television and internet media, hoping to interrogate why new media wasn't providing the space for marginalized voices excluded by traditional media and I applied media literacy frameworks and interdisciplinary approaches to reading online media. However, while the courses were popular among students, it was tough to have this academic approach taken seriously. This frustration, shared by many in my field, shaped how we critiqued media that resisted categorization. I was fortunate to establish and lead an internet studies degree at a small college and there I honed my critical eye for civic engagement, creative production, and the issues of bias in code and the need to critique Silicon Valley's "move fast and break things" mentality. We learned far too late that things broken by this ethos cannot be fixed easily. Further, to paraphrase Bo Burnham, we were witnessing the flattening of the human subjective experience as tech companies were converting xii *Preface*

it into exchange value. As the 2010s unfolded and a global rightward shift emerged in politics around the world, finally people were paying attention to the media effects of internet content and their creators. Safety, once an administrative concern, became an important part of social media policy and initiatives. The door for critical internet literacies was more acceptable in education, even though internet-based topics were hard to work with due to the nature of borderline harms and inappropriate content.

In the 2020s, following a period where everyone was thrust online without being given any digital literacies to do so, my eyes were opened to more nuanced aspects of content, creator work, and safety. I was asked to do talks for teachers for their professional development as well as talks for parents in communities. Along with some former students, we created a collective to share internet literacies with the public called Digital Void and we were offered a residency at a comedy club in downtown New York City. We misused the space and invited internet culture journalists, academics, and scholars to share their critical work in a lighthearted way, making information entertaining. As attention to internet culture grew, I was invited to give talks about meme and internet culture at the FBI, the World Health Organization, Google, and the Salzburg Academy on Media and Global Change. Many of these talks are now included in this book in text form. It has become my goal to make internet literacies accessible and increase our ability to discuss internet ephemera maturely, especially with young people and students.

This book is a primer. While I hoped to include more international examples, the main case studies are Western based and hopefully, you, as the reader, may apply the overall ideas to other examples. As this book is only a starting point, there are many avenues to continue to interrogate, critique, and analyze internet media. Further, this book pushes back against moral panics and any calls for "banning" social media and making legislation to block people from using internet tools. As of this writing, ByteDance has been ordered to divest from TikTok, their US-based version of its Chinese product Douyin, or be banned. Jason Koebler of *404 Media* explains better:

> A TikTok ban will have the effect of further entrenching and empowering gigantic, monopolistic American social media companies that have nearly all of the same problems that TikTok does. A ban would highlight, again, that people who use mainstream social media platforms run by corporations do not actually own their followers or their audiences, and that any businesses/jobs/livelihoods created on these platforms can be stripped away at any moment by the platforms or, in this case, by the United States government.[1]

As anywhere between one-third and one-half of young people wish to be creators some day and over 200 million people consider themselves creators, it is irresponsible to apply any blanket legislation to such an immense part of culture.[2]

Most importantly, this book is about finding ways to detect the bad actors who game the system for their benefit. Like a multilevel marketing scam, some of these users take advantage of the vulnerable (which to be honest was all of us at some point) to make a profit. Better internet literacies make us more resilient, more productive, and enable us to find the space for fun. Writing this book has also been a space of learning for myself, especially identifying the privilege I have to take the time to analyze this digital world. From learning about the joy of Black Twitter to witnessing the pain from influencers reporting from war zones, I've come to see the internet as human. Things may feel chaotic, and maybe that's why people fall down rabbit holes, but we need to take a step back every so often and recognize the systemic issues in which the internet replicates. We can make changes, albeit a little at a time, but only if we are given the tools, the knowledge, and the power to reconsider these issues and reframe how we use the world's most important tool.

Notes

1 Koebler, Jason. "The U.S. Wants to Ban TikTok for the Sins of Every Social Media Company." *404 Media*, March 13, 2024. https://www.404media.co/the-u-s-wants-to-ban-tiktok-for-the-sins-of-every-social-media-company.
2 https://linktr.ee/creator-report/.

1 Introduction

A Call for Internet Literacies

We are always online even when we are not "using" our devices. The culture we interact with online *is* our culture. On a global scale, new economies have emerged that shape markets and brands have shifted their techniques to attract new and unique consumers, and in general, our interactions with one another are guided by the overlapping of our off-platform and electronic lives. The internet operates on an "attention economy" where time spent online translates to better extraction of user data to convert to more precise targeted advertising. Underneath this structure are the reasons we use the internet: to interact with new forms of entertainment, consume news, connect with friends and followers, participate in fandoms, and to share content. However, *Critical Internet Literacies* argues that we are also participants in market flows, trends, economics, corporate hostility, and reactionary culture, all for the sake of a Silicon Valley ethos of scale and profit, where new opportunities for creative media production are coded as resisting corporate structures while simultaneously reproducing former media models.

This book begins with an interesting anecdote, a month-long event that combines all facets of the internet in its current form. While the internet has existed for over 60 years and the World Wide Web for over 30, it is our current era, that of the 2020s, we are in a unique position to critically engage with the internet, its content, its participants, and its user experience to better understand the way it has changed and will continue to evolve. With over half the planet connected in some way, we no longer "go online" as there is no "offline." Our first case study reveals the importance of critical internet literacies, especially to increase our language in discussing cultural shifts and safety. In just one event, we may see how teen anxieties and peer pressure mix with digital cultures, FOMO (fear of missing out), and media spectacle and moral panic. Under the surface of the event are structural issues at play like algorithmic boosting, digital

DOI: 10.4324/9781003483885-1

2 *Critical Internet Literacies*

trends, misinformation, and wasted resources. Even deeper, we will see how Silicon Valley's tech behemoths face existential issues, sometimes taking advantage of sensational news reporting and information flows in acts of corporate sabotage that sidestep legal issues and congressional oversight.

This book is a culmination of nearly two decades of critical internet research, scholarship, and pedagogy. Over that time, the internet has been both molded by its users while also shaping culture, all while we pay little attention to its externalities, extractive processes, and its nuanced operations as a never-ending archive. Reconsidering our digital worlds helps expand our knowledge of the new systems of content creation and content consumption and helps us better read the structures that support them. This project places academic texts, scholarly articles, and internet culture journalism in dialogue within a critical technocultural discourse analysis to interrogate the evolving subject of internet media and its creators. Critical internet literacies increase our ability to interact with our world with agency and help us develop a new language to discuss ongoing shifts that leave us with little consumer choice because our internet is a constant background utility. The goal of this book is to help us look at sensational events that seemingly "come from the internet" and adjust our reaction to regain control over the tools that have become so indispensable, especially when so much is at stake.

Caught in the Machine: The "Slap a Teacher" Challenge Hoax

On September 1, 2021, just days into the return to school effort, a seriously problematic video was uploaded to TikTok by a high school student in California. @jugg4elias recorded himself opening his backpack to show off his theft of a box of disposable safety masks. At that point in the pandemic, masks were fairly easy to attain, but the uneven safety restrictions at each school across the country caused stress among the typically forgetful teenagers as they made their way back into the classrooms for the new school year. That September should have been a moment of exuberance and joy, considering students hadn't been in their school hallways for over a year, and while mask mandates, social distancing, and strict health mandates were in place, an attempt was made to restart the school year in a positive manner.

Unfortunately, the pandemic "pause" and stay-at-home period resulted in many students missing their graduation ceremonies, school proms, important social events and many lost their internships or sports scholarships. More serious was the realization that a vast number of students lost a year of meaningful education, many unable to access to their online courses easily or safely. Far less understood in this period was how much the students had spent their time "extremely online." The phrase "extremely online" or "very online" is a term for internet users who can "read" internet media with a high level of fluency, negotiating new slang terms, connecting to esoteric cultural events, creating content for social media platforms in the proper "grammar," and understanding nuance and references so outside the mainstream it sometimes feels like a different language.

No matter how much students were physically present in the hallways and their classrooms, they now are always very much online. By the time of this incident, internet culture had been shifting and expanding its influence for nearly a decade, not to mention the impacts of the 2016 US presidential election and the global cultural politics affected by online behavior, but the pandemic set in motion a new shift, sometimes referred to as a "vibe shift" that resulted in internet media becoming far more prominent in our lives – especially meaningful to teenagers and new users logging onto social media sites. Young people enter a digital world built by others, one based on commodification, exploitation, and a runaway attention economy, with little control aside from creating content. Once back in class in September 2021, some felt the need to rebel – and document it.

According to KnowYourMeme's archive,[1] @jugg4elias may have launched the "devious licks" challenge. He captioned his video "a month into school absolutely devious lick. Should've brought a mask from home." Devious licks referred to an illicit or wildly inappropriate theft or vandalism of school property. While the videos contained no specific call to action, its mere existence on TikTok and its viral spread encouraged memetic remixes, each time upping the danger to gain additional views. Trends like devious licks fall into the category of "IRL memes" and while the vast majority of this type of meme are fairly harmless (for example: "Owling," "Planking," or even the ALS challenge) devious licks was more akin to destructive memes that emerged more publicly during the pandemic like "gallon smashing" (where people would destroy milk cartons in grocery stores on camera) or "ice cream licking" (opening a container of ice cream, licking it, and returning it to the store shelves).

Devious licks felt different. The pandemic caused deep anxiety among young people across the globe, increasing psychological stress and depression.[2] A great deal of people died needlessly, and mixed safety messages confused more than helped. Teens, who have always been the affected by life stress in their developing years, had never previously encountered this combination of forces in their life. In the age of social media, influencers, FOMO, YouTube, and memes, the pandemic stay-at-home period was an unprecedented event – add to that the power of mediatized rebellious acts broadcast on a platform that rewards more extreme content, and you have an unpredictable outcome. The trend spread and metastasized like a cancerous tumor inside of TikTok.

Days after @jugg4elias uploaded his video, another user named @dtx.2cent recorded himself unzipping his backpack to reveal a hand sanitizer. This wasn't the small bottle of liquid sanitizer you could find at a pharmacy, but the actual large wall unit that was, until @dtx.2cent removed it, bolted to the wall in his high school bathroom. As the trend grew online, the vandalism led to destruction of school bathrooms, safety equipment, and property – all captured on camera and uploaded. With no surprise, the devious licks trend created a moral panic and was lifted into the mainstream news cycle.

By mid-September 2021, the *New York Times* reported there were "tens of thousands" of videos using the #deviouslicks hashtag and its derivatives.[3] Students like TikTok user @mr.epicsinger used TikTok's duet feature to remix @dtx.2cent's video with his own: the theft of a school microscope. It was no longer isolated to bathrooms, but theft in general and the public was taking notice. In dozens of schools around the United States, arrests were made, bathroom breaks were eliminated, and school administrations met with faculty to understand the trend and quell the acts of destruction. Devious licks was a disaster, fostered by TikTok's participatory

Figure 1.1 The aftermath of the "devious licks" trend, captured by a TikTok user.

Introduction 5

environment, vicarious viewers, and shameless students rebelling for likes, and the trend resulted in handwringing, general anxiety, and speculative accusations of doom.

***

Even before the pandemic, TikTok had grown in influence. As the fastest growing social media app between 2018 and 2024, more than a billion people downloaded the app globally and over 150 million US users consider the app part of their social media diet. TikTok has been especially important for teenagers as they develop their identities and seek meaning. As far as content, it completely changed the online media environment, mimicking the earlier app Vine more than its social media predecessors like Facebook, Instagram, or YouTube. TikTok's features include easy to use editing tools, methods of remixing others content (called "duets"), and a content aware algorithm that customizes every For You Page (FYP) for each user to show them *exactly* what they want to see. TikTok is reminiscent of a television screen with the remote built directly onto its surface. Each flick upward brings a new piece of autoplaying media to the viewer. Its ease of access makes TikTok the technological equivalent of the participatory culture we've believed the rest of social media to be from their inception.

More than any other demographic, teens found TikTok to be their digital home – it launched as Gen Z was entering high school and early college. There's an exciting and controversial feature that also dominates TikTok: its content aware artificial intelligence algorithm. Unlike the recommendation systems of YouTube and Instagram, TikTok's algorithm "watches" the content and feeds it to users to enable what may be called "dwell time," or extended time spent on the app. When a user uploads a video, the AI system visually analyzes and listens to the video, using its systems to categorize, sort, and most importantly boost content it wants people to watch. The dwell time feature calculates how long a user watches any video and shifts their feed in response to show more of that type of content.

TikTok is just one product of the company ByteDance, a Chinese company that absorbed Musical.ly in 2017 and merged it into their TikTok product, the Western version of the Chinese Douyin app. As a popular social media founded outside the US, Silicon Valley executives and government legislators have always been somewhat nervous of TikTok's influence. These companies treated TikTok's algorithm and a trend like devious licks like an insurgency from a foreign government. While nearly all the internet operates like a "black box," meaning productive proprietary software designed for tech companies to remain competitive, TikTok's technology acts less like a culture factory and more like culture itself.

6 Critical Internet Literacies

"TikTok favors whatever will hold people's eyeballs, and it provides the incentives and the tools for people to copy that content with ease," Jia Tolentino writes in the *New Yorker* in 2019. [4] Tolentino continues: "The algorithm gives us whatever pleases us, and we, in turn, give the algorithm whatever pleases it. As the circle tightens, we become less and less able to separate algorithmic interests from our own."

We must continually remind ourselves that predictive algorithms can only use our past data to anticipate future interests and these systems do not operate in a vacuum: they are competitive and always shifting, reliant on previous iterations to maintain their hegemony over their users. For its part, TikTok banned the #deviouslicks hashtag, removed videos, and started redirecting videos of the vandalization to its community guidelines pages.[5] TikTok's trust and safety teams were in constant communication with schools and administrators and worked hard, albeit reactively, to calm the situation down and disincentivize the creators from participating in the trend. TikTok believed that if it lowered the visibility of the trend, the popularity of the destructive challenge would fade away as the fickle audience moved onto the next popular meme.

While the trend slowly diminished online, the reactivity of mainstream news reminded viewers of the dangers that lay just beyond teenagers' fingertips. The moral panic that surrounds apps like TikTok is a result of low internet literacies and a willful ignorance to what apps like TikTok – or really any social media – do to their audiences and participants. However, in late September, an ominous rumor emerged on Facebook that caused schools to become far more alert. October 2021 was going to be the start of the next TikTok challenge – called the "slap a teacher" challenge.

The slap a teacher challenge was part of a lengthy list of month-by-month TikTok challenges. It was spread across Facebook pages and leveraged by influential members of town communities. According to *Business Insider*,[6] an Idaho-based School Resource Officer shared the list on his Facebook page which was followed by over 30,000 people. The Facebook users who followed the Officer shared it in their own parent/teacher groups, in text messages, and on their own Facebook accounts. The rumor even led to a strange, niche creator market where several teachers produced their own TikTok and Instagram videos that warned students not to participate in the new trend.[7]

On the evening of October 5, *CBS News* Sacramento broadcast a report on the "disturbing challenge" that had allegedly surfaced on TikTok. The news reporters explained that superintendents of several school districts in California were warning parents about the trend.[8] The California Teachers Association posted "Educators beware!" on a lengthy Facebook post followed by a long description of the disturbing new trend and included a warning about an incident in South Carolina where a student hit a teacher.

Introduction 7

Parents expressed their outrage at TikTok and placed blame directly on the platform and news reports layered on more critical press about TikTok's influence.

However, the more journalists and savvy users investigated the threat, the more it seemed odd. Both disinformation researchers and teens expressed doubt that this challenge either existed or originated on TikTok.[9] In a rare case of platform *proactivity*, TikTok publicly responded that no such challenge existed, but if it showed up, the platform would ban the videos and remove any hashtags associated with the challenge. Neither the researchers nor TikTok's response assuaged the administrators and parents worried about the threats. It was just a month into a return to school and nerves were frayed with an unease of what had transpired and what students learned online in their year out of the classroom. *Could it get worse?*

The lack of internet literacies enabled fearmongering and hype-based reporting about the influence of TikTok challenges and persuaded people to take the supposed threat against teachers seriously. There is no arguing that the removal and destruction of bathroom supplies were real; the videos on TikTok were literally the evidence. But across the country, several schools heeded the warning of the slap a teacher challenge and closed their doors for a day or two in early October to throw water on the possible dangerous trend that threatened safety in their school hallways. The widespread threat never emerged.

In fact, the slap a teacher challenge did not exist. It never existed. It was just an intense rumor spread on Facebook that manipulated parents, teachers, and communities through fear-based tactics. However, this was worse than a rumor: it was a *hoax*. Who would perpetrate a hoax like this? This hoax amounted to an abuse of resources requiring schools to increase safety, send kids home for a day or two, and upended the trust that students were regaining after returning to school. While nowhere near as dangerous or disastrous as devious licks, this hoax could have manipulated the public in ways unknown. Disturbingly, this was not an organic hoax; it was not accelerated by students seeking to cause chaos. It was a hoax created by a consulting firm hired by *Facebook itself.*

The slap a teacher challenge was a well-produced hoax that leaned on anxieties about school theft, all too common violence in the US, and the pervasive nature of online trends affecting young people's everyday lives. In March 2022, the *Washington Post* reported that Facebook had hired Targeted Victory, one of the biggest Republican consulting firms in the US, to "turn the public against TikTok."[10] The hoax wasn't just the list shared on Facebook by unsuspecting administrators, the stunt included op-eds, letters to the editors of many news outlets, and an increased set of rumors warning of dangerous trends on TikTok to the public. How did Facebook, a platform worth a trillion dollars, successfully manipulate the

8   *Critical Internet Literacies*

public through the media and through its own platform? How does Meta remain free of accountability for the waste of money on public resources across the United States? And most importantly, what could we have done, as concerned citizens, to prevent this from happening?

This anecdotal incident presents us with an opportunity to examine the constitutive elements that require internet literacies. The internet and social media are not just pervasive in our lives as an ever-present access point to the world's creative output and collective knowledge, but have immense tangible effects. As the world's biggest social media company waged a public war against its competitor in plain sight, it used children, parents, teachers, and schools as its proxy – all by taking advantage of the public's low level of information and internet literacies. It is with this example that we may lead into the important discussion on how to better interact with similar incidents, build our resilience, and critique these infrastructures and communication systems we take for granted.

The Internet, The Content, and The Creators in the 2020s: An Overview

The internet, specifically internet media and its content, is cumulative and reactionary. No other previous system of communication, media, or production is similar in these foundational structures, and therefore no other medium offers a specific or holistic critical framework to analyze online content. The internet and the collective of all its content, though subject to platform colonization by Silicon Valley's technological innovations, are much more than the popular websites and massive social media networks that inhabit the 2020s user experience. The internet is designed to scale at all costs and requires an expansion of labor in all aspects of its use, encouraging users to create as well as consume, brands to develop multilayered advertising, and political parties to engage with more diverse communities than ever.

The internet is not beholden to any state or government actor, nor representative of an overarching authority, or even a single oversight committee, but fully functions as a super structure within capitalism and its market values. Its creators, its users, and its media are fully framed by a unique form of commodification, transposed across both digital and physical spaces, from like counts on a post to social clout in influential communities. The internet is also a culture industry that is better described as culture itself. The internet in its entirety is inconceivable, much the way we may not understand the sheer volume of stars in the sky. In its inter-objectivity, nearly everything on the internet contains multiple meanings. As such, it can only be viewed and investigated by its elements as it exerts influence on other things proving its existence; the internet is a hyperobject.[11]

Introduction 9

What the internet enables is a participatory mechanism on a machine that continually scales in all directions, encompassing labor (both hidden and visible), exploitation and externalities (like environmental impact), and sociopolitical influence (both soft and hard power). The internet, over the last four decades, has been a place where new language has been forged and pushed outward, overlapping common vernacular, through its textual, visual, and auditory elements. Functionally, internet-born aesthetics change visual grammar, fashion, and marketed products, simultaneously overwriting previous iterations and unused styles. Even more unique, the internet is self-healing, like end-grain wood on a cutting board. Cultural shifts on one part of the internet may "heal" over time through market forces and lapses in cultural memory, all enforced by the power of the never-ending presentness of its use.

The internet is also a de facto host of the fringe. It is a place that enriches, or maybe even enforces, extremism as it slowly normalizes malicious material and harmful content by absorbing the volume of media into its array of predictive algorithms, language learning models, and archived datasets. As bad faith actors shift their discourse to avoid content moderation, the Overton window widens just a bit more until it is unable to contract further. Encoding harmful speech is an ongoing game played by those most interested in disrupting conventional conversation in politics and social environments, and promoting a perverted version of civic engagement. All culture is cumulative, but the internet doesn't forget – it builds upon itself in a never-ending scaffolding and construction. Each day you use the internet is the cumulation of every day the internet has been active. There is no turning off parts of the internet's past: it uses all that has ever been created purposeful to the present.

The result of decades of cumulative interaction and reactionary content creation has resulted in the development of internet culture, including a possible infinite number of subcultures. Internet culture is the creator, the content, the critic, the commenter, and the code. It is the video that does not work without a caption; it is the image that contains a multitude of references and nuance; it is media shared among those literate enough to receive the messaging within; it is the young person who wishes to be a creator and the seasoned chef making videos of new recipes on TikTok. Internet culture is the user watching a helpful YouTube video while on the side of the road fixing a tire and the mom sharing a funny image with her friends. Internet culture is a power dynamic that cannot be contained, nor explained easily, but affects everything around us in our mediated realities.

Importantly, internet culture is also built on elision, and it is paramount to confront the ideas of access, exclusion, and inequality inside both the mechanics of the internet (such as code, algorithms, and platform structures) and the attention given to the media creators (popularity, implicit

10   *Critical Internet Literacies*

or explicit censorship, income distribution, and privilege). Like other communication systems, we may also define internet culture by what it is not by interrogating why some people do not have the opportunity to express themselves equally or use the systems tactically. And unlike traditional media systems, we also must acknowledge how internet culture can be a space for the support, uplift, and growth of vulnerable communities, increasing the overall safety and exposure of LGBTQ+ people and trans rights, but unfortunately simultaneously exposing them to malicious actors who may attempt to put them in harm's way.

It is no longer cute or novel to refer to the internet as a *place to go*, but rather an all-encompassing immersive environment. Political and activist movements have been forged in online spaces and permeated hundreds of times onto the streets around the globe and up the US Capitol steps. We experience these movements as distinctly physical – happening "in real life" – rather than seeing nearly everything as an overlap of the digital on the physical. While today we are not directly driven by the predictive algorithms, we are somewhat passive participants in the engagement systems on our ubiquitous devices and social media sites. The internet is always on even when we are off.

Further, the media created online has developed an economy of its own, existing solely in reaction to media that precedes it while simultaneously supporting the inequities and hegemony of those systems. This in turn has enabled some media to devolve into grifts, misinformation, conspiracy, rabbit holes, and fascistic behaviors, many of which result in real-world complications with consequences far beyond the control of regulation, law, and education. In many ways, the only way to manage these spaces is to negotiate our role within them, understand the cultures, and apply a moderate amount of fair necessary criticism to the power structures that enable, reinforce, and maintain hegemonies of traditional media structures.

Now this said, in its three decades since the launch of the web browser, the internet is visibly aging. Due to the overabundance of advertising in search and the intrusion of artificial intelligence and bots, Google search no longer functions the way it was intended.[12] TikTok has leaned into shopping, like its Douyin version in China, making the interface nearly unmanageable. Tech reporter and author Cory Doctorow refers to this process of degradation as "enshittification."[13] In addition, Elon Musk's takeover of Twitter has gutted the platform's integrity, incentivizing outrage bait, and meaningless chum to dominate the site where innumerable racists, antisemites, bigots, and bad actors to swarm anything they deem "anti-free speech." And overall, the internet is rotting.[14,15] As journalists are laid off en masse and local news dries up, links have stopped working,

Introduction   11

unarchived websites have disappeared into the ether, and valuable cultural artifacts are no longer accessible in context.

This book is an attempt to critique parts of the present extant internet, read events more fully, and reconsider how internet media operates in our daily lives and how we may use our knowledge to empower more intentional use, increase our collective safety, and inspire young people to manage the growth of the internet as new apps and platforms emerge. To apply critical literacies of the internet is to recognize its role in the hegemony of traditional media while recognizing its role as both a reactionary space and a tool of cultural atomization.

There is no way for any book on this subject to be fully comprehensive, it would take eons to catalog the material and contextualize the evidence. This project was conceived as a way to make discussions surrounding the internet and its media more accessible, less novel, and more part of our daily conversations. The most important part is to push back against a dualist mindset where the internet is a separate space and recognize we exist on the internet even when "offline." This project also hopes to destigmatize the concept of internet culture and the creators who produce internet media who simultaneously navigate the shifts in digital environments they have little control over.

The impetus to begin this project is to recognize that the shifts which occurred in the early 2010s, especially in 2014, that have vastly altered the culture of the internet and the industries that rely on its existence.[16] Internet culture flourished within these formative years while the utilitarian internet concretized globally. This book aims to look at the way the internet has influenced its consumers to move beyond the idea of the "prosumer" and accept a commodified user experience, where each user is a potential "creator," and in a world where about 50 percent of young people wish to be a creator of some sort, it is our responsibility to have a nominally approachable language to discuss digital culture and its effects.

This book is broken into eight chapters, each representative of a major aspect of internet media, the creators, and the ways we moderate and maintain safety in the present and into the future. The first half is an overview of the widest accessible sectors of the internet, its culture, and the environments. We'll interrogate the "creator economy," the visual language of memes and their resounding political power, and how we develop new language. The second half introduces critical approaches to boundary content and awareness media, enabling us to better read coded messages and agenda-based propaganda disguised as entertainment and also introduces new ways of understanding content moderation, safety, accessibility, and community growth. The overall goal is to increase our comfort when discussing how the internet operates, what it does to ourselves, our

12   *Critical Internet Literacies*

relationships, and to young people. Culture is shaped by the power dynamics around us, and internet culture is a dominant structure that requires an investigation.

Extending Critical Media Literacies to Internet Literacies

After this diagnosis, how may we apply current models of criticism to online content and internet culture? If each piece of internet media is diverse and variegated like ornate foliage at the ends of hundreds of branches, what tools may we use to reconsider creativity, content, and safety online? This text encourages an interdisciplinary approach to critiquing online events, media, and artifacts. However, we may apply media literacy to the content because this project argues that online content perpetuates the models, codes, tropes, and the inequities and biases of traditional media hegemonies. Aside from some prominent outliers, a great majority of online media relies on the visual grammar developed, codified, and utilized since radio, early cinema, and television and therefore these analyses are useful.

Media literacy scholar Renee Hobbs has explained that media literacy education can be traced back to the practice of rhetoric in Ancient Greece "to teach the art of politics through the development of oratory and critical thinking."[17] Today, media literacy helps educate people about film, television, and commercials in depth, analyzing key features of visual and auditory storytelling embedded within the codes of communication, as well as how images are framed on screen. Media literacy also covers how and why edits are motivated to hidden agendas and cultural politics weaved into storylines. With critical thinking at the forefront, the aim is to educate media consumers to apply some level of healthy skepticism and better "read" media as to not fall for propaganda or disturbing rhetoric, critically interrogate representations of race, class, gender, and identity, and better detect hidden advertising.

Due to its extraordinary novelty, online media has been analyzed through a vast array of a critical approaches – each valuable, though many approaches are tied temporally to the extant knowledge we had at the time. Some of these approaches, like any that utilize a dualistic framework of online versus offline, are no longer usable in the 2020s, as online media's influence and presence overlaps our everyday realities in more immersive ways than television or cinema can structurally allow. The idea of a "life on the screen," while conceptually an easy scapegoat, is outdated and downplays the methods of media creation that inhabit waking life.[18] Over the past 30 years, analyses of online content have evolved through several phases from "tool use" and skills[19] to participatory culture[20,21] to theorizing concepts of new media and digital production.[22,23,24,25]

Introduction 13

In 2007, Douglas Kellner and Jeff Share proposed a type of critical media literacy that combines previous iterations of media literacy education, tool competency, and critique that embraced critiquing ideology and politics of representation, applying the use of textual analysis to include context, society, and control. Kellner and Share write, "critical media literacy brings an understanding of ideology, power, and domination that challenges relativist and apolitical notions of most media education in order to guide teachers and students in their explorations of how power and information are always linked."[26] Calling for an incorporation of cultural studies, citing Stuart Hall and Ien Ang, they argue that the audience is active in the process of meaning making and benefit from a "multiperspectival critical inquiry of popular culture and the cultural industries that addresses issues of class, race, gender, and power and also promotes the production of alternative counter-hegemonic media."

Following YouTube's growth as a dominant media distribution outlet, there was a major shift in online media creation, content production, and internet culture. Communities began to concretize, emboldened by reactionary environments made up of affinity groups who used in-group memes, messaging, and visual grammar. Sites like Tumblr and Reddit rose to prominence by their creative output and their internal moderation methods and became a reactive space where users police other users through commentary aggression. This was a benefit to platforms as they recognized a boon of use when users felt an ownership over their communities and increased their time spent online. The rise of the influencer and the creator gave way to an organic competitive space, separated from traditional notions of media business and in protest of the "gatekeeping" models (agents, managers, producers, studios) that excluded independent producers lacking resources necessary in legacy media systems.

The platform colonization of the web dictated the new media markets. Nick Srnicek writes in *Platform Capitalism* that collective cooperation and knowledge become a source of value when the product of work becomes *immaterial*: "cultural content, knowledge, affects, and services. This includes media content like YouTube and blogs, as well as broader contributions in the form of creating websites, participating in online forums, and producing software."[27] Srnicek makes note that this is an illusion. Underneath any act of immaterial labor is the layers of connective tissue that operate silently behind the system – the workers at the platforms and the underpaid labor moderating the content on the screen all the way to the people who operate the extraction process of fossil fuels to burn to generate the electricity to maintain the "always on" experience of the internet and its super sites.

Creators, enamored by the prospect and possible uplift from regular blogger to endorsed millionaire influencer, unwittingly (and willingly)

14 *Critical Internet Literacies*

became part of the extractive process, drawing users into their space, building community, and occasionally bending ethical rules of engagement by responding to comments, and creating media in a feedback environment. It wasn't just creating content from their own creative idea space anymore either, they could use the immense amount of data provided to them from the platforms and their endorsers. Under the umbrella term of "surveillance capitalism," nearly every user of the internet was part of the system. Shoshanna Zuboff argues in her 2019 book *Surveillance Capitalism* that the phrase "if it's free, then you are the product" is incomplete because we are not surveillance capitalism's "customers," rather as Zuboff writes, "We are the sources of surveillance capitalism's crucial surplus: the objects of a technologically advanced and increasingly inescapable raw-material-extraction operation. Surveillance capitalism's actual customers are the enterprises that trade in its markets for future behavior."

The concept of future behavior is knowledge that the algorithm is cumulative, a learning machine designed to enhance decision-making by organizing your past activity into content suggestions and targeted advertising that slowly becomes more and more specific. Online content is more distinct than any other media with its technical layering, cumulative memory, and lack of any dualism. As there is no longer an offline and online and we are always online the trope of "real life" versus "online" is a disservice to readers as it lacks the criticality necessary to really read internet media. Online creators, whether consciously or not, have learned media techniques that require new methods of media literacy.

How may we read media techniques invented by influencers that game the algorithm with tactics like "retention editing," thumbnail techniques, screen within screen environments, vertical video, and algorithmic bias and audience manipulation? Online content is altered by platforms with proprietary codecs that sort uploaded material based on their own set of rules and content moderation boundaries that often harm vulnerable communities and lean into racialized and discriminatory practices locked in through the lack of diversity from the founders to the engineers and developers at the social media behemoths. On top of all that, the media created may also be reread through the production techniques to the referential layering and the nuance of in-group messaging embedded into the content.

We must also consider the media effects of rabbit holes and hyper-niche content that persuade users to take civic action. On January 6, 2021, as Donald Trump's supporters stormed the US Capitol, a man wearing a Pepe the Frog mask and "Kekistan" flag as a cape was seen climbing the steps. Reporter Kevin Roose noted on Twitter, "Hard to overstate how online this mob is" (tweet deleted). Many rioters carried cellphones, live streaming to their followers. In the following years, Elon Musk, one of the world's wealthiest billionaires, purchased Twitter and converted it into X,

Introduction 15

disabling and disincentivizing safety on the site. Twitter, once a space for important communities like Black Twitter and political organization, is now a haven for white supremacists and "free speech" warriors. These digital media effects have revealed the structural parts of the internet enmeshed in the hegemony of the traditional media that precedes them.

As André Brock Jr. writes in his 2020 book *Distributed Blackness: African American Cybercultures*:

> Despite protestations about color-blindness or neutrality, the internet should be understood as an enactment of whiteness through the interpretive flexibility of whiteness as information. By this, I mean that white folks' communications, letters, and works of art are rarely understood as white; instead, they become universal and are understood as "communication," "literature," and "art."[28]

The internet, its content, and its creators are part of the white supremacy that undergirds and scaffolds nearly all parts of the growth and treatment of the internet. It results in deep blind spots in the reporting, research, and journalism that surrounds the subjects.

It is here then where we may incorporate Brock's methodology of critical technocultural discourse analysis (CTDA) into critical media literacy approaches to read online media. A critical technocultural analysis means we will read the case studies throughout this book as artifact, converting them into text to analyze. As Brock explains, CTDA enables an "analysis of discourses across websites, services, and platforms – published by the technology's users about their wielding of the technology – but also to its holistic approach to analyzing technology as discourse, practice, and artifact."[29] Most of the case studies in this text are focused on internet media and culture in the late 2010s and early 2020s, and these approaches will be applied to the readings and reconsideration of the online product. In addition, we will apply diverse approaches to internet culture and content by Charlton McIlwain, Legacy Russell, Ruha Benjamin, AJ Christian, Laura Bates, and Whitney Philips among many scholars of internet and digital culture.

Finally, we will also consider the incredible work by internet culture journalists and disinformation researchers who often find themselves as the vanguard of public understanding of internet media. In 2020, journalist and author Jamal Jordan tweeted: "We have to admit that the rise of disinformation is due, in part, to the fact the journalism industry didn't take covering internet culture seriously until 2016" (@lostblackboy, October 18, 2020. Tweet deleted). While reporters had been covering internet phenomena for decades, the idea of internet culture as a "beat" took hold after Donald Trump's election and the rise of populist leaders across the

16 *Critical Internet Literacies*

globe. Taylor Lorenz's work is useful in this book following the publication of her 2023 book *Extremely Online: The Untold Story of Fame, Influence, and Power on the Internet* which recenters the history of the "creator economy" on the contributions of women creators and bloggers.[30]

This book is primarily focused on the years following the pandemic when online media went through a rapid growth and evolution which now influences nearly all other media. Our responsibility of understanding these changes helps reverse the runaway power dynamics of venture capitalists, founders of social media platforms, and creators who manipulate their audiences through unethical production techniques and storytelling. In the 2020s, large shifts in internet media have relied on nostalgia, aesthetic prominence, and a disregard for safety in lieu of marketing, hype, and profit. As users age and children learn about internet content, it is up to us to apply the necessary criticism in a hope for more just and equitable futures.

A Reverse Analysis of a Hoax

Facebook is no stranger to controversy. Meta platforms have defended themselves in the court of law over 60 times since its founding for causing employees PTSD,[31] failure to keep children's data safe,[32] abetting a genocide against the Rohingya in Myanmar,[33] and various antitrust issues. The slap a teacher challenge did not result in any legal cases, but the moral panic that ensued continues to enable fearmongers to blame TikTok and social media for the behavior of students. To be clear, TikTok is not a neutral platform, and it will not be referred to as a victim, but in this case, Facebook paid a company to undermine TikTok's brand and turn the public against the app. According to the *Washington Post*, who attained internal emails from the firm Targeted Victory, the firm was hired to deflect concern away from Meta's antitrust and privacy concerns.[34] Facebook, Meta's primary property, was also facing an existential threat from TikTok. An internal document discovered in the massive leak of the Facebook Papers by whistleblower Francis Haugen explained that teens were using TikTok "2–3x more" than Facebook or Instagram. The internal memo was dated back in March 2021 and the leaks occurred during September 2021 as Facebook rebranded to Meta.

The leak of the Facebook Papers were damning evidence of a company full of fear and hubris. They revealed the company had been aware of many issues for years (like mental health damage to teenage girls or optimization for radicalization), even though journalists and researchers were told the opposite. The threat of TikTok's popularity coincided with a report that Facebook had an aging user base and was unable to attract younger users to the platform.[35] Targeted Victory was hired to do the dirty work

Introduction   17

and malign TikTok. Targeted Victory is a Republican public relations firm (whose leadership team desperately lacks diversity[36]) that spends many of its earnings on Republican candidates like Senator Mitch McConnell, Congressman Steve Scalise, and organizations like the NRA.[37] They are not subtle about their tactics and claim success stories on re-election campaigns and lobbying tactics.

The slap a teacher challenge was a completely fabricated hoax and news incursion designed by a PR firm which affected students and communities around the United States. It's important to start this book with this anecdote to frame the necessity of increasing our internet literacies. This event contains multitudes of layers that prove we may need new approaches to interrogating and critiquing online media, their producers, the platforms, the consumers, and the media. It also provides an opportunity to reconsider the theoretical and critical approaches of the internet in over the last two and half decades. The following is a list of the constitutive elements of the example we used to start this book:

- Teenage anxiety and culture
- Peer pressure
- Covid-19 societal effects
- Participatory challenges
- Online trends
- Community pressure
- Silicon Valley
- Law and Congress
- Lack of internet literacies
- Misinformation
- Corporate sabotage
- Influencer creep

- Fear of missing out (FOMO)
- Digital cultures
- Viral videos
- Algorithmic boosting
- Fearmongering
- Child safety
- Platform existentialism
- Whistleblower Leaks
- Sensational news reporting
- Wasted resources
- Media spectacle
- Moral panic

This singular event that spanned over two months displays how elements of the internet exert soft power on civic life and media reporting. The Silicon Valley ethos of growth at any cost scales without concern or empathy for the users that support the structures. Many of these platforms, especially the platforms we'll refer to as "mainstream," are reliant on advertising to stay solvable and profitable. Their proprietary "black boxes" of code and user data can only be seen by their effects, leaving many people to speculate the nature of machines and their role in society.

This book is an attempt to reread major events at the overlapping environments of internet and everyday life and propose a way of discussing these issues with far more nuance and depth. The goal is to resist the urge to participate in moral panics and generate a language to discuss internet-born content and their creators with those who still may consider

18 *Critical Internet Literacies*

the internet another place. We have the responsibility to incorporate civic values and creative approaches to critical media literacy to help inform young people of the world they inhabit: one that is both online and offline simultaneously all the time.

Notes

1 "Devious Licks Trend." *KnowYourMeme*, September 8, 2021. https://knowyourmeme.com/memes/devious-licks-trend.
2 Fortuna, Lisa R, Isabella C Brown, Gesean G Lewis Woods, and Michelle V Porche. "The Impact of COVID-19 on Anxiety Disorders in Youth." *Child and Adolescent Psychiatric Clinics of North America* 32, no. 3 (July 2023): 531–42. https://doi.org/10.1016/j.chc.2023.02.002.
3 Heyward, Giulia. "TikTok's Latest Craze: Stealing Stuff From School." *New York Times*, September 17, 2021, sec. U.S. https://www.nytimes.com/2021/09/17/us/devious-licks-tiktok.html.
4 Tolentino, Jia. "How TikTok Holds Our Attention." *New Yorker*, September 23, 2019. https://www.newyorker.com/magazine/2019/09/30/how-tiktok-holds-our-attention.
5 The entire archive of #deviouslicks TikTok videos embedded on KnowYourMeme are inaccessible as of the writing of this book. Each of the videos archived by KnowYourMeme and all the videos embedded in news articles are ghostly black boxes, devoid of their original media.
6 Haasch, Palmer. "Schools Are Cautioning against a 'Slap a Teacher' TikTok Challenge, but It Appears to Be a Rumor Spread on Facebook." *Business Insider*. Accessed March 7, 2024. https://www.businessinsider.com/slap-a-teacher-challenge-tiktok-october-trend-2021-10.
7 "Dr. Sewell on TikTok." *TikTok*. Accessed March 7, 2024. https://www.tiktok.com/@drsewelllcms/video/7013139204230089989.
8 *Schools Warning Of Slap A Teacher TikTok Challenge*, 2021. https://www.youtube.com/watch?v=LeQGrirwwHU.
9 Gilbert, David. "The 'Slap a Teacher' TikTok Challenge Is a Hoax." *Vice* (blog), October 6, 2021. https://www.vice.com/en/article/3aq3e5/slap-a-teacher-tiktok-challenge-hoax.
10 Lorenz, Taylor, and Drew Harwell. "Facebook Paid GOP Firm to Malign TikTok." *Washington Post*, March 30, 2022. https://www.washingtonpost.com/technology/2022/03/30/facebook-tiktok-targeted-victory/.
11 See: Morton, Timothy. *Hyperobjects: Philosophy and Ecology after the End of the World*. University of Minnesota Press, 2013.
12 Brin, Sergey, and Lawrence Page. "The Anatomy of a Large-Scale Hypertextual Web Search Engine." *Computer Networks and ISDN Systems* 30, no. 1–7 (April 1998): 107–17. https://doi.org/10.1016/S0169–7552(98)00110-X.
13 Doctorow. "The 'Enshittification' of TikTok." *Wired*, January 23, 2023. https://www.wired.com/story/tiktok-platforms-cory-doctorow/.
14 Pegoraro, Rob. "The Internet Is Not Forever: 38% of Web Pages From 2013 No Longer Exist." *PCMAG*, May 20, 2024. https://www.pcmag.com/news/the-internet-is-not-forever-38-of-web-pages-from-2013-no-longer-exist.
15 Zittrain, Jonathan. "The Internet Is Rotting." *The Atlantic* (blog), June 30, 2021. https://www.theatlantic.com/technology/archive/2021/06/the-internet-is-a-collective-hallucination/619320/.

Introduction 19

16 Cao, Steffi. "How 2014 Changed the Internet Forever." *The Ringer*, May 1, 2024. https://www.theringer.com/tech/2024/5/1/24144418/modern-internet-2014-anniversary.

17 Hobbs, Renee, and Amy Jensen. "The Past, Present, and Future of Media Literacy Education." *Journal of Media Literacy Education* 1 (2009): 1–11. https://doi.org/10.23860/jmle-1-1-1. p. 2.

18 See: Turkle, Sherry. *Life on the Screen: Identity in the Age of the Internet.* Simon & Schuster, 1995.

19 Holcomb, Julie L. "Kathleen Tyner's Literacy in a Digital World: Teaching and Learning in the Age of Information." *Journal of the Association for History and Computing* (November 1999). http://hdl.handle.net/2027/spo.3310410.0002.317.

20 Jenkins, Henry. *Convergence Culture: Where Old and New Media Collide.* New York: New York University Press, 2006.

21 Jenkins, Henry. *Confronting the Challenges of Participatory Culture: Media Education for the 21st Century.* The John D. and Catherine T. MacArthur Foundation Reports on Digital Media and Learning. Cambridge, MA: The MIT Press, 2009.

22 Manovich, Lev. *The Language of New Media.* A Leonardo Book. Cambridge, Mass.: MIT Press, 2001.

23 Wardrip-Fruin, Noah, and Nick Montfort, eds. *The New Media Reader.* Cambridge, Mass: MIT Press, 2003.

24 Chun, Wendy Hui Kyong, and Thomas Keenan, eds. *New Media, Old Media: A History and Theory Reader.* New York: Routledge, 2006.

25 Cohen, James, and Thomas Kenny. *Producing New and Digital Media: Your Guide to Savvy Use of the Web.* Second edition. London New York, NY: Routledge, 2020.

26 Kellner, Douglas, and Jeff Share. "Critical Media Literacy: Crucial Policy Choices for a Twenty-First-Century Democracy." *Policy Futures in Education* 5, no. 1 (March 2007): 59–69. https://doi.org/10.2304/pfie.2007.5.1.59. p. 61

27 Srnicek, Nick. *Platform Capitalism.* Theory Redux. Cambridge, UK; Malden, MA: Polity, 2017. p.38

28 Brock Jr., André L. *Distributed Blackness: African American Cybercultures.* Critical Cultural Communication. New York: New York University Press, 2020. pp. 6–7.

29 Brock Jr., André L. *Distributed Blackness: African American Cybercultures.* Critical Cultural Communication. New York: New York University Press, 2020. p. 2.

30 Lorenz has been the target of far-right reactionaries as her work illuminates and critiques through a journalist lens some of the more insidious behaviors of online personalities including Elon Musk, Chaya Raichek (LibsOfTikTok), and Tucker Carlson.

31 Garcia, Sandra E. "Ex-Content Moderator Sues Facebook, Saying Violent Images Caused Her PTSD." *New York Times*, September 25, 2018, sec. Technology. https://www.nytimes.com/2018/09/25/technology/facebook-moderator-job-ptsd-lawsuit.html.

32 McCallum, Shiona, and Tom Gerken. "Instagram Fined €405m over Children's Data Privacy," *BBC.* September 5, 2022. https://www.bbc.com/news/technology-62800884.

33 Milmo, Dan. "Rohingya Sue Facebook for £150bn over Myanmar Genocide." *The Guardian*, December 6, 2021, sec. Technology. https://www.theguardian.

20 *Critical Internet Literacies*

com/technology/2021/dec/06/rohingya-sue-facebook-myanmar-genocide-us-uk-legal-action-social-media-violence.

34 Lorenz, Taylor, and Drew Harwell. "Facebook Paid GOP Firm to Malign Tik-Tok." *Washington Post*, March 30, 2022. https://www.washingtonpost.com/technology/2022/03/30/facebook-tiktok-targeted-victory/.

35 Heath, Alex. "Leaked Files Show Facebook Is in Crisis Mode over Losing Young People." *The Verge*, October 25, 2021. https://www.theverge.com/22743744/facebook-teen-usage-decline-frances-haugen-leaks.

36 https://targetedvictory.com/team/.

37 https://www.opensecrets.org/campaign-expenditures/vendor?cycle=2020&vendor=Targeted+Victory.

2 Critical Perspectives on Digital Cultures

From Digital Culture to Internet Culture

Digital cultures emerge as communities inhabit spaces of expression, coalescing around likeminded individuals with similar interest and passions, where participants both curate material and create new media, encoded with the values of the group. These digital cultures are identified by their tactility and connection to the technologies themselves, occasionally gaining influence and growing outward into internet culture at large. The etymological roots of the word digital come from the use of digits, or fingers, to interact with their media and therefore, the tools, though made invisible in their media output, are part of the way digital cultures codify their forms of expression and cannot be discounted in their analyses. What structures make up a digital culture at its time of existence are representative of the digital cultures themselves, same with their tools for creativity (i.e. message boards, websites, social media sites, and video creation). In other words, digital cultures are a symbolic derivative of their moment.

This chapter is both a literature review and a retrospective reconsideration of several digital cultures as they developed into creator cultures, economic spaces, and influencer markets as well as a model we may utilize to analyze them in their time of existence. Over the past 30 years, there have been many definitions of digital cultures, but here it may be best to synthetize definitions from Martin Hand (2016), Saskia Sassen (2017), and Paul Mihailidis and Samantha Viotty (2017): Digital cultures are affinity groups online that emerge from the digital environments and contain their own political economy, history, lore, expression of identity (through media), and maintain and police their own ethical and moral boundaries among their participants.[1,2,3]

Consider digital cultures to be the building blocks of internet culture at large. Digital cultures are representative of their members, but also must be willing to mature, include more people, and attempt inclusion rather

DOI: 10.4324/9781003483885-2

22 *Critical Internet Literacies*

than exclusion as culture inevitably shifts. Digital cultures can be based on fandoms, collective movements, political ideologies, autonomous zones of expression within a platform, creative misuse of technologies, and collaborative creator movements, to name a few. If we are to increase our internet literacies, we need to recognize that nearly every digital culture has strong, occasionally intense, feelings of belonging but also offers spaces of resilience and expression that connect diffuse users over large distances into an organized space (for better or worse), but also may exert power by creating viral trends, controversial moments, or spreading emotional media outward to unfamiliar audiences.

Digital cultures vary from global sites of participatory engagement to site specific, locative, or geographically regional when they cohere around a specific interest or act of participation. Fan fiction sites like Archive of Our Own (AO3) are representative of non-geographic digital cultures whereas the "private publics" of Pakistani digital social spaces to discuss local television are site specific.[4] Current digital cultures benefit from their structural origins that date back over three decades. These original digital cultures – and their documentation – supply evidence of how much progress has been made in online spaces. When immersive digital environments first emerged in the late 1980s and early 1990s, they were primarily used by those who were privileged enough to have access to a computer consistently and had excess leisure time that enabled them to build online communities (in text-based or computer-code environments). They also maintained a collective power over the future growth and development of their communities. The existence of digital cultures always raises curiosity, especially when they exert influence on commercial activities or develop distinct externalities worth examining. However, when digital cultures are analyzed in their respective times of influence, these texts are often published within the same market, one that occasionally displays an overall bias toward a white, heteronormative sense of computer use. These early critiques also deserve analysis to help us read contemporary literature on digital life. Those able to write about internet and digital culture in the early days may have benefited from a normalized privilege within a biased media environment. Revisiting some of these texts helps our awareness of the temporal environments and hopefully encourages us to prioritize the diverse perspectives of the 2020s.

Today, digital cultures are so profuse online there's no way for anyone to catalog and analyze all of them (or even a nominal percentage), especially when new trends and new access points, particularly in the Global South, are constantly shifting. But what we can analyze is a way to better read the effects of these digital cultures and their influence on culture at large through their conversion to internet culture, a more recent term to describe the flow of culture as it overlaps our everyday lives, considering

Critical Perspectives on Digital Cultures   23

the ubiquity of mobile devices, profuse digital surveillance, extractive applications, and especially the reliance on search engines for mundane tasks.

This chapter describes how digital cultures exist as reactionary environments – not to say these are neccesarily negative in the sense that fandoms are reactionary to the content or celebrity in which they exist. As an electronic media space built upon data, digital cultures cumulate over time, building off previous iterations and metatextual in-group references. Some exert power on other digital cultures, acting like a cultural pendulum that increases its size exponentially. As the pendulum gains critical mass, it emerges into mainstream news coverage, resulting in a media and content feedback loop. Finally, we also should interrogate who may have been able to create digital cultures and whose voices were not part of the development. Finally, using a pragmatic heuristic like "who is left out?" may assist in the scholarship, reporting, and research that informs the public (through either the news or through education) on the crucial influence of internet culture on everyday life.

Early Cultural Developments

While there is no distinct "beginning" of digital cultures, several foundational details of the current internet environment were shaped in the 1980s and 1990s when the internet was considered a separate place. We logged on. We went to the computer room. We connected to the "net." It was ecologically different from our physical reality. Early communities formed when the privileged few who had access to the network splintered into subcultures of affinity groups and considered their digital spaces "local." Likely, these members carried their digital passions with them to work, school, or leisure, but could not easily identify other members in public.

Much of the early writing on internet culture and screen-based activities wasn't really framed around a culture deriving *from* the internet, but rather being *on* the internet, relating their effects to those of traditional media (specifically research on fandoms, fashion, artistic movements). In the mid to late 1980s, an "underground" culture emerged made up of tinkerers and technologists who sought to create a computerized community for the exploration of psychedelia and a space for unregulated freedom of expression. At that time, the term "cyberspace" was given to the mostly imaginary spaces that existed at the end of the modem phone line. The term, coined by William Gibson in his dystopian 1984 science fiction novel *Neuromancer*, gave a noun to an ephemeral space, made up of code and messages sent via internet relay chat. The "console cowboys" in Gibson's novel were people who could navigate the digital world with acuity and vigor, often breaking the rules to get access to parts of the internet beneficial to their digital adventures.

24 *Critical Internet Literacies*

This underground culture developed its own offline aesthetic, language, and community as well and many of these people referred to themselves as "cyberpunks." (The leather-clad characters in the Wachowski's 1999 *The Matrix* are the image we conjure, but many cyberpunks didn't express themselves in that specific style of fashion.) In 1991, journalists Katie Hafner and John Markoff covered the topic in *Cyberpunk: Outlaws and Hackers on the Computer Frontier* explaining that cyberpunks had been inspired by the "change in the way computers were being used" especially among "young people for whom computers and computer networks are an obsession, and who have carried their obsession beyond what computer professionals consider ethical and lawmakers consider acceptable."[5] In this early framing, computers were a device to be used by the few (professionals), had to be used in a standard way (ethics, law), and there were a minority of people who could exploit the technology (cyberpunks) for their own use. This us/them framework was a standard way thinking when computers were wildly inaccessible due to cost and lack of access for personal use.

The advent of the World Wide Web in late 1989 and the birth of the web browser in 1993 completely shifted the way people interacted with the digital "underground." The cyberpunks who tinkered online had developed their own space and came to know each other by their usernames considered their frequently visited bulletin board services (BBS) as if they were "locals." In an early example of the reactionary environment these online spaces were to become, BBS users would often become agitated each September as an influx of amateur users logged onto the internet for schoolwork at their universities. The browser and the access to the personal computer altered a near decade-long underground culture and in September 1993, the term "Eternal September" was coined by BBS users. In her 2014 essay "Eternal September: The Rise of Amateur Culture," Valentina Tanni writes:

> 1993 was the year in which big providers such as AOL (America Online) began offering Usenet access to all their customers. Before then most users were university students: a population that grew a little every year in September when the new intake of freshman accessed the net for the first time. Every time another set of newbies joined the network, the community had to cope with their "net illiteracy" and general lack of netiquette; their behavior was in fact considered annoying and potentially dangerous for the quality and content and discussion. After 1993, this influx of users became permanent and the "Eternal September" is still ongoing today, at an exponential rate.[6]

The term originated on a Usenet group by a user named Dave Fischer who wrote: "September 1993 will go down in net.history as the September that never ended."[7]

Critical Perspectives on Digital Cultures   25

From a critical perspective, these calls for "net literacies" and "netiquette" were heavily coded in a "native" versus "immigrant" mentality. These are not the literacies we are focused on in this book, but rather a set of standards developed by early "netizens" who deemed themselves the arbiters of what roles users should play in relation to the more native users who "grew up" on the net. It's important to remember these factors as we go through the case studies presented in this book, as many of the original frameworks, mindsets, and pronouncements concretized into a philosophy of identity and movement.

"The New Home of the Mind"

By the mid-1990s, internet media, including rudimentary video streaming, amateur journalism, early blogging, and linked websites like GeoCities, revealed that the web was expanding exponentially and bringing on millions of new users. While unprovoked or unthreatened, much of the content was produced in opposition to mainstream media messaging to prove that the hegemony of corporate and regulated media can be countered by a rebellious group of ragtag tinkerers willing to create for the sake of creation rather for some invisible executive beholden to advertisers and media distributors. While the internet was a "freer" space, internet service providers (ISPs) are corporations, and these ISPs would eventually be sustained by the very corporate systems these early users felt they were rebelling against. Operating the internet is very costly.

The cyberpunks had always felt that corporations, advertising, and governments get in the way of unrestricted expression and true "freedom." By 1990, the hype around commercial immersive technology like virtual reality combined with the advances on hypertext and the development of the web. This resulted in conferences, touring events, demonstrations, and gatherings. One of the earliest of these was "The First Conference on Cyberspace."[8] In attendance was John Perry Barlow, the occasional Grateful Dead lyricist and libertarian thought leader, tech historian Howard Rheingold, academics like Michael Heim, Meredith Bricken, AR Stone, Nicole Stenger, as well as early adopters of the virtual reality and the nascent web. The topic of cyberspace, which covered the internet and the early versions of commercial virtual reality, led to discussions on nearly all aspects of the digital landscape unfolding in front of them, from gender identity to virtual lives to immersive experiences. Notably missing from the talks and publications are discussions about race and exclusion; nearly every single attendee was white.

In a fateful coincidence, days after the end of the conference, a widescale governmental raid on hackers called Operation Sundevil took place throughout the United States. Barlow became incensed by the lack of rights many from the cyberpunk subculture maintained during the arrests.[9] In

26 *Critical Internet Literacies*

reaction, Barlow met with venture capitalist and founder of Lotus, Mitch Kapor, and libertarian activist John Gilmore, and together they founded the Electronic Frontier Foundation, or EFF. Even before the browser existed, Barlow and Kapor had discussed writing a "Constitution for Cyberspace" to establish a set of rights for digital participants to defend the "civil liberties in the digital world."[10] Five years later, in an obvious tell of the future developments of the internet and its structural quest for scale and profit Barlow ended up delivering his constitution at the 1996 World Economic Forum in Davos, Switzerland.

Barlow's manifesto, titled "A Declaration of the Independence of Cyberspace" opens:

> Governments of the Industrial World, you weary giants of flesh and steel, I come from Cyberspace, the new home of Mind. On behalf of the future, I ask you of the past to leave us alone. You are not welcome among us. You have no sovereignty where we gather.[11]

Arguably, Barlow's "A Declaration" is one of the most consequential and reactionary texts in the history of tech and media. Framed from a completely libertarian perspective, delivered among the titans of capitalism, the essay is foundational in the evolution of the development of the web, social media, and digital cultures. It's a text seeping with anger and leans into threats several times: "You are terrified of your own children, since they are natives in a world where you will always be immigrants."[12] This prideful take of ownership at the exclusion of governmental oversight expectedly resulted in the unprecedented inequality that cumulates to this day.

Media theorist Douglas Rushkoff, who had witnessed and documented digital cultures since the early 1990s, states this more succinctly in 2016:

> What those of us unversed in Marxist theory at the time didn't realize was if you get rid of government you create a very fertile soil for the unbridled growth of corporations. Government and corporations tend to balance each other out like fungus and bacteria might in a human body. When you get rid of one, you get overgrowth of the other.[13]

Barlow and the EFF may have been sympathetic to the cyberpunk cultures that were possibly targeted unfairly, but in his reactionary stance, spoken loudly at Davos, he set the tone and mantra for the way we would interact with the technology and its content, mostly through commodification or corporate counterparts, systems that built on exclusivity and marginalization in their operations.

Critical Perspectives on Digital Cultures 27

Early Critical Work on Digital and Internet Culture

By the mid-1990s, digital cultures had concretized into forums, fandoms, and gaming communities. The launch of the Mosaic browser in 1993, followed by its stunning IPO and conventional name change to Netscape, created one of the most outstanding examples of corporate intrusion in history. Seeing the success of the tool that could read hypertext markup language and convert it to images, Bill Gates and Microsoft developed Internet Explorer and packaged it with their Windows Operating System. The event – known as the "browser wars" – showed how low corporate entities would go to get involved when it came to providing the access portal to the internet. The browser wars would later resolve in Microsoft's loss after Gates had threatened to withhold Windows to schools if they used Netscape and the courts argued this was monopolistic. Meanwhile, users were immersing themselves more and more though direct connections and newly launched portals like Prodigy, CompuServe, and America Online (AOL).

Even with slow internet speeds, creativity was at a flurry online, especially for those who had the access. In 1995, MIT researcher and scholar Sherry Turkle published *Life on the Screen: Identity in the Age of the Internet* which examined the "rapidly expanding systems of networks collectively known as the internet" and studied how the technologies were changing thought, sexuality, communities, and most importantly, our identities.[14] From Turkle's mid-1990s perspective, her research was prescient, noting how virtual spaces changed the users' behaviors in physical environments. However, Turkle's status as an MIT scholar inadvertently created an issue for further research as her prominence sets the standard for critical references (similarly to the way Richard Dawkins is still mentioned in meme scholarship).

Turkle's work, like many others at the time, focused on the spaces of creative freedom, especially the most unique and weird for their time. Turkle investigated multiuser dungeons (MUDs) games and their players, virtual avatars, "cyberspace marriage," and psychotherapists who use the computer to communicate. Three decades on, these novel examples are normalized in gaming, artificial intelligence, relationship apps, and the all-to-common telehealth systems. Fortunately, Turkle's examination recognized the "story of the eroding boundaries between the real and the virtual, the animate and inanimate, the unitary and the multiple self" but given the time it was written, Turkle described a system of duality, one in physical space, one on the screen. This dualist viewpoint was often repeated and used as evidence in further research even after the advent of social media, commodification, and recommendation algorithms; even worse, the dualist approach occasionally enables people to use the internet as a scapegoat in moral panics.

28   *Critical Internet Literacies*

In 2011, theorist Nathan Jurgenson wrote that the omnipresence of cell phones, extractive surveillance data, and cultural overlap negate any possibility of a digital dualist approach.[15] In his critique of anthropologist Amber Case's use of Turkle's term "second self," he argues that we must be wary of considering the "false binary" of online versus offline. Jurgenson argues that digital cultures extend and enmesh into our living lives, as the digital impacts our *offline* experiences. Jurgenson recommends using the term "augmented" rather than the binary suggested by many authors who continued using a dualist approach in the 2000s in texts by authors like Nicholas Carr, Jean Twenge, Mark Bauerlein, or Jaron Lanier. Further, in the 2020s, following the pandemic stay-at-home period, we now exist online all the time.

Further examples of this critique are supported by curator and scholar Legacy Russell in her 2020 book *Glitch Feminism: A Manifesto*. Russell grew up in the East Village of New York City as it was growing more affluent, and writes, "Away from the keyboard (or 'AFK'), immersed in a rapidly gentrifying East Village, faces, skin, identities like my own and like the mixed communities I had been brought up in were slowly disappearing."[16] As a young, queer, woman of color, Russell was using an internet that was gentrifying (or already gentrified) as well. The structural binaries of the web – from the code to the construct – undercut her ability to express herself freely, so she was "never being fully seen." While Jurgenson used the term augmented to describe how identity is not online/offline, Russell calls it a "glitch." "Within glitch feminism, glitch is celebrated as a vehicle of refusal, a strategy of nonperformance. This glitch aims to make abstract again that which has been forced into an uncomfortable and ill-defined material: the body."[17]

The body, meaning your physical self, is often detached when we interrogate the digital spaces that develop cultures. While we may interact at the tips of our fingers and our eyes, we inhabit a body that is affected by the pressures of the world. On the internet, those vulnerable bodies, trans bodies, or Black bodies coded as carceral, have moments of reprieve, but are never detached and therefore digital cultures are evidence of the bodies of the physical being as well. In Turkle's book, she considers digital gender swapping in gaming and concludes it is novel and "easy" to do in digital spaces, with little recognition of expression or gender identity, calling it "virtual cross-dressing."[18] Some latitude may be provided due to the time of Turkle's writing, but it could also be part of the systemic issues of MIT. In Charlton McIlwain's 2020 *Black Software*, he explains that MIT decided only in1964 that they could invite a small number of Black students to enroll at the esteemed school.[19]

The normative stance for technology and digital cultures were encoded as "neutral," which did not require any labeling or categorization. It was

Critical Perspectives on Digital Cultures   29

just how the internet was used and little critical pressure was necessary. To repeat what Dr. André Brock Jr. clarifies in *Distributed Blackness*:

> Despite protestations about color-blindness or neutrality, the internet should be understood as an enactment of whiteness through the interpretive flexibility of whiteness as information. By this, I mean that white folks' communications, letters, and works of art are rarely understood as white; instead, they become universal and are understood as "communication," "literature," and "art."[20]

It isn't just that the machines, code, and software were primarily designed by white people, it's that digital culture itself was encoded with the status of white cisgendered normativity. Any aberrations require labeling or unique cultural makers to define their presence by comparison to other digital cultures. The othering that takes place then becomes part of future code, future mindsets, and future political outcomes.

Social Media's First Success was Community

In 1999, founders Omar Wasow and Benjamin Sun launched the early social media site BlackPlanet. Years previous, projects like NetNoir on AOL and GoAfro on CompuServe proved that Black communities were interested in connecting online within a space of safe expression. Unfortunately, building media environments required an immense amount of capital. According to Hannah Giorgis's long-form essay about BlackPlanet for *The Atlantic*, the "team faced a major challenge in launching Black-Planet: the perception that Black people simply didn't use the internet. It was true, around the turn of the millennium, that white households were significantly more likely to have internet access than Black ones."[21] Wasow and Sun's insistence paid off: they developed a platform that enabled Black folk of all walks of life to join and by May 2001 – surviving the dotcom bust completely – BlackPlanet had 2.5 million users. Wasow helped develop the space for Black internet culture and design a platform in the pre-algorithmically optimized era that would set the stage for social media communities and creators, especially the connective underpinnings of what would later become Black Twitter.

According to Giorgis, BlackPlanet was a smaller social media than we'd expect today; it was also fairly racially homogenous, aiming to onboard as many Black folk as possible to use the site. BlackPlanet was forum based, with a range of topics, some which veered into being controversial. Whereas today, we see users intentionally gaming the feed or baiting users into rage responses, this was not rewarded on BlackPlanet as it lacked the "like" button or any form of retweet or repost features.

30 *Critical Internet Literacies*

Giorgis continues: "BlackPlanet users talked candidly about politics, debated sports, and engaged in conversations about what it meant to be Black across the diaspora." One of the features of BlackPlanet that some readers may find familiar was the access to customization on the site where users could change their profile page with colors, music, and gifs, with basic coding, something that MySpace pilfered quite readily.

André Brock Jr. notes in *Distributed Blackness* that the rise of MySpace and Facebook pushed the success of BlackPlanet into the background.[22] Investors started to back away as the site was unable to scale financially and they saw little value in the idea of community and trust over the financial rewards of young people joining social networks where they may connect, but also see advertising. Sites require server maintenance and infrastructure support, and BlackPlanet unfortunately dwindled. On the other hand, the existence of Black Twitter is directly correlated to the digital spaces of NetNoir and BlackPlanet. Black culture resists the co-option of its platforms and while BlackPlanet was a nearly completely homogenous culture, it was a success – all the way to Barack Obama's presidential campaign.

Some Origins of the Problematic Web

In the background of the 1990s was a growth of interest in Japanese culture and technology. Inside the cyberpunk cultures, there was a subculture of "otaku," meaning young people who became *obsessed* with being online and using new technologies, especially fetishizing culture and technology developed in Japan. The subculture was difficult to explain to the lay person, but their presence was exceptionally influential online. While there are no mentions of otaku culture in Turkle's *Life on the Screen* aside from mentioning that one of the largest attended MUDs was a Japanese simulation, the subculture had existed throughout the 1990s. In the United States, young men found the web to be the perfect medium to lean into their obsession, and as Dale Beran writes in his 2019 book *It Came from Something Awful*, these men were similar to the Japanese hikikomori. Beran writes, "'Hikikomori' literally meant 'pulling inward,' and it describes the sociological phenomenon of older children refusing to abandon the comfort of their parents' home or seeking extreme isolation in apartments."[23]

In 1999, a young Japanese man named Hiroyuki Nishimuru fulfilled the demand of this subculture and coded a forum site with default anonymous usernames, threaded replies, and almost no rules, and named it 2channel (named after the way gaming consoles needed the television to be set to channel two or three to work). The site, hosted in Japan, gained interest from local users who wanted some anonymous use of the web as well as attracting otaku, mostly young men, from all over the world. One US user in particular, an otaku named Richard "Lowtax" Kiyanka developed a

Critical Perspectives on Digital Cultures   31

similar site called "Something Awful" which was a humor website (with a better aesthetic than 2channel's) where Kiyanka believed people could get "weird" on the internet. Beran writes:

[Something Awful's] nerdy content quickly attracted the cynical, pop-culture-obsessed 90s adolescents who were clambering onto the web. All forums suffered from the same systemic problems since the days of Usenet: flame wars, obsessive users, and rude comments. This behavior seemed to come more easily when people were safely separated by their computers. But what set SA's forums apart was its attitude toward all of this. Rather than strip out all the bizarre aggression that inevitably accompanied forums, SA simply let it grow as a grotesque experiment, cultivated it even.[24]

The site permitted users to post nearly everything and was only moderated by Kiyanka. Though he hated anime, he eventually created a channel for anime (the name will not be repeated here). There, a young, 14-year-old boy with the username "moot" was searching for porn and would get an idea for another site: 4chan. Following the closure of 2channel in Japan due to controversy and the uplift of hate, moot, whose real name is Christopher Poole, copied the code and developed a space that had even fewer rules than Something Awful.

The Long-Lasting Spectacle of 4chan

In October 2023, three weeks after the Hamas attack on Israel, AFP photographer Joseph Eid attended a pro-Palestine protest in Beirut, Lebanon and captured an image of a group of young boys wearing plastic Guy Fawkes masks with their hands making the "V"-shaped peace gesture.[25] A day later and a world away, in Eugene, Oregon, US, a masked counter-protestor named Jonathan Wisbey violently drove his GMC pickup truck through a crowd of pro-Palestinian protestors at the Free Palestine march. His truck was adorned with several right-wing flags and the Gadsen Flag. Wisbey was wearing the Guy Fawkes mask during his attack.[26]

In fewer than two decades, the plastic mask from James McTeigue's 2006 Hollywood film *V for Vendatta* has become iconic and ubiquitous wherever there are protests, direct action, and disruptive events. But this mask is not a mask, it is a metonym for the influence of the internet in reactionary settings. The simple and cheaply made plastic mask is a replica of V's, the protagonist of *V for Vendetta*, a film produced by the Wachowskis. The presence of the mask is clear evidence that memes from internet culture have influence on our everyday realities and have become normalized. It's a global product that now represents the concept of anonymity, but its origins are not revolutionary – the original meaning is *failure* mixed with a perverse view of retribution based on the real failure of Guy Fawkes mixed with the success of the V icon from the film.

The meme character "Epic Fail Guy" predates Pepe the Frog, troll faces, and Wojaks (explained next chapter) and is often accompanied in posts where a user would share a story that depicted an awkward situation or a failure of some sort. (In one of the earliest posts archived, Epic Fail Guy discovers his mask in a garbage can.) The mask contains multitudes. When wearing it, *the wearer* makes the decision on which meaning it represents to themselves. But likely, when it comes to protests, 4chan users chose to wear the Fawkes mask because of their meme rather than the film representation or the historical figure. The digital cultures that enable this type of behavior are characteristic of online affinity groups that develop their own language, aesthetics, activist stances, and iconography. On the other hand, every time a Guy Fawkes mask is purchased, Warner Brothers Studio makes some amount of money from the sale.

4chan is a unique digital culture, one that is more representative of the web than we like to think. Made up of mostly young, white men, the users gather on the site to express themselves in ways that are nearly impossible off that platform. 4chan, as we know it, is usually confused with its more aggressive boards like /b/ (random) or /pol/ (politically incorrect), but 4chan has dozens of affinity sites that range from music to pets to anime (of course). However, the boards that express the most influence on the rest of the web are usually /b/ and /pol/. Harmful language, hate speech, and derogatory messages are nearly de rigueur for the users. Many of the young men who gather on the site do so knowing that the site maintains their anonymity and it auto-deletes it old posts. (After 10 pages, the site purges posts with little or no engagement.) The site, which attracts lonely men or so-called "NEETs" (not in education, employment, or training)

Figure 2.1 The "Epic Fail Guy" meme wearing the plastic Guy Fawkes Mask.

and has inspired hate-based activities off-platform. Driven into a lifestyle like the hikikomori, these users really only have each other in a world that is changing around them. With little guidance, the site is the space for the fringe to be all encompassing and immersive, slowly shifting these mindsets so only this version of reality – one of perceived victimization and retribution – exists. If you pay attention to something like the Guy Fawkes mask as a symbol of their culture, you can track how these users can develop what may look like collective movements.

A Collective of Mistrust and Missed Opportunities

The Guy Fawkes mask has been a strategic tool for protestors seeking to disguise their identity since 4chan's 2008 "Operation Chanology." According to Gabriella Coleman in her exhaustive 2014 book on Anonymous, *Hacker, Hoaxer, Whistleblower, Spy: The Many Faces of Anonymous*, before 2008 4chan, specifically its random board /b/, was mainly known for its "internet motherfuckery," trolling, doxing, mischievous behavior, posting horrific content, and malevolent online attacks and brigading.[27] Operation Chanology was a reactionary event founded in internet spaces that bled out into physical environments when /b/ users decided to protest the Church of Scientology both online and at the front door of various Scientology locations around the US.

The birth of Anonymous (capital A) transpired as a chaos-driven troll division within the spaces of anonymous (small a) posters on the forum. To converge off-platform, or IRL, anonymous users chose the Guy Fawkes plastic mask to be their collective symbol of organization and performance. In short, 2008's Operation Chanology was a reactionary event designed to heavily troll the Church of Scientology after the organization successfully had YouTube remove an internal video clip that featured Tom Cruise. Two years earlier, 4channers had learned how to use their collective activism when they attacked – for the "lulz" – the Finnish website The Habbo Hotel. The site was a somewhat cute virtual haven for teenagers that looked like a primitive environment as seen in "The Sims." The members of /b/, for lack of a better term, invaded the space with hundreds of avatars, each a similar black persona wearing a grey suit. They coordinated their moves to have their avatars form swastikas and bullied regular users on the site. As a result, Fox News reported on the event calling Anonymous an internet hate group. When the 4channers responded to Fox News via a low-resolution YouTube video, they appeared as a headless man in a black suit.

The members of 4chan continue to believe they are the arbiters of the internet and its content. Their digital culture holds a belief that the internet enables an absolutist view of free speech, meaning that everything – *literally everything* – should be allowed on the internet, regardless of harm. When

34 *Critical Internet Literacies*

Scientology, which the online collective considered a cult, successfully petitioned for the removal of their internal video, Anonymous turned toward digital and direct action. Online, they attacked Scientology websites with directed denial of service (DDoS) attacks (meaning they overloaded their servers with too many website visits), ordered pizzas and prostitutes to Scientology churches, and made hundreds of phone pranks to the Dianetics hotlines.[28] Then, on February 10, 2008, Anonymous appeared in public on the streets to protest in front of Scientology churches in 127 cities in the US. The images are visual evidence of a spectacular event as nearly every protestor donned the Guy Fawkes mask.

In 2011, 4chan founder Chris "moot" Poole delivered a TED Talk to explain the platform's influence. He'd been invited to speak after he had been voted one of the Time 100 in 2009, although arguably gamed by 4chan users. Poole was especially proud of the /b/ forum, which he described as the "beating heart" of the website, where new memes were forged, new linguistic markers were developed, and a reactionary powerhouse primed to attack their supposed enemies of the internet. Poole says an interesting phrase in the talk that was underreported at the time: "The internet, my community, decided to do something about it."[29] The idea of the *internet* being a community seems like an odd statement considering it is accessed by over half the population of planet Earth. But this community is made up of digital cultures, many that feel a specific way about defending their way of life online.

Missed in many discussions about 4chan and its users is their ability to cohere collectively, a tactic that is difficult for most activist movements, but 4chan motivates unlike any other. In their ability to collectively challenge their supposed enemies, they miss an opportunity to develop systems of resilience that could counter the systemic issues that bring them to the site in the first place. But perhaps, that isn't their goal anyway. It just may be their way of managing the growth of the web as the world changes around them. Facebook has never competed against sites like 4chan, but has slowly opened the door to their membership. There has been an overall "4chanification" of the web, meaning we've gradually become adjusted to some of the more abhorrent things that happen in the dark corners as they happen both with more frequency and more in the open as a reactionary stance. The combative nature of the 4chan users resulted in a two-decade long project of reactionary pendulum swings, each time pushing the boundaries of the Overton window slightly more open in every direction. The reactionary branches of our current internet environment exist *because* of 1990s commercialism, early 2000s forums and mommy bloggers, and social media's libertarian stance on regulation and oversight. Any reading of the internet today requires us to interrogate the branch all the down to its roots.

Creator Cultures, Communication, and Commodification

Some people unfamiliar with its forum-based predecessors, found the internet valuable because it empowered regular people to speak directly with creators themselves, feeling as though they had a say in the development of the creator's media. Taylor Lorenz argues in *Extremely Online* that early "mommy bloggers" were partly responsible for this new market. "Throughout the early 2000s, frank parenting talk was hard to come by," Lorenz writes, "Women's magazines pushed an idealized, often misogynistic version of motherhood that was less and less relevant to modern mothers."[30] In 2001, Heather Armstrong (who died by suicide in 2023) started Dooce.com, a site that enabled Armstrong to share the reality of parenting with other moms.

The ability to retain an audience was a valuable opportunity and growth was important to Armstrong, but it didn't pay the bills. Dedicating your life to content creation requires some sort of income. In 2004, Armstrong began running advertisements on Dooce.com to draw income from her content, but there was backlash from her fans, wondering why she was monetizing her blogs; her blogs weren't paywalled, Armstrong just added advertising. This reaction may be tied to an early audience's expectation of content online being "free" or it's possible that this was a misogynistic response, but either way, Armstrong decided to keep ads on her site. The ads on her blog enabled Armstrong to create a business for her content and she was later able to support her family based on her work. This model of placing ads on personal blogs was one of the earliest forms of commodification in the creator space. First, you needed an audience, but then you had to convince companies to invest in your product.

As a reactionary environment, there is always an opposing force on the internet. On the other side of the spectrum from mommy bloggers, the creator economy also finds its roots firmly situated in content developed inside what we now call the "manosphere," a space where disaffected men, some from 4chan, some from other sites, share their woes and gripes about society with one another. While Armstrong's audience was interested in her tales of parenting and personal stories, there was a rapidly growing space for unkind content, misogyny, and "pickup artistry" type of blogs that went under a genre known as PUA. These "online seduction community" blogs run by "pickup gurus" lured young men by convincing them there was a "game" to seduce any woman into dating them. The few "gurus" were well-known influencers and drew the attention of *New York Times* writer Neil Strauss who immersed himself in the PUA movement and in 2005 published *The Game: Penetrating the Secret Society of Pickup Artists* which in turned launched some of the more insidious parts of internet culture into the mainstream.

While Armstrong influenced the growth of the mommy blogger industry, empowering women like Rebecca Woolf who started the blog "Girls Gone

36   Critical Internet Literacies

Child" in 2005. Whereas these women expressed their raw emotions in ways that traditional media could not or were considered taboo at the time, the men of the manosphere felt emotions were useless. *The Game* taught men to bury their feelings and use tactics to get women rather than connect to their personal being. PUA and the manosphere were deemed to help with male loneliness and the confusion of a changing world where women were becoming more empowered in their individuality. However, the PUA masterminds had little care for the uplift of young men, they wanted their tactics to generate a profit. As you may imagine, the PUA game does not work nor cannot scale, meaning that *if* it worked for some, there was no way it was truly a tactic. While women increasingly became more comfortable with expressing emotions of their postpartum experience and child rearing lives, young men reacted in quite an impressively terrible way.

Believing that "the game" doesn't work for some young men, due to a number of reasons, whether it be low social skills or attachment to gaming communities or online forums, some young men became concerned that they may be "involuntarily celibate," or "incel" for short, a qualifier that soon became a cynical badge of honor. Without guidance, coaches, or social assistance online, bad faith users took advantage of these young men, insisting that *their* strategies worked and often for some cost. Many PUA creators relied on their disaffected audiences to sell their books, guides, and videos and failure was built into their process. The entire project was a grift; success would mean that the young men would move on.

The modern creator economy lives on the branches on a massive tree whose trunk is strengthened by advertising, reactionary ideologies, and invisible labor. The roots date back to these years before YouTube where foundational creators developed interactive tactics – both healthy and harmful which taught future founders what to include in their social networks. We cannot uproot this organism that has now transformed our world and the lives of millions of creators and we have these early models to thank for their current success. Current movements, like "tradwife" content to masculinity influencers like Andrew Tate to the current lucrative mommy blogger influencer space are all connected to these early roots. We need to remind ourselves about these origin marketplaces because it's easy to forget that women set the stage for the idea of influencers while some of the earliest grifting was created by taking advantage of vulnerable people thinking they were being helped.

The 2000s: Hype, New Media, Participatory Culture

In the early 2000s, a shift in academic approach tended to lean into the novelty of the media, retitling the industries under the blanket terms "new media" and participatory culture. In media theorist Lev Manovich's 2002

Language of New Media, Manovich compares the production, creation, and communities of the digital to the traditional media marketplaces, to the avant-garde editing and montage styles of Russian cinematographer Dziga Vertov's work. Soon after, media theorist Henry Jenkins popularized the use of the term "participatory culture" to encourage new forms of media literacy education within digital spaces – which were optimistic, but difficult to spread at scale.

New media is a space of experimentation, alternative media making, and unregulated (and non-unionized) products and productions. Manovich argued that if we'd known in 1895 that a new medium (cinema) was being created, we could have used the opportunity to interview audiences, develop narrative strategies, and build a language of media making – but Manovich fails to ask *who* gets to develop the language. Who has the privilege to publish and do so? Who is being interviewed? Who gets to do the interviews? It seems a blind spot in early work that missed the fact that we were unfortunately, and unknowingly, reproducing the advent of cinema, radio, and television in new media environments and platforms. With the inherent privilege built into the growth of the web, financial support in the form of venture capital leaned into white entrepreneurs and scalable projects. It's no wonder Mark Zuckerberg relentlessly developed programs and algorithms with little or no consideration of diversity. Not only were there very few texts providing students with diverse stories of digital experience, but commercial systems were designed specifically to react *to* diversity.

While BlackPlanet was a stable community, it had virtually plateaued and had little interest in the scale that Silicon Valley entrepreneurs were obsessed with at the time. MySpace emerged as a new social media network and millions of teens flocked to the site where they developed their own communities, spaces of play, and experimentation. It was participatory user-generated media in a controlled digital environment. Until it wasn't. After Mark Zuckerberg launched Facebook and opened the gates beyond dot-edu addresses, many US teens left MySpace to join the gleaming white and blue social media. In 2011, danah boyd published the outcome of over four years of ethnographic research on teens and social media use. boyd found that teens' preference for either site was more than just interest, "it reflected a reproduction of social categories that exist in schools throughout the United States."[31] Some teens who had left MySpace referred to the site as "ghetto" (more the slang term than racial, a teen explains).

boyd relates the exodus and migration from MySpace to Facebook to "white flight," the period in the early 20th century when white urban city dwellers left for suburbia to avoid racial integration. A similar effect can happen in digital spaces, segregating into what we may call communities, but are really segregated consumer categories and expression zones that thrive on exclusion. Further, as digital cultures increased, they concretized and created their own exclusivity *within* the social media sites, making it difficult for outsiders to participate in fandoms or for people to join social movements without full participation in the cause. As digital cultures matured, so did their language and their ability to evade traditional media literacy, slowly becoming dependent on their own cultural markers to be used as referents of expression. Standard codes of semiotics were no longer a tool for interpreting these in-groups because signs themselves were entirely dependent on digital cultures redefinition of their meanings.

The Mobile Web and Atomization of Culture

When the iPhone was launched in 2007, it was not the first smartphone. Its ubiquity today is a result of incredible marketing and a dominance in the tech market due to boosterism and uncritical reporting (which are sometimes the same). At the time, mobile smartphones were not exactly great portals to the internet, but soon proved useful as a storytelling device that valued immediacy. On January 15, 2009, a man named Janis Krums

Figure 2.2 A recreation of Janis Krums's famous 2009 tweet and photo taken with his iPhone 3G of Flight 1549 in the Hudson River in New York.

Critical Perspectives on Digital Cultures   39

was on a New York river ferry on the Hudson River when US Airways Flight 1549 crash-landed in the river. Krums took a photo from a few hundred yards away through shoddy ferry glass and sent the image to Twitpic, a third-party service used by Twitter to host images. Krums tweeted: "There's a plane in the Hudson. I'm on the ferry going to pick up the people. Crazy."[32] along with the photo of survivors standing on the wing of the plane. Scooping journalists, Krums instigated a reactionary movement inside of journalism called "citizen journalism" where *anyone* – in theory – could be a journalist.

In December 2010, Mohamed Bouazizi self-immolated in Sidi Bouzid, Tunisia. His act was captured on a mobile device and shared on social media. After Tunisia's President Zine El Abidine Ben Ali visited Bouazizi in the hospital, the image of the burning and the burnt man are amplified by aristocratic young students in Tunis, the capital of Tunisia, which causes the reaction resulting in the Arab Spring. The Occupation of Tahrir Square in Egypt the following summer, captured on mobile phones, attracts the world's attention. Unlike all previous global events, images from the conflicts that later resulted in the toppling of three governments (and the ongoing civil war in Syria), appeared in the same feed as our thoughts, tweets, posts, and responses. The strife of the world was part of the digital interface.

At the same time, both Instagram and Snapchat were founded as mobile-first technologies, and it was soon clear that mobile-first social media was going to become the priority for developers. Twitter benefited from a mobile-first interface and arguably it helped concretize Black Twitter's presence on the site. Tumblr's mobile interface let people find their communities and develop real-time fandom interactions in second screen environments. However, the biggest asset to social media was not the interactivity, response time, or the content, but the enormous amounts of data that could be extracted from user devices and the surveillance of our user habits to construct customized feeds. While the mobile phone empowered users to become first responders, witnesses, and storytellers from wherever they could get signal, the explosion of information resulted in atomization of information into particulate and cultural detritus, refusing a collective narrative. Algorithmic customization was learning in real time that engagement mattered more than a coherent narrative of objective reality.

Anonymity for the Rest of Us: Tumblr, Teens, and Memes

Tumblr launched in 2007 as an alternative social network, one that merged the concepts of forums, social media, and blogging. A year earlier, Facebook launched its most successful product, the News Feed, which centralized the posts of everyone you follow. Tumblr, on launch, built something

40   Critical Internet Literacies

called a Dashboard, a space where you can see a never-ending scroll of posts from anyone you follow. While the Dashboard is where Tumblr users spend the majority of their time, there was a distinct focus on curation and brand-building, leaning on anonymity as the top feature. Tumblr wasn't a blog, but used blogging tools and allows users to mark up their text and use italics, bold, fonts, and colors. Tumblr wasn't a forum though it allowed "reblogs" where people could repost anything and add their own notes. These features aren't what made Tumblr popular, it was the fact that teens were jumping onto the site. By 2010, millennials, the newest generation on the web since its inception, used Tumblr to define the web their way, with twee language, new memes, and relatable humor.

In many ways, Tumblr is a reactionary site developed by teenagers. Whereas sites like MySpace, Facebook, then Twitter courted users of all generations, Tumblr settled on letting the teenagers (late millennials) define their environment. Teen culture had very little space to go in the late 2000s and early 2010s. Facebook was bringing on more and more parents, Twitter was occupied with news, and Instagram was too pretentious. It was Tumblr that allowed awkward people like Pizza to develop her identity. In Elle Reeve's 2016 essay "The Secret Lives of Tumblr Teens," Reeve attempts to find Pizza, one of the most popular Tumblr users of the early 2010s and discovers how teens operated a site like Tumblr. Reeve interviewed Danielle Strle, Tumblr's head of culture and trends, who explained that the site was best defined as connecting the smart weird kids from all over the world. Because of Tumblr's creative flexibility, users could post images, gifs, or witty jokes like, "*looks in mirror* you again." Reeve explains:

> This brand of Tumblr humor often focuses on what I think of as micro-humiliations, tiny moments of social awkwardness that can feel absolutely crushing for a teenager figuring out how to be a person in the world. Anonymous kids with witty usernames like Larsvontired or Baracknobama post incisive one-liners confessing their most vulnerable moments of social mortification. Sometimes those one-liners spread across continents, tweaked by thousands of other teens who add their own jokes as they reblog the original.[33]

Pizza, whose real name is Jess Miller, had a knack for making quick jokes and replies, using the mobile app to make sure she was able to catch anything she felt she could use to boost her followers.

Tumblr, like 4chan, was a space to express sadness, but unlike the dark, sardonic irony-bro mentality of 4chan users, Tumblr was explicit, putting the vocabulary together to describe emotions to an internet audience. It was anonymity for everyone else. Users could change their name, which

Critical Perspectives on Digital Cultures 41

would change their URL, any time they liked. Jess Miller was originally iwantmyfairytaleending.tumblr.com before becoming pizza.tumblr.com. The goal of Tumblr was to create and curate the most niche content possible, or as Reeve writes, "Here is a feeling you thought only you felt but is actually universal." The downside of Tumblr was its reactionary stance to outsiders, people who didn't cohere to the vernacular, language, or understand the grammar of the space. This was intentional, but also problematic as it perpetuated some of the more insidious methods of self-policing that emerged in the early 1990s message boards – you're either with us or against us. In addition, the expressive freedom of Tumblr, along with its progressive stance, upset the trolls of 4chan and they saw Tumblr as a corporatized environment that competed against their meme factory. The new niches of Tumblr developed their own memetic language, opening the door to more creativity and an expansion of memes (which we'll cover in Chapter 4) that were more public facing and appropriate to share.

In 2013, Yahoo bought Tumblr for $1 billion and introduced ad sharing. Unfortunately, this commodification led many Tumblr users to shift their brand into a far more influencer-centric directions. For a brief period of time (2008–2012), a micro-industry of Tumblr-to-books was common as well, with books like *Hipster Puppies* or cookbooks like *This is Why You're Fat* or *Minus Garfield* (which was a Tumblr where the creator removed Garfield from comic frames making it look like Jon was insane). Luke Winkie describes the time, where blogs were bound into books and sold at Urban Outfitters, as a "publishing feeding frenzy" as all industries were trying to find how to connect to teenagers in the social media era.[34] This frenzy also led to a reactionary stance by the darker corners of the internet when they felt excluded from yet another model of income. The importance of Tumblr outweighs any of the issues it carried and represents a small section of the awkward internet in action. While users were anonymous, many found their communities through their common reblogs, connecting with people they may never have met otherwise or anywhere else.

Digital Cultures of Conspiracy

Unfortunately, there are now dozens of books, podcasts, and documentaries on the digital cultures of conspiracy. While conspiracy theories and theorists existed long before the internet, the web is often the center of blame for its expansion into our everyday lives. Rabbit holes, radicalization, and reactionaries are inherent parts of online environments, as conspiracy theorists are drawn to the act of "discovery" and "research" that the internet affords them. On the other hand, it goes without saying that

42 *Critical Internet Literacies*

many conspiracy-minded folk are being horribly manipulated by bad actors aiming to onboard new members to a grift or even platforms subtly shifting content recommendations to increase engagement, retention, and time spent online. Conspiracy cultures sit at the borderlands of harm, remaining online as long as the members are "just asking questions" or expressing their opinions, however, their cultures encourage others to act. Digital cultures of conspiracy, as all the extant texts agree, are spaces of extremism, where answers are ever enough, the rabbit hole must go deeper.

The act of "taking the red pill" has become a call to join conspiracy cultures online. It should be well known by now that the reference comes from *The Matrix*, an overall allegory film about identity, but one which leans on conspiratorial concepts to drive the plot. As Neo takes the pill that lets him open his eyes to see how "deep the rabbit hole goes," he emerges into a world of destruction, where *everyone else* is enslaved. This has become a mantra for conspiratorial types, egged on by their community members, that they're the ones that are correct, not the masses of delusional people who have cloaks pulled over their eyes. Unfortunately, conspiracies are limited by reality itself. As David Neiwert writes in his 2020 book *Red Pill, Blue Pill*, conspiracy theories are unhealthy and damaging to democracy as they cause their communities to disengage from meaningful civic connection which leads to self-disenfranchisement. Neiwert explains that belief in conspiracy theories has a "uniquely unhinging quality" where "regardless of the direction of the theories, right or left or utterly idiosyncratic, the absorption of such beliefs into [conspiracists'] worldview has a singular ability to separate people from their contact with reality."[35] Typically, believing in one conspiracy theory opens the door to believing in many more of them.

The larger issue of cultures of conspiracy online is their need to both retain members and grow their communities. In the chaos that makes up reality, cultures of conspiracy give people answers and someone to blame. As Brian Keely writes in his 1999 essay "Of Conspiracy Theories," "conspiracy theorists are some of the last believers in an ordered universe. By supposing that current events are under the control of nefarious agents, conspiracy theories entail that such events are capable of being controlled." In our internet era, a larger danger has appeared: the internet exposes users to the more chaotic parts of reality and without internet literacies, some users fall down rabbit holes seeking answers. On the other hand, as journalist Ben Collins writes,

> The world is big and scary. It's much easier for these people to believe nefarious agents are wreaking havoc than to come to grips with the randomness of their lives. Blame the false prophets who are in on it, who have made supplement empires out of the violence.[36]

Critical Perspectives on Digital Cultures   43

Like the PUA grifters of the early 2000s, conspiracy grifters like Alex Jones and Tucker Carlson know better, but willingly profit from vulnerable folk.

"One of the insidious aspects of conspiracism is that it has a built-in immunity to what might be a normative means of drawing people out of that belief system – namely, a rational and reasoned application of factual evidence and logic," David Neiwert explains.[37] There is no "blue pill" anecdote to becoming "pilled" online. Researchers, journalists, and scholars have consistently found that people who become pilled have difficult lives, sometimes falling apart at the seams. They may be of any age, but off-platform strife contributes to a willingness to join cultures of conspiracy and occasionally act on the calls to action demanded by the conspiracies themselves, asking members to take solutions into their own hands. It is a systemic issue, one that requires major changes, increase in explanations, and most importantly, compassion. While it sounds weird to extend compassion to those most "pilled to the gills," as host of the QAA Podcast would say,[38] we need to understand they are humans as well. Collectively, we have to increase our literacies for the sake of users who struggle to make sense of the world. The more we learn to read the internet and its nuanced vernacular, symbols, and memes, the more we can discuss online culture maturely.

Black Twitter and Digital Migration

While Chris Poole feels the need to describe 4chan as the "beating heart" of the internet, arguably Black Twitter is more important. Black Twitter, so named by its space within a space, is an in-group digital culture that has shown resilience in the threat of the ongoing 4chanification of the web. While Elon Musk has shown himself to be open to racism, misogyny, and conspiracy theories, the inhabitants of Black Twitter refuse to leave the site, even as it devolves and transforms around the members. Black Twitter is a community aware of itself and its community, one that itself defines the optimism of the internet. In the July 2021 issue of *Wired Magazine*, Jason Parham takes on Black Twitter, from origins to current struggles under Elon Musk's ownership. *Wired Staff* summarizes Parham's piece here:

> No other subsection of social media has produced ideas and movements as influential or as dynamic as those that have come from Black voices on Twitter. In the early days, it existed as a space where Black people could connect, bat around some jokes, and share their experiences. Over time, Twitter's Black community grew to become a driving force of real-world social change. It catalyzed culture and led to important movements like #OscarsSoWhite, #MeToo, and, of course, Black Lives Matter.[39]

44 *Critical Internet Literacies*

Parham explains that the subsection community of Twitter organically developed, almost like a backyard conversation, but all of that changed after the killing of Trayvon Martin in 2012.

Parham explains that "a Black kid getting killed is not news, it happens literally all the time in America, this is just sort of the America we live in and the reality we live with but it was something about this moment that catalyzed Twitter in a way that hadn't happened before." People were searching for news on Google, but only found links to information on Black Twitter's corner of the internet. The hashtag #BlackLivesMatter appears for the first time as a result. Unlike the anonymous communities of 4chan and far-right hate spaces, Black Twitter members are proud of their identities, forging relationships, that André Brock Jr. – who has researched Black Twitter since before it was called Black Twitter – explains: "Black Twitter users intentionally signal their cultural affiliations to a like-minded audience in a space where, until recently, racial identity was considered a niche endeavor."[40]

When Elon Musk purchased the site, there was a clear shift away from the community-driven focus the site enjoyed (though arguably it was never run well). The threat of Elon's conversion to X threatened the existence of Black Twitter. Following the takeover, Chris Gilliard and Kashonna Gray debated the merits of sticking around. Gilliard writes:

> If people want to stay on Twitter to debate fascists, more power to them, but there is a danger in conflating Twitter the technology and digital space with Twitter the people. The platform is made up of people. Elon Musk bought Twitter, but he did not buy the communities that exist on the platform.[41]

The article points out an unfortunate reality for non-cishetero-white spaces online, they are precariously supported and rely on their members to continue the digital culture. Gray explains that migration is nothing new to Black folks, "digital or otherwise," and debates the merits of where to go:

> The exodus from Twitter has given rise to discussions about what's next and who will be welcomed there. No one wants to return to Facebook, which has become a kind of digital sacrifice zone: a term used by Black women to define their realities in online spaces because unfair policies and practices leave women and folks of color exposed to the adverse environmental conditions of the digital public. Borrowing from environmental justice, *sacrifice zone* implies tainted and poisoned grounds, polluted air, and a host of other environmental and climatic atrocities. On Twitter, the reality is also that only a subset of the user base is impacted by pollutants. [Italics Gray's.]

Critical Perspectives on Digital Cultures 45

There is no doubt Black folk have had to display resilience within communities for far too long, and this shift is unfortunately another example of harms that we may not consider "harm," though it is a sign of the value of digital cultures. The story of Black Twitter has been updated and Parham's piece was adapted into a Hulu Series and is discussed further in Chapter 6.

The Rise of the Internet Culture Beat

By the mid-2010s, there was no longer any question of the influence of digital culture and internet culture as it impacts everything around us. Still waving the libertarian flag hoisted by Barlow in 1996, most social media executives rely on their freedom from laws to experiment at will on their users, nudging social trends and enabling spaces for people to express harm. The rise of the internet culture beat within news agencies has helped people to understand how and why certain aspects of the internet operate as they do. The issue of course, is the difficulty of explaining any specific issue in brevity, while holding a critical lens to their material. Writers like Taylor Lorenz, Ryan Broderick, Rebecca Jennings, Jason Parham, Ben Collins, Rusty Foster, Kat Tenbarge, Kelly Weill, and Edward Ongweso, Jr. (to name only a few) have spent most of their career focused on helping the public understand how internet culture operates.

Writing about internet culture and online media is a precarious job. On one hand, reporters consider their career as a responsibility to inform the public of issues difficult to understand. Financial journalists explain the nuance of banking and trading, sports journalists delve into critical aspects of athletes and their industry, fashion writers go beyond aesthetics into cultural influence. The strange part of covering the internet is that it contains everything and influences nearly everyone with its soft and hard power. When billionaires like Elon Musk purchase entire social media sites and young media savants like Jimmy "MrBeast" Donaldson upend our known media flows, we need internet culture writers to report on that beat. However, the internet is a non-place, or better perhaps every place. Journalists who cover the internet have a task that is typically more difficult than most beat reporters who can "go" to the story and capture its elements.

The best internet culture reporters must be fluent to do their work, and that means immersion in their environments, expertise, and a willing detachment to tell the story. Internet culture reporting also helps bring the issues of the online world into view, helping people become aware of the shifts in culture as they happen. In the early 1990s, as the web was starting to cohere into digital cultures, *Village Voice* music journalist Julian Dibbell started covering digital cultures. In 1993, Dibbell wrote one

46 *Critical Internet Literacies*

of the most important articles about early internet abuse in his piece "A Rape in Cyberspace." Dibbell writes about a male-presenting malicious user in a MUD, or in this case a "MOO," which meant that it was more than just text-based gaming and allowed the game to take place in a virtual "space," who forced a female-presenting user into non-consensual cybersex.[42] While it took place over text, the victim was traumatized and told her story to Dibbell who published the piece in the paper. The piece is filled with lexicon and online jargon of the online world since Dibbell was trying to express the story in terms of the digital space, but it still stands out as one of the most important pieces of online culture journalism.

Three decades on and the entire internet culture beat is responsible for helping us make sense of the overwhelming deluge of events. There is always a threat of being accused of "astroturfing" or "parachute" reporting since the stories take place in a digital realm. Astroturfing is the laundering of messages from the subject, often enabled by "access" or the fear of never being able to speak to the subject again and astroturfing is occasionally conflated with boosterism and support writing, more like public relations than reporting. Parachute reporting is when a reporter parachutes in to capture the details, leaving as soon as the story is filed. In the churn of a shifting news environment, these stories are often part of a content farm or framed solely around novelty, lacking any critical perspectives. As journalist Morgan Sung writes in her piece "In Defense of the Internet Culture Beat":

> Internet culture, as a beat, is frequently overlooked as fluff. Talk about it with someone who doesn't wake up and immediately check Twitter, and they'll be as condescending as they are bewildered. Although the beat has developed enough for legacy newsrooms to prioritize covering it in recent years, internet culture still can't shake the connotation that it revolves around whatever trend the Youths are into.[43]

What makes internet culture reporting even more difficult, as we'll cover in Chapter 5, is the need for keen detection of whether a subject may be acting in good faith when interacting with the reporter. Irony, in the form of sardonic responses, or trolling are often part of the internet persona. Further, a good reporter must understand whether the story is "real" or just part of a "bit," meaning made up to catch a reporter's attention so harmful, coded information may be laundered into the mainstream. Sometimes, internet culture events are directly correlative to mass shooting events, harassment campaigns, or even the 2021 US Insurrection. In a lengthy thread on Twitter in 2019, Ben Collins expressed his frustration with covering

Critical Perspectives on Digital Cultures   47

internet media, explaining that it often takes quite a toll on the reporter, but journalists must hold the powerful to account. Collins writes:

> Absolutely nobody is taking this seriously enough, especially the people running the platforms that have created this sort of guerrilla basement platoon of empathy-free children who think school shootings are false flags. Social media execs will never take their role in radicalization seriously for a simple reason: It's a defense mechanism. They did not intentionally create something that is used as a weapon of division and violence. They'll accept any alternate explanation that works as a balm.[44]

As the internet culture beat was finally taken more seriously in the 2020s, news outlets like NBC News, *Rolling Stone*, and *Business Insider* have dedicated journalists on the beat. In 2022, Karen Maniraho interviewed five internet culture journalists for the *Columbia Journalism Review* in a long-form piece titled "Very Online." Maniraho writes:

> The best of these journalists are immersed in the internet but do not obsess over viral moments, which fly by too fast and seem, in isolation, to be trivial. By focusing on creators, communities, and the algorithm-based platforms that drive trends, these writers find ways to cut through the noise – and surface a deeper understanding of life, online and off.[45,46]

When Maniraho asked Lorenz, Broderick, Jennings, Parham and Foster how to define their beat, it ranged from tech reporting to culture reporting to pop culture to creator economy reporting and all were aware that the readership is not only passionate and protective about their spaces, but highly critical of reporters themselves. Unlike reporting on a celebrity, online celebrities and influencers have rabid fanbases that can form collective resistance. For example, the *Washington Post*'s Taylor Lorenz is also a victim of several smear campaigns because she writes about powerful figures like Elon Musk or MrBeast. *Vox*'s Rebecca Jennings is very aware of her privilege in the reporting space, explaining:

> the space of internet culture reporters is very white, very middle class – you know, one segment of the population that is in no way representative of the actual population. I think there needs to be way more people covering this beat that are not middle-class white women and white men that live in New York or LA, or wherever. That's for sure.

Lorenz explains that internet culture reporting is extremely "under-resourced" and this is an issue for civil society. Digital and internet cultures

48 *Critical Internet Literacies*

affect our world around us and have casually blended themselves into our waking lives. Ryan Broderick, who runs the *Garbage Day* newsletter, has a more concrete concern:

> The American right has had so much success with internet culture, or like memetic political movements, because of Trump. They've leaned into it very fully now. And by doing so, it means that it takes like thirty minutes to explain why they're doing anything. But the emotional information is immediately understandable to their base. I don't see political outlets trying to explain any of this, because traditional journalism doesn't really have the room to explain, you know, nine months of lore.

The restrictive speech of public broadcasting also limits our ability to learn about digital cultures, many of which have embedded deep racism and misogyny into their messaging. It is difficult for a reporter to explain the word "groyper," no less how to explain the influence of the popular hate-mongering podcaster Nicholas Fuentes.

As you may imagine, this becomes extremely problematic for vulnerable publics, especially when people like Chaya Raichik, who runs "LibsofTik-Tok" (explained in Chapter 5), express victimhood while also acting in bad faith and harmful ways against the LGBTQ+ community, especially against trans youth. Cultures online are more important than most people currently understand. Our interest in the novelty or our willingness to listen to those who thrive on moral panics often overwhelms our senses as to the value of digital cultures. *Wired* journalist Jason Parham's coverage, especially that of Black Twitter, is representative of reporting that helps us understand those values. Parham explains: "Culture sometimes is an afterthought, when so much of what we see today or what we talk about today is driven by communities that I find are important – and that are deserving of validation."

Perhaps Morgan Sung summarizes this best:

> All aspects of internet culture are worthy of coverage, from the political theater of tech CEOs testifying before Congress to the weird little communities that form around hyperspecific interests. The internet, in all of its dazzling, hellish glory, will always shape how we interact with the real world – the boundaries between internet culture and life offline evaporate a little more every day. The influence that it has on every facet of our lives, online or not, is undeniable.[47]

Conclusion

Digital cultures often cohere after what Taylor Lorenz calls a "breakout moment" that shows people "how to post" and how to interact with the

Critical Perspectives on Digital Cultures   49

community.[48] These cultures then create a feeling of belonging. Building off Ryan Broderick's point about lore, digital communities have history and moments of memory that can be referred to by other members of the group. Digital cultures then emerge as the communities grow and develop their own passionate ways of expressing themselves – and feel the freedom to do so. While vulnerable people are more visible thanks to the internet, their existence faces more threats as a result, but we must celebrate the optimism while being critical of the systems in which we all engage. 4chan's influence on the web is a product of longitudinal commodification as anger is a guiding model for retention and engagement, but other methods of belonging exist and should be uplifted. What we need is an ability to properly express our thoughts about the culture we share on- and off-platform as our identity is constantly under construction and our use of the digital is part of the rest of our lives, and as Morgan Sung writes, "Isn't that worth exploring?"

Notes

1 Hand, Martin. *Making Digital Cultures: Access, Interactivity, and Authenticity*. 1st ed. Routledge, 2016. https://doi.org/10.4324/9781315593289.
2 Sassen, Saskia. "Digital Cultures of Use and Their Infrastructures." In *The Sociology of Speed: Digital, Organizational, and Social Temporalities*, 72–85. United Kingdom: Oxford University Press, 2017.
3 Mihailidis, Paul, and Samantha Viotty. "Spreadable Spectacle in Digital Culture: Civic Expression, Fake News, and the Role of Media Literacies in 'Post-Fact' Society." *American Behavioral Scientist* 61, no. 4 (April 2017): 441–54. https://doi.org/10.1177/0002764217701217.
4 Hashmi, Mobina. "Private Publics: New Media and Performances of Pakistani Identity from Party Videos to Cable News." In *Global Digital Cultures: Perspectives from South Asia*, 245–60. University of Minnesota Press, 2019.
5 Hafner, Katie, and John Markoff. *Cyberpunk: Outlaws and Hackers on the Computer Frontier*. New York: Simon & Schuster, 1991. p. 9.
6 Tanni, Valentina, Smetnjak, and Domenico Quaranta. *Eternal September: The Rise of Amateur Culture*. Brescia: Link Editions, 2014.
7 Fischer, Dave. "Longest USENET Thread Ever." *alt.folklore.computers* archive, January 25, 1994. https://groups.google.com/g/alt.folklore.computers/c/wF4CpYbWuuA/m/jS6ZOyJd10sJ.
8 The proceedings are published in Benedikt, Michael, ed. *Cyberspace: First Steps*. MIT Press, 1994.
9 Levi, Ron. "Malicious Life Podcast: Operation Sundevil and the Birth of the EFF." Accessed June 24, 2024. https://www.cybereason.com/blog/malicious-life-podcast-operation-sundevil-and-the-birth-of-the-eff.
10 https://www.eff.org/about.
11 Barlow, John Perry. "A Declaration of the Independence of Cyberspace." *Electronic Frontier Foundation*, January 20, 2016. https://www.eff.org/cyberspace-independence.
12 This notion was furthered by Marc Prensky in his 2001 essay, "Digital Natives, Digital Immigrants" where Prensky used this framework to argue that education was threatened by a digital immigrant class of instructors who refuse to adapt to the new world creeping behind the modems.

50 *Critical Internet Literacies*

13 O'Keefe, Andrew J. "Staying Human in the Machine Age: An Interview with Douglas Rushkoff." *Singularity Hub* (blog), June 17, 2016. https://singularityhub.com/2016/06/17/staying-human-in-the-machine-age-an-interview-with-douglas-rushkoff/.

14 Turkle, Sherry. *Life on the Screen: Identity in the Age of the Internet*. New York: Simon & Schuster, 1995.

15 Jurgenson, Nathan. "Digital Dualism versus Augmented Reality." *Cyborgology* (blog), February 24, 2011. https://thesocietypages.org/cyborgology/2011/02/24/digital-dualism-versus-augmented-reality/.

16 Russell, Legacy. *Glitch Feminism: A Manifesto*. London; New York: Verso, 2020. p. 5.

17 Russell, Legacy. *Glitch Feminism: A Manifesto*. London; New York: Verso, 2020. p. 8.

18 Turkle, Sherry. *Life on the Screen: Identity in the Age of the Internet*. New York: Simon & Schuster, 1995. p. 212.

19 One of those first Black students at MIT was Dr. Shirley A Jackson, the first African American woman to earn a PhD at MIT; Jackson's degree is Theoretical Elementary Particle Physics.

20 Brock Jr., André L. *Distributed Blackness: African American Cybercultures*. Critical Cultural Communication. New York: New York University Press, 2020. pp. 6–7.

21 Giorgis, Hannah. "The Homepage of the Black Internet." *The Atlantic*, April 12, 2024. https://www.theatlantic.com/magazine/archive/2024/05/blackplanet-social-media-history/677839/.

22 Brock Jr., André L. *Distributed Blackness: African American Cybercultures*. Critical Cultural Communication. New York: New York University Press, 2020. p. 18.

23 Beran, Dale. *It Came from Something Awful: How a Toxic Troll Army Accidentally Memed Donald Trump into Office*. First edition. New York: All Points Books, 2019. p. 31.

24 Beran, Dale. *It Came from Something Awful: How a Toxic Troll Army Accidentally Memed Donald Trump into Office*. First edition. New York: All Points Books, 2019. p. 43.

25 https://www.gettyimages.co.uk/detail/news-photo/boys-wearing-guy-fawkes-masks-gesture-and-hold-palestinian-news-photo/1734759025.

26 https://doublesidedmedia.com/2023/10/21/photos-masked-counter-protester-arrested-after-stopping-shooting-at-free-palestine-rally-and-march/.

27 Coleman, E. Gabriella. *Hacker, Hoaxer, Whistleblower, Spy: The Many Faces of Anonymous*. London New York: Verso, 2015.

28 Coleman, E. Gabriella. *Hacker, Hoaxer, Whistleblower, Spy: The Many Faces of Anonymous*. London New York: Verso, 2015. p. 14.

29 Poole, Christopher "moot." "Christopher 'Moot' Poole: The Case for Anonymity Online | TED Talk," February 2010. https://www.ted.com/talks/christopher_moot_poole_the_case_for_anonymity_online.

30 Lorenz, Taylor. *Extremely Online: The Untold Story of Fame, Influence, and Power on the Internet*. New York: Simon & Schuster, 2023. p. 20.

31 boyd, danah. "White Flight in Networked Publics? How Race and Class Shaped American Teen Engagement with MySpace and Facebook." In *Race After the Internet*, 203–22. Routledge, 2011.

32 Janis Krums [@jkrums]. "http://Twitpic.Com/135xa – There's a plane in the Hudson. I'm on the ferry going to pick up the people. Crazy." Tweet. *Twitter*, January 15, 2009. https://x.com/jkrums/status/1121915133.

Critical Perspectives on Digital Cultures 51

33 Reeve, Elspeth. "The Secret Lives of Tumblr Teens." *New Republic*, February 17, 2016. https://newrepublic.com/article/129002/secret-lives-tumblr-teens.

34 Winkie, Luke. "Urban Outfitters Literature." *The Dirtyverse*, March 14, 2023. https://dirt.fyi/article/2023/03/urban-outfitters-literature.

35 Neiwert, David A. *Red Pill, Blue Pill: How to Counteract the Conspiracy Theories That Are Killing Us*. Guilford, Connecticut: Prometheus Books, 2020. p. 7.

36 O'Neil, Luke. "Reporter, Dystopia Beat." Substack newsletter. *Welcome to Hell World* (blog), August 28, 2018. https://luke.substack.com/p/reporter-dystopia-beat.

37 Neiwert, David A. *Red Pill, Blue Pill: How to Counteract the Conspiracy Theories That Are Killing Us*. Guilford, Connecticut: Prometheus Books, 2020. p.149

38 https://soundcloud.com/qanonanonymous

39 Wired Staff. "Why the History of Black Twitter Needed to Be Told." *Wired*. Accessed June 26, 2024. https://www.wired.com/story/gadget-lab-podcast-514/.

40 Brock Jr., André L. *Distributed Blackness: African American Cybercultures*. Critical Cultural Communication. New York: New York University Press, 2020.

41 Gilliard, Chris, and Kishonna Gray. "For Black Folks, Digital Migration Is Nothing New." *Wired*. Accessed June 21, 2024. https://www.wired.com/story/black-twitter-social-media/.

42 Dibbell, Julian. "A Rape in Cyberspace: How an Evil Clown, a Haitian Trickster Spirit, Two Wizards, and a Cast of Dozens Turned a Database Into a Society." Blog Archive. *JulianDibbell*, December 23, 1993. http://www.juliandibbell.com/texts/bungle_vv.html.

43 sung, morgan. "In Defense of the Internet Culture Beat," February 13, 2024. https://www.rat.house/p/in-defense-of-the-internet-culture.

44 Tim Onion [@oneunderscore__]. "Absolutely Nobody Is Taking This Seriously Enough, Especially the People Running the Platforms That Have Created This Sort of Guerrilla Basement Platoon of Empathy-Free Children Who Think School Shootings Are False Flags." Tweet. *Twitter*, January 25, 2019. https://twitter.com/oneunderscore__/status/1088610165862133760.

45 Note the dualism that still factors into the explanation of the web.

46 Maniraho, Karen. "Very Online." *Columbia Journalism Review*, July 19, 2022. https://www.cjr.org/special_report/internet-online-culture.php/.

47 sung, morgan. "In Defense of the Internet Culture Beat," February 13, 2024. https://www.rat.house/p/in-defense-of-the-internet-culture.

48 https://www.threads.net/@taylorlorenz/post/C9F4dtwvBuz?xmt=AQGzMFqiiiks39eHpFhu2uZGVT0ejGy3pC6aPn11PCJLSw.

3 The Creator Economy and the Hyper-Niche

The Beastification of YouTube

In early November 2023, YouTube's biggest star, 25-year-old Jimmy Donaldson, tweeted, "I already know I'm gonna get canceled because I uploaded a video helping people, and to be 100% clear, I don't care. I'm always going to use my channel to help people and try to inspire my audience to do the same" followed by emojis that signaled sweating and love.[1] Earlier that day, Donaldson, best known as MrBeast, uploaded the video "I Built 100 Wells in Africa"[2] and he was already playing defense to his critics. For someone as immensely popular as MrBeast, starting on the defense seems odd, but it's also part of the role he plays within the creator space. Either Donaldson doesn't fully understand why his "kindness" content could be considered exploitative, shameless, and occasionally problematic, or it's part of the reactionary game that must be played in these internet venues. MrBeast is the most subscribed channel on YouTube with over 300 million subscribers and growing, and for a guy who's pretty plain, he's a cultural icon that represents homegrown success earning over $80 million in 2023.

According to *Forbes*, Donaldson likely brings in far more than $80 million. In fact, it's likely nearly a billion dollars a year from advertising, endorsements, and views, most of which he reinvests directly into his projects or philanthropy.[3] Donaldson's tweet is a quandary: while he says he doesn't care, his post shows he's most definitely concerned by the feedback, especially by those critical of his creative approach. For a celebrity of his stature, he's surprisingly sensitive and supposedly genuinely nice, part of the endearing qualities necessary to succeed in the precarious space of independent online creator. On the other hand, MrBeast is an entrepreneur. His company has about 250 employees and his productions are spectacular, some sets cost in the hundreds of thousands of dollars.[4] In 2024, Donaldson was named one of the Time 100 Leadership Series highlights and appeared on the cover of *Time* magazine. His videos use techniques that

DOI: 10.4324/9781003483885-3

The Creator Economy and the Hyper-Niche 53

are not quite television and not quite YouTube, somewhere in the realm of surreal early MTV mixed with reality television and Donaldson plays the vlogger version of Ed Harris's god-like director in the film *The Truman Show*.

"MrBeast videos could best be described as stuff an imaginative 9-year-old boy would try if he had, like, a gazillion dollars. Donaldson crushes expensive cars, gives strangers life-changing amounts of money, holds contests to see who can do a dumb thing the longest," *Time Magazine*'s Belinda Luscombe explains of Donaldson's work.[5] Within that content, MrBeast has also developed an editing technique called "retention editing," which keeps viewers glued to the screen by using "loud sound effects, fast cuts, flashing lights and zero pauses" and other YouTubers who use these frenetic techniques call it the "Beastificaton of YouTube."[6] Donaldson is also obsessive about the YouTube thumbnail, making dozens of variations until he reaches his goal which is to make someone "feel something" like "How did they do that?" or "Is that real?" or "What the fuck?" One of those three makes someone click to watch.

The majority of MrBeast's programming is similar to spectacular television game shows, but reimagined through a Willy Wonka-like lens, like "Ages 1–100 Fight For $500,000"[7] or "Anything You Can Fit In The Circle I'll Pay For"[8] or "Survive 100 Days in a Circle, Win $500,000."[9] In that latter episode, Donaldson invited a fan to live in a house the MrBeast team built in a field for 100 days – all while MrBeast taunts him and eventually tears the house down around the man. Donaldson compresses 100 days to a 17-minute show, and while it contains no commercial breaks, Donaldson reads an ad for Venmo near the end of the video just as a wrecking ball destroys the house.[10] Donaldson tells Luscombe it could be 12,000 hours of footage for a 15-minute clip. (For comparison, this is like a high-end reality show with multiple cameras like *Survivor*.) What was it about his "I Built 100 Wells in Africa" video that made him preemptively defensive?

MrBeast represents more than editing techniques, manipulative advertising, and spectacular programming, he represents creator culture itself, a space that exists in reactionary defiance against "the gatekeepers" of industry, defining itself by *not* being television. In that way, it's remarkably difficult to do public critical work about Jimmy Donaldson. His fandom is not just rabid, they are a digital culture and resemble the fandoms or "stan armies" of the K-pop music group BTS or Taylor Swift's Swifties and criticism of MrBeast often leads to groans or "pile-ons" in the comment sections on Elon Musk's X. Luscombe explains that much of MrBeast's criticism does not come from any of the visual tactics MrBeast employs in his work, but rather from his philanthropy content. In the 2020s, one of the quickest ways to get an enormous number of views is through "kindness" content, where the host films themselves "giving away" something,

54   *Critical Internet Literacies*

Figure 3.1 MrBeast stands alongside his contestant, who watches helplessly as his house is torn down, while MrBeast reads a Venmo advertisement on-screen during the demolition.

but it benefits the host, not the receiver. According to Brad Podray, a former orthodontist-cum-TikTok star who formerly went by the online name Scumbag Dad, the draw for kindness content is the use of reactions to draw in viewers, even if it's done unethically.[11] The online audience enjoys seeing reactions and smiles, even if it's in bad faith.

About a third of MrBeast's content is kindness or philanthropy content. In one video, "1,000 Blind People See for the First Time," MrBeast subsidizes the cost of eye surgery for hundreds of people, converting their disorder into entertainment fodder while missing an opportunity to critique access to Western medical treatment. In addition, MrBeast was criticized for the thumbnail of the video where he is seen wide-eyed, mouth agape, gripping a young boy's shoulder who was seemingly dazed with gauze being lifted over his eyes and smiling into the camera. (The thumbnail was shifted to an elderly man after the controversy.) As Max Read writes for the *New York Times*, the criticism helped MrBeast gain more attention. Read writes,

> To Donaldson's fans, who view the phenomenon through the distortion field of YouTube's incentive structures, this criticism seems basically incomprehensible. Within the world of YouTube, the most "demonic" content is often the most successful, and what makes Donaldson stand out is not that his videos make you feel "icky" (as another streamer put it), but that he puts that ickiness to work.[12]

The Creator Economy and the Hyper-Niche 55

In the *Time* article, Luscombe points out to Donaldson that videos, like the eye surgery video or the wells in Africa video are criticized because it frames Donaldson as the hero rather than tackling the systemic inequalities that enable MrBeast to step in with his philanthropy. In addition, Donaldson seems to have some moral flexibility with where his funds come from as well. According to reporting by Ryan Broderick for *Fast Company*, MrBeast's "We Schooled Hundreds of Teachers" video in April 2024 worked with Charles Koch, whose personal philanthropy has been used to "dismantle public education" in the US.[13] Donaldson defends himself by both explain his attempt to be a better role model for teens and reminding his audience that his charity channel gives away $100,000 a month.

Regardless, MrBeast's fandom seems to strengthen with every criticism, his fans digging into their support; reporting on MrBeast is a chore for many journalists. MrBeast's most viewed video, "$456,000 Squid Game in Real Life!" (with over 625 million views) drew a lot of critical attention because of Donaldson's shallow approach to the reimagining of the Korean horror-thriller series on Netflix. The original *Squid Game* was a disturbing and uncomfortable series about the lengths people would go to pay their financial debts. In the *Squid Game* series, contestants literally fought for their lives in an immersive game set built with tarrying versions of basic children's games where nearly half the contestants die in the first round. MrBeast spent millions recreating the sets and invited 456 contestants to play the same game – without any of the critique on capitalism.

Vice reporter Gita Jackson wrote at the time:

As a feat of production, it's not just admirable, but enviable in how perfectly MrBeast recreated the sets of the show. As a piece of media, it's perverse. This doesn't just badly misunderstand the anti-capitalist message of *Squid Game*, it's a literal recreation of the villain's ultimate desire to watch desperate people compete for money purely for his amusement.[14]

Jackson's tweet was inundated with angry replies by MrBeast fans who complained Jackson misunderstands MrBeast and his content.[15] On the other hand, MrBeast is not a burgeoning creator, he is a veteran of the site and creates content with a YouTube fluency and he's been on YouTube creating since he was a 12-year-old making Minecraft videos. In Donaldson's words, "I can make almost anything go viral."[16] As of the writing of this book, that holds true, but the "creator economy" is fickle. Aside of YouTube, Donaldson also owns a line of chocolate bars and cookies called Feastables, a sports drink line, and a new restaurant chain in New Jersey called MrBeast Burger; Donaldson was number 46 on Fast Company's "World's 50 Most Innovative Companies of 2023."[17]

56 Critical Internet Literacies

From MrBeast's productions to his fandom to his critical reception to his defensive victimhood to his success are all part of a three-decade long evolution of the creator economy, a term coined by the venture capitalists, advertisers, brands, and banks looking for a new way to dynamically invest in multilayer niche media, diversify their campaigns, and build on robust data to prove their return on investment. There are few boundaries for this economic model; if you are willing to commodify yourself as a "brand" on a commodified platform (meaning ad supported), then you may earn the trust of brands who may be interested in collaboration. The more natural and "authentic" the collaboration, the more likely the creator may leverage future profits and brand endorsements and increase their influence and clout.

Goldman Sachs (who primarily funded Facebook before it was publicly traded) has estimated that the current creator economy is valued at $250 billion and will potentially reach half a trillion by 2028.[18] In a study by Oxford Economics in 2022, YouTube's creative ecosystem contributed over $35 billion to the US GDP and supports more than 390K full-time equivalent US jobs.[19] It's no wonder that private equity is interested in this form of entertainment; unlike television or traditional media systems, the consumer data acquired through platform advertising, influencer endorsement deals, or subscriptions are so granular that profit seems inevitable. The downside of course, is the more capitalism adjusts to a new market, the space for safety and play is reduced for the sake of profit. We must also remember the creator economy is also resource intensive, growing exponentially, and all that content needs to be stored, using immense amounts of energy and carbon.

There's evidence of the creator economy evolving into its own industry that works alongside traditional models of media programming. The Nielsen Gauge chart, which keeps track of viewing trends, notes that streaming (38.5%) is catching up to the traditional media distribution points of broadcast (22.5%) and cable (28.3%).[20] From 2023 to 2024, YouTube dominated the top spot on the Gauge chart (9.7%) and according to the *Hollywood Reporter*,[21] this is in due part to ongoing series on YouTube like Sean Evans's *Hot Ones*, Michelle Khare's *Challenge Accepted*, and Ms. Rachel's children's programming; other programs are leveraged by MrBeast's immense popularity among a youth audience. Creators are still resisting the gatekeepers but often want to be recognized as television stars. They may well get their chance, because YouTube – and nearly all video apps – are turning into television, whether they like it or not. Unfortunately, that means the structural hegemony of the past continues to haunt the creator economy present.

By comparison to MrBeast, Michelle Khare runs a YouTube series titled "Challenge Accepted" where she performs stunts and accepts challenges from her fans. While she has nearly 5 million fans, her shows, like her

The Creator Economy and the Hyper-Niche   57

episode "I Tried Houdini's Deadliest Trick,"[22] gained 4.5 million views with production quality that rivals traditional television programs. In May 2024, the *Hollywood Reporter* explained that Khare's productions, like Donaldson's, may take up to a year from conception to production and therefore should be eligible for television awards like the Emmys. Rhett McLaughlin and Link Neal, who host the long running show *Good Mythical Morning* on YouTube, explained to *THR* that they don't consider their work user-generated content, but rather "independent television."[23] YouTube operates as a space for independent television and is celebrated as such, however, unlike television, who may someone like Donaldson or Khare go to when they need to hold someone accountable? Who is their boss? What rights may that have for their employment? And most importantly, what power or role do they have in YouTube's evolution?

While MrBeast, Rhett and Link, and Michelle Khare represent the peak of the creator economy, we need to understand that the techniques developed to produce content in this space date back to the 1990s. The early creators not only developed the grammar but the business model that YouTubers use and TikTok, Twitch, Instagram, and OnlyFans creators inherited. The creator economy is "passion industry," not unlike the "gig industry" of the 2010s and subsists by onboarding new creators and believing in collective support while struggling for individual success. It's a tough environment with odds stacked against the creators. This seems to be of little concern for young people – between 33 percent and 50 percent of young people hope to become creators as a career.[24] Whether they know it or not, creators share a reactionary ideology that comes into play in the content they produce when it comes to their overt defense of their work. In addition, joining the creator economy in the 2020s means they are participating in a structure concretized by three decades of participation.

It is difficult to explain the odds stacked against the average creator if they are interested in becoming as successful as MrBeast. Of the billions of channels on YouTube, there are only a handful of creators making over six figures a year with more than 1 million followers. According to a vast study by Linktree, the social app that enables creators to list their digital properties on one link, of the 4.2 billion users on social media, approximately 200 people million consider themselves "creators."[25] This means that almost 5 percent of all users consider themselves a creator, regardless of model of production or platform. To sustain a career on the internet is extremely precarious and requires an immense amount of labor and platform expertise. Of these millions of creators, there are so many genres and meta-genres, it's impossible to catalog them all. Their externalities range from extreme fandoms to persuasive civic action to fast fashion and consumer waste. To be a creator is to be both independent and part of a large systems operation.

58 *Critical Internet Literacies*

The creator economy is a bustling industry with insiders, managers, agents, and networks of opportunistic business partnerships and affiliations for mutual benefit. Large segments of the creator economy work collaboratively, hoping to increase the following of a new, popular entrant into a genre, or at least are aware of their "colleagues'" career and project endeavors. These connections happen through direct message rather than traditional communication methods, something some news editors must get used to when their journalists are using communication techniques of younger generations. Most importantly, creators are aware of their competition in both the sense of a competitive edge and a chance to share the screen with another creator, hoping to merge their audiences and attract new markets. It is consistent work, requiring full-time labor and upkeep, knowing the other person to hold accountable is themselves.

According to the US Census Bureau, "social media" is not considered one of the 22,607 industries it categorizes.[26] Creators use social media to distribute their content, yet they have no significant way of being recognized for their labor. Even "micro-creators" (meaning those with fewer than 100,000 fans) are making some type of income for their media productions, but that apparently is not enough to qualify the market as a legitimate industry. Even so, the creator economy is alluring for a variety reasons, from creator independence to reactionary expression to the possibility of mass influence. But as culture shifts, so does the model of income and many creators find themselves unable to conform to new algorithmic normalizations. On the other hand, a new platform like OnlyFans, which started to get exclusive content from a creator, is now a creator site that ranges from extra fan material to hardcore pornography. Whereas YouTube shares 55 percent with their creators, OnlyFans shares 80 percent. Sex work *is* labor as well, and the content produced for OnlyFans, whether risqué or not, can be a profit stream.

Further, these creators can also be considered employers like Donaldson. Tech reviewer Marques Brownlee has an office in New Jersey where he employs editors, producers, researchers, and a creative director.[27] Brownlee's work is so well researched, his reviews have changed the way several tech products market their products. For example, in April 2024, Brownlee reviewed the Rabbit R1 artificial intelligence tool calling out the tech industry for "selling a product today based on the promise of features to come in the future."[28] His acuity in the review nearly caused the product to be shelved. In other words, Brownlee, while the influencer on screen, is really part of a team, one that not only entertains an audience but influences the entire tech market. Further, many OnlyFans creators have found that they do not have the time to run their account alone and hire "chatters," people willing to pretend they are the creator talking to their fans.[29] This extension of labor is obviously even lower compensated that the precarious job

The Creator Economy and the Hyper-Niche 59

of creator, but arguably the chatters are part of the creator economy as well. Applying critical internet literacies enables us to look at this industry from other perspectives.

This chapter primarily focuses on YouTube as its origin, growth, and existence are representative of Silicon Valley's overt role in the creator economy and while US use is second to India's, it represents the cultural hegemony of the platform. On the *Forbes* list of top earners on YouTube, nearly all are white men from the United States.[30] (Nastya, a young girl YouTuber, is originally from Russia but her parents moved their family to Texas in 2015; TikToker Khaby Lame is an Italian citizen and migrant from Senagal.) India's T-Series channel continues to grow and over the past decade, both Felix Kjellberg, better known as PewDiePie, and MrBeast have celebrated their subscriber numbers in comparison to the T-Series channel, which is known for music videos, trailers, and spectacular Indian programming. While TikTok and Meta products are part of the creator economy, YouTube continues to represent the space through its corporate maturation and structural incentives and its slow transformation into mainstream media. We need to apply criticism to the online creator economy as we do to television, film, radio, and legacy media, and we need to look *through* internet media to see why it operates the way it does.

Delineating Between Content versus Creator Media

In his 2023 book *The Gutenberg Parenthesis*, Professor Jeff Jarvis argues we shouldn't use the term "content" to describe media, writing, "Content is a passive word, as is audience, for those who consume it. Content is commodity. Now it is no longer scarce. It is abundant, unlimited. Thus, is has lost value."[31] Jarvis's argument is strong because on sites like YouTube, content *is* commodity as the site exists nearly entirely as a commodified space. On the other hand, Nick Srnicek argues this is the basic premise of "platform capitalism," where these sites convert the immaterial of "cultural content, knowledge, affects, and services" into material in the form of data.[32] With that said, content makes up most of the media hosted online, archived, stored, and on-demand, and although very little of it may ever to be seen by more than its necessary audience it is valuable in its own way. The content that rises to the masses is usually algorithmically boosted, amplified by users, or in the extreme minority, part of the creator economy. So how much media is on YouTube?

In 2023, researcher Ryan McGrady and his team at University of Massachusetts, Amherst published a paper estimating that YouTube hosts over 14 billion videos.[33] Due to the opaque nature of YouTube's infrastructure and their lack of data transparency to regulators and researchers, it's very difficult to determine the vast quantity of content on the

60   *Critical Internet Literacies*

site. Typically, YouTube statistics are shared by their press department and released as part of promotional events. McGrady's team used a technique they called "Dialing for Videos"[34] where they randomly generated a code extension that may be a unique video identifier and captured the results if a video existed at the end of the randomized link. (For example, /watch?v=0e3GPea1Tyg is MrBeast's "$456,000 Squid Game In Real Life!") The importance of McGrady's project cannot be understated: YouTube is the second most used search engine, the largest video repository in existence, and could be worth $400 billion.[35] The authors of the paper even concede that YouTube, though incredibly popular, is a "critically understudied platform."

YouTube and the variety of other video hosting sites (DailyMotion, Vimeo, Rumble, SproutVideo) and apps like TikTok, Instagram, and Facebook contain millions more pieces of content that are not part of the creator economy's market. At its core, YouTube is a video repository and the advertising models that overlay the platform enable it to scale its technology and infrastructure – to say little of their profit-sharing model. To delineate, we recognize nearly all the content within the creator economy are produced intentionally, leaning into platform's creator network, collaborating with other influencers, and managing to fall into the recommendation algorithm system that serves users with new videos. The rest of the content falls into what Ryan McGrady and his team calls "Deep YouTube," which includes most of the content that is not uplifted by the algorithm.

> So much of YouTube is effectively dark matter. Videos with 10,000 or more views account for nearly 94 percent of the site's traffic overall but less than 4 percent of total uploads. Just under 5 percent of videos have no views at all, nearly three-quarters have no comments, and even more have no likes. Popularity is almost entirely algorithmic: We found little correlation between subscribers and views, reflecting how YouTube recommendations, and not subscriptions, are the primary drivers of traffic on the site. In other words, people tend to watch just a sliver of what YouTube has to offer, and, on the whole, they follow what the algorithm serves to them.[36]

McGrady's study helps us set up the framework in which we will delineate what's included in the creator economy from raw content, though both deserve critique and analysis. McGrady also expresses a similar interest central to the core of this project: "Changing the language we use to talk about YouTube allows a discussion based on its real place in the world." McGrady recommends that we talk about the use of YouTube as institutional, knowing that the uploaders themselves have a variety of intentions

The Creator Economy and the Hyper-Niche   61

when putting their work online. Each of the methods have long lineages of development, new entrants to the space have different goals, all while brands and advertisers struggle not only to keep up but figure out who to trust and how to manage their investments.

Early Foundations of the Creator Economy

In 1995, interactive producer Scott Zakarin developed a project for AOL called *The Spot,* a dramatized version of an AOL chat room in the form of television; sort of a *Melrose Place* (1990s standard soap opera) meets MTV's *Real World.* At the time, chat rooms were a dominant example of digital culture: real-time communication with groups of people from anywhere based in thematic rooms. Zakarin was enamored and excited by the existence of these communities and like someone whose worked in an office or restaurant too long, believed the setting would make great alternative television. *The Spot*'s story is documented in John Geirland and Eva Sonesh-Kedar's 1999 *Digital Babylon: How the Geeks, the Suits, and the Ponytails tried to bring Hollywood to the Internet.* Geirland, a journalist, and Sonesh-Kedar, a venture capitalist, put the book together to tell a story of new possibilities.

Digital Babylon is one of the very few texts documenting the new environment and the book's plot signifies the extent of the exclusivity in this creator space. Their book, like many texts of that period, celebrates Zakarin's attempt with little or no critique of the structures, though they do introduce the three pillars of the mid-1990s creator economy: the geeks, the suits, and the ponytails. The geeks were the programmers like Marc Andreesen, founder of Netscape (and someone with great influence today), the suits were the venture capitalists, and the ponytails were the creatives. While ponytails may be gendered in the feminine, here it refers to men – likely white men – who wore their hair long in the 90s.

In a similar story, the eccentric[37] computer analyst Josh Harris was directly responsible for launching some of the more risqué chat rooms on Prodigy, AOL's primary competitor. Harris was well ahead of his time and founded the metrics company Jupiter Communications in 1986. In 1993, he founded Pseudo.com, one of the first streaming media channels. Documented in Ondi Timoner's 2008 documentary *We Live in Public*, the story follows Harris through his foundation of Psuedo and his projects "Quiet" and "We Live in Public" – both are extremely voyeuristic experiments that abuse the participants; Harris believed he was creating a physical version of the internet. Harris self-funded these latter projects through his earnings from the sale of Jupiter Communications, but Pseudo, at its peak, was a multichannel streaming website with 10 channels and produced 60 programs produced a week.

62 Critical Internet Literacies

Instead of a platform product, Zakarin and Harris shared the same libertarian mindset and created their projects with a reactionary rhetorical flare. AOL had funded Zakarin's *The Spot* because internet executives believed the web would topple traditional media hegemony. Harris was so adamant the internet was the future that he threatened Bob Simon of CBS's *60 Minutes*.[38] When Simon asks Harris his goals toward the end of the piece, Harris responds emotionally, "I'm in a race to take CBS out of business. That's my focus. That's what my bankers are telling me to do. The race is on. We're in the hunt."[39] A skeptical Simon plays the role of the general public's reaction to internet-born projects at the time. Bob Simon's eyebrows raise, but he's clearly aware Pseudo didn't have the infrastructure to compete with CBS. His skepticism turns to cynicism as Simon ends the segment telling the audience Pseudo just had to lay off many of its staff.

Notably missing from these early tales of internet video content is the contribution by Black creators. In 1995, the same year as the launch of Zakarin's *The Spot*, AOL signed Farai Chideya, the founder of one of the earliest blogs, PopandPolitics.com, to produce content for AOL's site. Chideya tells her story in Charlton McIlwain's 2020 *Black Software: The Internet and Racial Justice, from the AfroNet to Black Lives Matter.* Chideya recognized that AOL was a walled garden – "an internet within the internet" – and Chideya converted her blog to make weekly videos for NetNoir, AOL's "first on-line service devoted exclusively to Afrocentric material."[40] Representation mattered as the internet of the 1990s lacked diversity. McIlwain explains that sites like NetNoir worked because Black people "could connect with people whom they never had the opportunity to otherwise" and AOL was at least attempting to make investments in projects like Chideya's.[41]

NetNoir established a liberal approach to content creation and allowed users to curse and respond more openly than any of the extant competitors and NetNoir allowed participants more flexibility with their expression, a lesson Twitter benefit from in the late aughts as Black Twitter thrived on its social networking site. There were other attempts at developing spaces of Black expression like CompuServe's GoAfro, but GoAfro failed because it was too strict. Users wanted to meet each other and connect in ways that were not as possible in real life but resembled "real life." Digital cultures may develop on commodified platforms, but they need room to grow organically and set their own rules.

Broadcast Yourself

In the late 1990s, a group of Silicon Valley technologists and investors, led by Peter Theil, developed the banking product PayPal. When it went public

The Creator Economy and the Hyper-Niche 63

in 2002, the 19 founders, nicknamed the "PayPal Mafia" (which included Elon Musk), walked away with hundreds of millions of dollars. Three of the PayPal founders – Jawid Karim, Steven Chen, and Chad Hurley – had an idea for a "video site." On February 13, 2005, Karim sent an email to the other two locking in their idea and sharing some concerns. The email stated:

> I just talked to both of you on the phone. I'm 100% convinced that this can be HUGE if executed right. It's the kind of thing that will be picked up by MTV and Maxim right away. Timing is perfect because video digital cameras are exploding right now. Our site should be video-only to emphasize the unique aspect of our site.[42]

Karim's biggest concern was "web server scalability," especially in the case of success. The following day, the URL YouTube.com was purchased. On April 23, 2005, the trio uploaded the first video to the new site featuring Jawed Karim at the zoo (titled "Me at the Zoo"). He spends 19 seconds telling us about the zoo and the elephant's trunk, ending the video with the line that defines the space to this day: "And that's pretty much all there is to say."[43] The video is a perfect video origin story for YouTube: it would be a place to share nothing and everything.

At first, the site was unprofitable and the uploads to the site resembled all other platforms as people posted their pets, family tapes, copyrighted footage from television shows, music videos, and miscellaneous content. But two things differed: the founders wanted to create a community and prioritized guidelines with limits on what could be uploaded, and they also encouraged users to comment on videos. The onboarding was so slow at first that by November 2005, the site was giving away free 4GB iPod Nanos every day to bolster its use.[44] By the following year, the founders found themselves under a copyright lawsuit from Viacom as many of the earliest viral clips were from television shows. The success of the site attracted Google and even though Google had the resources to build their own video site by 2006 (they already had Google Videos), Google made an offer to buy YouTube for $1.65 billion and acquired it in October 2006. Google wasn't buying YouTube's technology; it was purchasing the userbase.

In 2006, *Time Magazine* declared the person of the year to be "You" (Yes, You) which included a shiny, mirror-like surface set inside a computer screen on its cover.[45] At the time, it was a novel step in the direction of web 2.0 innovations (MySpace was popular, and Facebook had just opened up to the public) and YouTube was not only centralizing the video experience online, but uplifting common video creators into the digital space. The section on YouTube, written by author Lev Grossman, considered the concept of YouTube and web 2.0 a revolution that fought back

64　*Critical Internet Literacies*

against the "Great Man" theory of history, acknowledging the populism of the web. Grossman may have been overly utopian:

> This is an opportunity to build a new kind of international understanding, not politician to politician, great man to great man, but citizen to citizen, person to person. It's a chance for people to look at a computer screen and really, genuinely wonder who's out there looking back at them.

Written before the launch of YouTube's recommendation algorithm, monetization features, or intrusion by bad actors attempting to grift off vulnerable users, Grossman's point was more utopian than history would allow. While the philosophy is correct as people uploaded content that spoke to no one and everyone all at once, YouTube needed to profit, and would do so by any means possible.

The advent of the video blogger, or vlogger, was revolutionary in many ways. For one, the vlogger emerges during the explosion of reality television programming. Reality TV is inauthentic documentary production, relying on layers of manipulation to present "reality" to a mainstream audience by uplifting the common person to celebrity through directed plots. The vlogger is a reaction to this shift in traditional media, presenting a more unvarnished and amateur presentation of self to extremely niche audiences. The vlogger also didn't exist in a world of contracts, their work is longitudinal. Whereas viral video and television programming drove conversation, vlogs are part of a long-term media project that in turn developed its own video grammar, methods of audience engagement, and viewer retention. The vlogger set the stage for almost all the current popular genres on TikTok and Instagram Reels and has created long-term success for hundreds of people who were otherwise unlikely to be visible media personalities. The vlogger is an opportunity for visibility to those truly excluded from the hegemony of media preference in the mainstream, enabling voices from LGBTQ+, Black, Brown, and less-abled communities to express themselves publicly through a mediated format.

On the other hand, when we consume vlogs or influencer videos, we often disregard the labor that goes into the development of each upload. There is prep, planning, video acquisition, post-production, uploading, marketing work, and sharing that goes unaccounted. However, as time goes on, the vlogger develops their own production methods, and these tools are unique to this type of media production. There was a low bar to entry to start vlogging and many early creators spoke directly to their web cameras. Before the ubiquity of cell phones, onboard editing software, and accessible wifi, the practice of the vlogger was a hobby of passion.

The Creator Economy and the Hyper-Niche   65

This said, any criticism of early YouTube should acknowledge the privilege of access, both in terms of connectivity and technology. Until 2014, a fair amount of retrospective work on early YouTubers would illuminate white vloggers and uncritically speak about their success without mentioning their privilege. (Even on the list of the top viral videos from 2006, only Tay Zonday's "Chocolate Rain" (a song about racial inequality) is representative of a Black person – the rest are white people, cartoons, and animals.)

The Rise of the Internet Personality

The concept of the vlogger and internet personality was not born on YouTube. The proliferation of small video cameras and computer-based editing software emerged in the late 1990s, though was far from accessible to the public. In 2000, a man named Adam Kontras posted his video diaries of a cross-country trip to his website 4tvs.com.[46] He spoke directly to the camera with no clear audience in mind. There's an unconfirmed digital legend that claims there were 17,000 YouTubes before YouTube, likely an expression for just how many places someone could upload clips to the web.[47] The vlogger became a style, a format, and an aesthetic for personalized storytelling. When YouTube launched, it centralized the space of web video and provided a host for content, with less fear of maintaining a server or file format issues.

In the early years, vloggers were disconnected and disparate, lacking community, but YouTube was a new tool. Here we'll focus on two creators that started in 2007, Tyler Oakley and Franchesca Ramsey. Tyler Oakley recorded a video diary note to his friends and uploaded it to YouTube a month into his freshman year at Michigan State University in October 2007. "Raindrops," Tyler's seventh video, begins with over 20 seconds of Oakley wiggling his nose and making faces in his dorm room before starting to speak:

> So today was the first day of school that it rained on my way to classes and I woke up to the thunderstorm and at first I was like "oh fuck". But then I actually went out in the rain and walked to class. It was... I liked it a lot.

Oakley mastered the vlogger style early on and used a mix of linguistic tricks with visual aesthetics like jumpcuts, music underlay, staged settings, and direct eye contact with the audience. Most important is Oakley's awareness of the viewer, almost as though he's edited the video to show how he's contemplating what to say next – remember, the vlogger *is* the director. It is all intentional. These are internet power dynamics.

Figure 3.2 Tyler Oakley in his college dorm room making faces on his early video "Raindrops" (2007).

At the time Oakley was uploading his videos, human curators were in charge of picking videos out of deluge of uploads and uplifting them onto the front page. Tyler's sixth video – now private – was one of them. Though he was speaking to his friends, the curators must have enjoyed his style. "Raindrops" is the first video Oakley made for both his friends and a new, unseen public that visited YouTube. In "Raindrops" we are introduced to Tyler Oakley the YouTuber, a performative version of himself aware of the community that exists on the site. There were no instructions on how to be a vlogger, it was an act of imitation: a mix of television skills and earnest attempts of candid expression to an audience where either no one or everyone may be listening.

That same year, Franchesca Ramsey also joined YouTube and used the site to create "how to" hairstyle videos for Black women with dreadlocks. Her account, chescaleigh, was a mix of hairstyle content and vlogging material. Ramsey grew in popularity with her audience through her positive and sarcastic approach to storytelling, her animated facial expressions, and her tutorials for Black women with natural hair. As a young Black woman online, she broke ground as a representative for a traditionally marginalized audience. Ramsey also benefited from a curator putting one of her videos on the site's front page, leveraging her into the creator space.

The Creator Economy and the Hyper-Niche 67

Ramsey's videos also unintentionally revealed some of the technical limitations of YouTube's platform. If you watch her early content, you can see that YouTube lacked proper encoding for people with dark skin. Even in low resolution and high compression, Tyler Oakley appears clearer than Franchesca Ramsey that same year.

In contrast to Tyler Oakley, Franchesca Ramsey dealt with issues of cyberbullying and hatred. In 2008, Ramsey won an internet contest and was chosen to do a red-carpet appearance for *People Magazine*. The attention brought in even more followers and Ramsey split her channel into two outlets: chescaleigh for vlogging content and chescalocs for natural hair content. Along with attention came a white supremacist stalker who used her comments section like a hate board. While YouTube was still figuring out its trust and safety measures, marginalized creators were often at a disadvantage on social media platforms. Her stalker was banned repeatedly but returned over and over to spread hate speech on her channel leaving Ramsey with no defense aside from a strong community of supporters and the block function.[48] That was... until she was valuable. In 2012, Ramsey produced a satire video "Shit White Girls Say... to Black Girls" which went viral during the heyday of viral media. Her value to the platform increased and more attention was paid to her safety.[49]

Both Tyler Oakley and Franchesca Ramsey represent early entrants into this space and though their aesthetics differed, they showed that authentic approaches were useful to platform success, but each vlogger's measure of "success" often differed wildly. The internet personality was a model that enabled thousands of other people to join, from the elderly users like Peter Oakley (unrelated to Tyler), geriatric1927, to young people like Brooke Brodack, known as Brookers. As Jean Burgess and Joshua Green write in their 2009 *YouTube: Online Video and Participatory Culture*, YouTube isn't *just* a video site, it is a community center and functions "as both a 'top-down' platform for the distribution of popular culture and a 'bottom-up' platform for vernacular creativity."[50] In addition, vlogging was an act of public intimacy and helped bring personal issues to a wider audience. As creators on YouTube reacted to the newfound power of having an audience, and soon grew a fandom, they developed an aesthetic that set their work apart from the traditional media apparatus. Their aesthetics and creator choices became a toolbox for future creators. What they didn't talk about very often was their precarity, a place to work with no boss means there's only one person to hold accountable for your trajectory.

The Foundational Video Codes of Creator Content

John Fiske writes in *Television Culture* that television audiences find meaning in their television programming by connecting to it culturally. He explains, visual "codes are links between producers, texts, and audiences,

68 *Critical Internet Literacies*

and are the agents of intertextuality" through which the media connects to meaning through culture.[51] Television is encoded through an ideological lens while also being a window to its representation of reality. Fiske acknowledged that reality itself was already culturally encoded, therefore television media relied on a general interpretation of reality since the mediums, like radio and film, were mass media. Fiske laid out a framework for the analysis of television by reverse engineering the codes, from their acquisition to their content delivery to the audience.

On the other hand, the internet is a cumulative technology that contains content unburdened by the need of pleasing a general audience, often produced in reaction to other media. Therefore, the visual codes of internet media are not guided by the semiotics of mainstream culture, though still derived from them structurally. While it still (for now) relies on the basic rules of visual media for a two-dimensional environment, web media's presentation of representation and ideology is fairly unique. At the most basic level, internet personalities shifted authority, breaking the fourth wall, and making direct eye contact with the audience. Vloggers leaned into this personal approach, adding a layer of self-effacing delivery, managing to present themselves as the authority while simultaneously making the viewer feel empowered. Though the direct address is normalized today, it continues to challenge the concept of authority and expertise.

Linguistic traits were also developed and now contain platform-specific slang and delivery nuance. There is a specific voice trick that many YouTubers use to connect with the audience called the "schwa." Linguistic professor Naomi Baron explained to Julie Beck of *The Atlantic* in 2015 that the schwa is the sound of an overstressed vowel that makes a "euh" sound.[52] Along with the schwa, vloggers would overstress consonants and sneak extra syllables into their sentences. The sound can be heard if you ask a someone to do "the YouTube voice" and you hear the sing-songy "*Hey Guys*" with the dull "euh" sound and longer "s" at it drags out longer than it should. This trick is an audio meme, a replicable tactic for engaging with users even when they're not watching directly. As ears do not blink, YouTubers and online video producers prioritize tricking the ear before working with the visuals.

Visually, vloggers understood that the background of their recording mattered and told some of the story unexpressed in words. Many viewers watch content with subtitles on and occasionally without audio. The setting (like the dorm room in Tyler's early videos to his bright large room and couch in more recent years) tells much of the story as well. We feel a sort of connection to the creator by seeing their environment. In Tom Ford's 2016 essay "The American Room," Ford inadvertently reveals the privilege that many creators benefit from: the suburban setting.[53] Perhaps boring, suburbanite walls, painted beige or grey, help the creator accentuate themselves

The Creator Economy and the Hyper-Niche   69

in contrast to their background. Ford writes, "all of their frolic is bounded by a set of conventions that are essentially invisible yet define our national physical and technological architecture. Their dancing, talking bodies are the only non-standardized things in the videos."

Hand gestures and over the top facial expressions also help deliver the content because the size of the screen is much smaller than that of the television. Music plays a significant role in burying edits and motivating cues at the beginning or the end of a video or for setting the stage for affective shifts in emotion. Finally, the most important tactic of the digital creator is the jumpcut. Used in television to manipulate edits, it's rarely seen openly in traditional settings and often covered by b-roll footage. Jumpcuts are standard in online media, providing YouTubers with the ability to compress time and eliminate mistakes, but have evolved in pace and jumpcuts are now used in a technique called "retention editing." Retention editing is when edits are rapid, shots are digitally pushed in for extreme closeups, whip-pans added for no reason, and the creator leans into accentuated moments with sound effects. These techniques and aesthetics are storytelling tools for this new environment. Just as the codes of television assist in storytelling (closeups for serious moments, wide shots for establishment, etc.), internet media developed its own codes for a small screen in its environment. While internet content may repurpose traditional media into digital spaces, it often doesn't translate the other way around.

Web Television and the Mis-Adventures of an Awkward Black Girl

Aside from vloggers, numerous creators utilized YouTube as their production outlet for more polished products that resembled traditional television. Like Zakarin's series from the mid-1990s, many creators wanted to bypass the gatekeepers of television and share their pieces directly to an audience without the burden of network notes and reconstruction for advertisers. Between 2007 and 2012, webseries and webisodes were a dominant feature of the creator economy. These series had a variety of economic models, from fundraising to personal bank accounts, but each were passion projects. Though the internet was a "democratic" space for creation, uplift tended to favor those biased by traditional media. Young white people dominated the webseries space: from *We Need Girlfriends* (2006–2007) to *Chad Vader: Day Shift Manager* (2006–2012) to *The Guild* (2007–2013), the endearingly awkward character was in demand as alternative television programming on the web.

In 2008, *New York Times* reporter Stephanie Rosenbloom interviewed the creators of *We Need Girlfriends* who expressed their desire to create an "anti-*Entourage*" (at the time, a popular program on HBO) and the trio pushed back against the "alpha males" of traditional media.[54]

70 Critical Internet Literacies

The article was titled "The Beta Males' Charms," uncritically discussing the nerdy, geeky guy who can succeed online. During the 2007 Writers' Guild strike, many creators used the web as a creative loophole. Joss Whedon, popular from the beloved series *Buffy the Vampire Slayer*, called in favors and produced a three-part multi-genre webseries with Neil Patrick Harris, Nathan Fillion, and Felicia Day called *Dr. Horrible's Sing-a-long Blog*. The musical-scifi-comedy-drama series uses all the "beta male" tricks of the vlogger and webseries, but with a very professional approach. Harris's Dr. Horrible is an endearing antagonist, framed as though he is the hero. (The final two seconds of the series reveal the truth.)

There were creators from marginalized communities producing web television as well, but the marketing systems that operated YouTube unfortunately resembled traditional and legacy media. YouTube uplifted what it deemed could be profitable. In 2011, around the time webseries were considered a sort of rite of passage for creators (especially in Los Angeles), then 26-year-old Issa Rae upload her series *The Mis-Adventures of Awkward Black Girl* to YouTube– soon just called *Awkward Black Girl*. Aymar Christian writes in *Open TV: Innovation beyond Hollywood and the Rise of Web Television*, "Awkward Black Girl's first episode is a delicate balancing act between universal and specific black women's experiences," where she encounters awkward moments successively, something that's not typically displayed in mainstream Black media. Christian continues, "Whereas legacy TV representations of Black women are constrained, the indie TV market features a breadth of representations of Black women, each differently tied to black feminist politics, across genres."[55]

Issa Rae represents another success model of the creator economy, one where the creator leverages their independent media to mainstream success. Issa Rae's *Awkward Black Girl* had a huge retention rate for her series, and she adapted the storylines into a book. From there, her show was adapted into the hit HBO series *Insecure* (2016–2021). Though the beta males of early webseries left their mark on the alternate media field, it was Issa Rae who became the anti-*Entourage* success story. These scenarios are representative of web television's plight – thousands of webseries were created, but only a few made their way to the mainstream. But if that was the creator's goal, they were unaware that the systems had not changed, the systems were duplicated on the internet.

The Soft Power of the Influencer

Vloggers are typically aware that they must use some parasocial tactics in their productions, leaning into audience capture, where they make content *for* their audience, recognizing the intimacy and faux proximity of their viewers. The audience capture also enabled viewers to believe that had

The Creator Economy and the Hyper-Niche   71

some control over the ongoing content made by their creator. Using these tactics, many vloggers expressed their vulnerable selves to the camera, more than they may have in person. For example, Tyler Oakley came out to his parents in high school as gay, but retold the story on his YouTube channel in 2008, acknowledging the difficulty of the decision and empowering others to embrace their Pride. In Chris Rojek's 2015 book *Presumed Intimacy*, Rojek explains that the development of parasocial connections occurred in early television settings, but today "it is too limiting to confine parasocial interactions to the relationships between media personalities and spectators." The medium itself has turned people into "screen presences with whom emotional relationships are built and developed in spite of the absence of physical co-presence."[56]

The benefit of these relationships develops into long-term attachment to your audience which provides statistical evidence of influence. Advertisers and brands are keen to notice this trait and have leaned into endorsement models that support creators as their emotional connection sells products to their followers. One of the most impactful forms of building parasocial relationships is through intimate storytelling models like makeup artistry or Get Ready With Me vlogs. These pieces show an influencer as "bare" and "real" as possible and invite the audience to watch them get ready and put on their makeup showing them their "vulnerable" state and uses manipulative video tactics to convert themselves from vulnerable to confident over the course of the video. Makeup artistry videos are also entry points for new creators and are successful due to their process-video and DIY styling.

On the other hand, there are only a handful of educational institutions that teach how to produce online media, create vlogging content, and how to manage audiences and comments. The self-taught mantra of YouTube and TikTok occasionally leads to abuse. For example, Colleen Ballinger, better known as Miranda Sings, used her influence to exploit her younger fans, some as young as 12 years old. In 2023, some of her former fans accused her of toxic and inappropriate sexual comments from when they were young.[57] Parasocial relationships could also develop the audience into a space of toxicity as well, as seen in the form of MrBeast's fans (or even Elon Musk's), where they feel such a deep connection they may act in irrational defense of their favorite star. Tyler Oakley witnessed his parasocial power in 2013 when he attended a One Direction concert and was shocked to discover that his fans overlapped the One Direction fandom; while he was in the audience the entire Staples Center started chanting his name before the show.[58]

As commodification became a primary motivator, parasocial relationships became part of the internet influencer toolbox. Along with the aesthetic choices creators use in their content, they also leverage their peer

72 Critical Internet Literacies

influence to attract brands and marketers. In 2014, Bethany Mota, one of the earliest makeup artistry YouTubers, leveraged her strong fandom to collaborate with the clothing company Aeropostale, creating one of the first brand partnerships. She was just 19 years old at the time and outside of YouTube was barely known. By the end of the year she was the most searched-for designer – more searched than Kate Spade or Oscar de la Renta.[59]

This trust was noticed not just by brands but by political figures and would result in a shift in political strategy. In 2013, President Obama developed an internet strategy team, composed mainly of popular YouTubers, to help him figure out strategies to promote the Affordable Care Act (known as "Obamacare").[60] The team was made up of 15 personalities including Oakley, Hannah Hart, Michael Stevens of VSauce, and the Fine Bros. Notably, the only non-white person was Iman Crosson, better known as Alphacat, who became famous as an Obama impersonator. The team inspired Obama to be a guest on Zack Galifianakis's *Between Two Ferns*, part of Will Ferrell's Funny Or Die web channel.[61] Obama crossed into the digital realm and promoted the ACA as the straight man to Galifianakis's ludicrous personality. The strategy worked: the episode increased visits to Healthcare.gov by 40 percent.[62]

Multichannel Networks: A Missed Opportunity

In 2014, *Variety* hired a firm to poll young people on their recognition of celebrities and found that of the top 20, the first five were YouTubers: Smosh, The Fine Bros, PewDiePie, KSI, and Ryan Higa, followed by Paul Walker and Jennifer Lawrence.[63] But this just shows the *most famous* and most recognizable of the creators – what about the tens of thousands of other popular, but not famous, producers? How do brands diversify their investments among lesser known but still wildly popular creators? YouTube is far too diffuse for a brand to work at a granular level and creators, along with their management and brand liaisons, came up with a solution known as "multichannel networks," or MCNs. These networks would band together thousands of channels to assist brands with their marketing, but also to uplift creators though profit-sharing incentives.

MCNs were sort of a collective inside the YouTube architecture, giving creators rights within the platform that verged on bargaining agreements. As YouTube and all other web platforms are structured on their libertarian philosophies, MCNs functioned as a content management system for brands rather than for establishing unions for the independent producer to benefit from; creators were proud of their (collective) independence.

The Creator Economy and the Hyper-Niche 73

Many early reports about MCNs come directly from strategists and banks, noting their early interest as a source of streamlined revenue. If creators can shift culture and move markets, a collection of channels would be much more valuable. The multinational accounting and auditing firm PricewaterhouseCoopers wrote at the time:

> Content on these networks is noticeably different from that on conventional video or YouTube channels. Although talent and shows are frequently organized in verticals or genres similar to those of cable networks – including news, comedy, and lifestyle verticals for cooking, beauty, music, gaming, and the like – the execution of the content differs in story selection, talent, voice, production style, and length. The tone, voice, and production all emphasize an unfiltered "authenticity" that is specially designed to appeal to a millennial or even younger-skewing demographic, as can be seen through the videos of MCN-based YouTube stars like teenage fashion sensation Bethany Mota, video-game critic PewDiePie, and Truth Mashup, an online comedy show.[64]

The firm notes that even "edgy" or controversial content produce value. Here is early evidence that engagement matters far more than safety (discussed further in later chapters).

The biggest MCNs were Vevo (which hosted music videos), Zefr, Fullscreen, and Maker Studios. These were mini corporations inside of YouTube and helped uplift smaller creators to work alongside larger creators. For example, Maker Studios relied on PewDiePie's success to scaffold the "trickle-down" incentives of the networks. MCNs *required* creators to create, regardless of time management for solo producers, and MCNs became content farms that guaranteed brands the outlet for endorsement material. These ecosystems were ripe for capitalist opportunism and in that same year, Disney launched an effort to acquire Maker Studios and spent nearly a billion dollars on the deal. As Brooke Barnes writes for the *New York Times*:

> the deal is about distribution and programming expertise. Maker manages roughly 55,000 YouTube channels, most of which provide a pipeline to young consumers for Disney's characters and franchises. Disney is also counting on Maker to help it learn how to best interact with the raised-on-the-Web generation.[65]

This micro-industry was framed as an economic model within the structure. Unfortunately, the stress of creation combined with the need to be seen created a model of one-upmanship against the platform itself.

74 *Critical Internet Literacies*

"If you do it right you get to quit the day job"

If there were to be a place to pinpoint the beginning of the current creator economy, it would likely be in early 2017 when Casey Neistat uploaded his call-to-action anthem "Do What You Can't." Neistat, who had been vlogging since 2010 and making activist videos, switched to daily vlogging in 2015, promising to make one video a day until he couldn't any longer. In just a few years, Casey was positioned as the gravitational center of the late-2010s creator market thanks to his transparency and interviews with creators. Casey's story, like Jimmy Donaldson's, is a story of creator success: persistence, patience, and production eventually lead to recognition. In 2017, YouTubers were a known value for marketers and brands, and many companies and agencies started investing in their specific online star, encouraging them to push back against the structural hegemony of television, disguising their advertising in embedded plugs and native programming styles. The main way the creator economy could operate wasn't just onboarding new creators but explaining the value of the industry.

Casey's call to action begins with him dangling off a rope ladder connected to a helicopter flying over the Hollywood sign. The monologue starts: "To the haters. The doubters. My seventh-grade vice-principal. To everyone who's ever told anyone with a dream: 'they can't.' This video is for you." The video cuts to his previous remarks, now scribbled on a mirror as Casey hits it with a bat as the techno-beat ("Carte Postale" by Sløve) drops. This nearly four-minute 2017 pump-up video "Do What You Can't" is stylized as an autobiography of Neistat but reframed as an optimistic collab video.[66] Upbeat music, rapid edits, and examples of influencers doing influential things (like Liza Koshy interviewing President Obama) set the tone, but the campaign here is to promote a sustained feeling of opportunity through the lens of a reactionary mindset:

> You don't need gear, you don't need trucks or a crane, you don't need some big expensive camera rig that never works. When you're a Creator you don't need someone in your ear telling you what you can and can't do, what you can and can't say."

According to Casey, all you need is your phone, an internet connection, and an idea. "Do What You Can't" features 39 YouTube creators, ranging from some of the earliest recognizable vloggers (Grace Helbig, Philip Defranco) to some of the more recent popular influencers from the Faze Clan to Mislav Mironovic. The featured talent are diverse, but represent only the most elite of the recognizable YouTuber class. And while the video includes Quentin Kenihan, the disability activist YouTuber who sadly passed away a year later, it still reinforces the unspoken perpetuation of

The Creator Economy and the Hyper-Niche   75

traditional media tactics of exclusivity. Missing from Casey's examples are any creators that function within the reactionary creator economy that also support YouTube's success. By 2017, many controversial heterodox creators also embraced a similar mistrust of traditional media and had similar competitive followings, though they often veered to the border of harm. Casey's overall message champions a similar mindset: join us to be liberated from traditional hegemonic rules through the freedom of the creator economy where you can live "a life moving so fast and so full, you won't even have time to process it."

"Do What You Can't" feels like YouTube propaganda: the ideological stance of making content seems to be the ability to resist that nebulous "someone" always telling you what you can and can't do, encouraging *you* to be the boss. But pay attention to the way the video is produced because it's sly in its messaging and rhetoric, designed to do many things at once. In a high-end video, you may find the creator (the brand) representing the platform (the brand) while spreading the message of the sponsor(s) (the brand(s)) combined with the message, the reference(s), the presentation style, the aesthetic, and the rhetoric. Depending on how niche the influencer, there may be multitudes of layers.

Casey Neistat has developed a knack for telling stories with multitudes, from crashing his bike repeatedly to share a civic message to the city of New York[67] to developing exposés about the tertiary markets of the tech industry.[68] Casey represents a perfect model for the creator economy and has finetuned his videos to circumvent the average consumer who may be enamored by his charisma and content quality over the advertising messages. He's been courted by brands for nearly his entire career (including for a similar commercial for Nike's short-lived Fuelband[69]). The "Do What You Can't" video is a bit more insidious than his previous work: while this is a promotional video for Casey (the brand) and YouTube (the brand), this time it's just a commercial for the sponsor (the brand), and in this case, it's Samsung. Unless you notice the Samsung products (shown twice) or wait until the credits, the ad is indistinguishable from a Casey Neistat hype video.

Samsung's "Do What You Can't" campaign used Casey Neistat for their YouTube version to make an ad in the model of what scholar Mara Einstein calls "black ops advertising," so well disguised that it's hard to distinguish between what is and *what isn't* advertising.[70] Neistat's script is intentionally vague, similar to the "The Old Spice Guy" commercials produced years earlier, and Neistat states exciting platitudes that directly speak to the aspiring creator. The multiyear "Do What You Can't" campaign was developed by Leo Burnett, one of the oldest ad agencies in the US, the agency displaying its agility with present-day marketing.[71] Each iteration of the ad campaign was designed in the aesthetic for each distribution

76   *Critical Internet Literacies*

platform. Neistat's version was two-fold: one for YouTube (which allowed curses, crude hand gestures, and reactionary rhetoric) and the other debuted the night of the Oscars in 2017 (Casey was dressed in the same tuxedo). The campaign extended to several television spots each featuring regular people that defied the odds. Neistat's willingness to make a viral collab video promoting YouTube's most insidious features – the embedded branded content – was a sign that the modern creator economy would not only be an economic profit model, but also structuralize into its own version of legacy media and production.

Algorithmic Normalization

Today, we're often focused on the ways in which artificial intelligence is trained through its large language models and machine learning. YouTube's algorithm that runs the recommendation system is based on what their engineers describe as a neural network, a massive machine learning structure with a primary goal of making the YouTube experience better for users. However, as a learning model, it normalizes content rapidly in its training. This means that if a YouTuber does something provocative and gains a lot of views in a viral moment, the algorithm sees that as the new upper limit of what is acceptable on the platform as well as what can be suggested in a feed. This means that creators often normalize their levels of "extreme" behavior. The term extreme is a paradox. Extreme acts are no longer extreme once normalized, therefore, extremism is in a constant state of becoming *more* extreme. Unfortunately, this results in terrible consequences for creators in the creator space.

While PewDiePie and Logan Paul stand out for their extreme antics, this issue extends to far-right provocateurs and children's content. Both PewDiePie and Logan Paul produced content so controversial the mainstream news had no choice but to talk about it. Felix Kjellberg, the Swedish "Let's Play" creator better known as PewDiePie, leaned into more extreme content to attract fans and increase followers. After he surpassed 50 million subscribers in 2017, he became one of the most popular creators in the world. Oddly, PewDiePie seemed to love using his channel to complain about the platform in which his career existed; to Kjellberg, the site was far too punitive and restricted his more risqué content and he accused the platform of restricting his content because he "was white."[72] His reactionary stance was due in part to the rising growth of social media movements and an increased discussion around equality as well as the ongoing and yet unexplained demonetization known as the "adpocalypse" that was going on in the background of the YouTube platform.

Kjellberg's reactionary mindset attracted new users, but probably not the ones that he was interested in and this resulted in a shift in his content

The Creator Economy and the Hyper-Niche   77

strategy. He found that disaffected young men would engage more often than passive viewers and leaned into their desires and his content slowly became more extreme. Kjellberg occasionally made content outside his genre and leaned into prank content that scored views. In one very notorious moment, Kjellberg hired gig workers on the platform Fiverr and asked them to hold a sign that said "Death to all Jews" – which they did. PewDiePie thought this was hilarious. Disney did not. Maker Studios soon dropped him from their MCN which in turn enabled him to repurpose his victimhood stance.

Logan and Jake Paul, who had migrated from Vine, were professionals at creating content on the extremes. Their short-form formats translated well to risqué content, and each gained their own respective fan bases. Logan Paul's "LoGang" were rabid followers of the creator, ceaselessly defending him and his crude antics. While PewDiePie's engagement with racist and antisemitic tactics marked a new low for mainstream YouTubers, Logan Paul made things worse. In his video "We found a dead body in the Japanese Suicide Forest" (now deleted), he shows exactly that. Wearing a green Pokémon beanie and traveling with friends, he shows the victim in the trees and says, "This marks a moment in YouTube history." His video was immediately admonished by the mainstream, excoriating the platform as an irresponsible space for children to inhabit. (They weren't completely wrong, but as we'll discuss, it's more complicated.) The event displayed a unique quirk about YouTube's role in the cumulative reactionary space: Logan Paul *gained* followers after his horrendous video.

As Vicky Osterweil writes in *Real Life Mag*:

> The Logan Paul incident has brought a spotlight to YouTube's negligence, but we should also be using it to shine a light on the fan armies YouTubers are amassing. While controversy occasionally leads YouTube to partially demonetize channels, YouTubers almost always continue to grow their subscriber base despite this.[73]

Osterweil writes about the way YouTubers, without the guardrails of regulation or advertising models, can repurpose the techniques media creators have honed over a century, now mixed with techniques of the vlogger including parasocial tactics and algorithmic amplification. Osterweil continues, "Around every popular piece of cultural production fan sites, conventions, wikis and other infrastructure bloom, reflecting an attempt to wring as much happiness and meaning as possible from what limited sources of pleasure our planet-destroying, inequality-magnifying capitalist culture provides."

YouTube, like other social media, is in a constant struggle against regulations, hoping to keep the governments of the world off their sovereign

78   *Critical Internet Literacies*

structures. On the other hand, advertisers are not interested in sharing their products on spaces where malicious content may be streamed, so advertising often seems like the only regulatory body. YouTube's response aided the advertisers, not the creators, and they began what would be called the adpocalypse, a multiyear shift in the rules of monetization for creators. Creating content that crossed the line into inappropriate harm would result in demonetization or inability to monetize a channel before outright removal. However, YouTube seemed to have different rules for different YouTube personalities. The authoritarian monetization rules hurt hundreds of other creators of lesser stature who mimicked Kjellberg's and Paul's tactics to increase their following after it was normalized by the entire system. The adpocalypse resulted not in a course correction for content creation, but rather a feeling of disenfranchisement. Many shifted rightward and fell down rabbit holes. The adpocalypse didn't affect users who hadn't monetized or weren't allowed to anyway because they'd already crossed the line. Some creators were self-funded or sold merch to compensate, knowing they could still use YouTube as a broadcast outlet, even if they couldn't profit-share.

The Populism Playbook

Donald Trump and populist leaders around the globe, like Marine LePen, Neandra Modi, and Jair Bolsonaro, promoted a form of new media populism that could also succeed in the highest levels of government. As a result, this led to a cottage industry of influencers who represented a form of personality that connected with their audience in similar ways to these leaders: as an avatar of their emotions. Trump's team used internet media to leverage his popularity which was also a boon to television ratings, as Trump's unpredictable ramblings and occasionally bigoted messaging created seemingly never-ending news cycles. Online, young, cynical white men who felt that the world was shifting away from their control, created content that represented a Trump-like ideology of victimhood and martyrs of media representation. These victim grifters were creators who felt the internet was the only place they could express themselves without getting in trouble. Mainstream media was far too restrictive for their heterodox views (which is a coded way of saying they were disallowed from saying bigoted or racist remarks in other spaces).

White nationalists, like Carl Benjamin, Stefan Molyneux, Brittany Sellner, and Mike Enoch, were welcome along with more conventional conservative influencers like Ben Shapiro, Jordan Peterson, and Steven Crowder. Young white supremacist firebrands like Nick Fuentes also took advantage of the reactive model that was growing online and in politics. The populist right leaned on these creators to spread their message to the

The Creator Economy and the Hyper-Niche   79

digital masses and many developed deep parasocial relationships with their fans. Far-right creators entered the space using the same tools developed by the original YouTubers. The rise of the media martyrdom ideology ("I got in trouble for saying *this* on television") mixed with the YouTuber mantra ("no one can tell you what you can and can't say") and the aesthetic grammar, resulted in a benefit for platforms. Far-right reactionaries were controversial, and their agitation resulted in engagement that increased profit for the platforms and their notoriety so they could sell merch or branded supplements.

Bad actors on these platforms engaged in tactics that encoded bigoted messaging and hate speech in meme-like trolling. Users, journalists, and reporters with low internet literacies would accidently amplify some of these messages and uplift them into the mainstream. (We will dissect several of these cases in Chapter 5.) Take creator Josh Feuerstein for example. Feuerstein is an online personality and, according to Colby Itkowitz for the *Washington Post*, Feuerstein is a self-described "disciple of Jesus."[74] In fall 2015, a Starbucks non-controversy became a funnel for attention and Feuerstein became a populist leader in response to the "politically correct culture" that was harming the spirit of Christmas. Starbucks' holiday red cups did not have the printed "Merry Christmas" on them and were accused of removing the text to appease secular audiences and support "PC culture." In truth, Starbucks never featured the text but did formerly include Christmas imagery. Feuerstein asked his followers to go to Starbucks and tell the barista your name is Merry Christmas and then take a selfie with the cup. Feuerstein's actions could amount to trolling, but his charismatic delivery encoded his call to action in creator grammar. Interestingly, Feuerstein did not call for a boycott of Starbucks, but rather to buy *more* Starbucks using his trolling technique. This is a form of attraction within the creator economy.

The goal of the populist YouTuber was to garner support for their cause and to enhance their brand persona. Speaking as if they are the spokesperson for the fictional "silent majority," they achieve brand awareness through their consistent messaging and willingness to go above and beyond the act of simply recording their message. If you mix the YouTube Playbook method with populist rhetoric and include agitation, you can see a new model of activism rapidly evolving. In the run-up to Donald Trump's presidency, these online personas were seen as the authentic voices, not burdened by the bias of mainstream media, untainted by corporate interests, and free to speak their minds.

As a result, you can see the truly dangerous aspects of this formula in YouTubers like Lauren Southern, the Canadian YouTuber who had become a self-funded warrior against migration, working alongside nationalists and "identarians" in Europe. Her goal was to "expose" the inadequacy

80　*Critical Internet Literacies*

of the local governments she feels are not protecting the citizens from an influx of migrants. In Ryan Broderick's 2017 *Buzzfeed* piece "Far-Right Activists Are Stealing Tricks From YouTubers And It's Going To Get People Hurt," he writes "A small group of far-right activists have figured out how to manipulate the media with viral stunts – and it's getting more and more dangerous." Southern was a Canadian political activist who became a provocateur and joined Rebel Media, a far-right media outlet and started calling herself a journalist. Her YouTube channel quickly gained attention as she leaned into her heteronormative and stereotypical looks as a young blond woman willing to express alt-right concepts to a more mainstream audience.

Southern had malleable beliefs, leaning often into the most reactive spaces, especially those with the best rewards of views and financial support. It would not be hard to describe Southern as acting in bad faith in many of her productions. Bad faith, as described by Lewis R. Gordon in his 2022 *Fear of Black Consciousness*, is an act of sincerity and belief. Gordon writes, "The concept of bad faith involves the ability to lie to oneself. Lying is something one does, which means it belongs to the agent who lies."[75] Southern's moral ambiguity and thirst for fame led her to believe her own narrative, even when it harmed others, and sell it authentically to her audience. She gained further attention by leaning into extreme acts of nationalist rage in the style of YouTube programming. Broderick writes, "Her videos are slick. The one about her time in Italy is titled 'HAVE I LOST MY MIND?' and it opens with 20 seconds of her riding around a boat full of flares with dubstep playing in the background." Southern's video shows her attempt to stop a migrant ship from docking in Italy in the name of anti-immigration. Broderick continues:

> Since then, she's adopted that playbook for her stunts on the road – show up with a camera, antagonize people, build it up on social media as a live event that her fans can follow at home, and then release a summary of the whole thing on YouTube the next day.

At the outset of this video, Southern interviews her guest Martin Sellner, one of the leaders of Austrias ultranationalist Identarian Movement, and explains that she's been accused of burning a migrant child.[76] While she did not burn a child, the fact she even defends herself against this horror means she has made some interesting life choices. The video is compelling, and the techniques are there – she's charismatic, smiling, and speaks in the bubbly sing-songy voice of "traditional" YouTubers. She just happens to be speaking about her populist agenda of preventing migration. Amplified by her desire to agitate on location, Southern's tricks are derived from the YouTubers who established themselves on the medium, but her desire to

The Creator Economy and the Hyper-Niche 81

increase the intensity is what makes her iconic. Southern obfuscates her definitions, trying not to relate to anything mainstream or traditional. She rearranges her references to attempt at authenticity solely available online. Southern, like YouTubers before her, was a medium for the ideology, laundering hate speech through YouTube to vulnerable viewers.

In 2019, *New York Times* reporter Kevin Roose profiled a young man named Caleb Cain in a long-form piece titled "The Making of a YouTube Radical" and revealed some of the YouTube rabbit holes that led him to becoming radicalized into far-right ideologies.[77] At 26 years old, Cain emerged from the radicalization of the alt-right which he believed started on YouTube. The far-right ecosystem acted as a funhouse mirror to the origins of standard YouTube media; the existence of far-right media and ability to provide immense amounts of engagement resulted in a slow takeover of the YouTube recommendation system, though safety was not a primary concern since the sector brought in immense amounts of profit. Cain provided Roose with his entire YouTube viewing history and something odd emerged – his suggestions that autoplayed in the "Up Next" feature were slowly getting more and more dangerous.

Cain admits that he was curious of some pseudo-intellectual content online and was unaware that some far-right creators embedded their hate speech in knowledge content. Cain specifically mentions consuming Stefan Molyneux, who described himself as an "anarcho-capitalist" but was very clearly a white supremacist. Molyneux's content managed to escape YouTube's terms of service policies by posing as help for young, disaffected men to make sense of the world. Cain tells Roose: "He was willing to address young men's issues directly, in a way I'd never heard before." This model will be copied by Jordan Peterson and Andrew Tate in years to come. Molyneux's content automatically shifted Cain's algorithm through its content inclusions. In other words, the fact Cain consumes Molyneux means that everything within bounds of Molyneux's ideologies is now part of Cain's feed. This included Lauren Southern, Paul Joseph Watson, Steven Crowder, and Carl Benjamin. All of whom preyed on vulnerable men like Caleb Cain.

However, Roose's article, and those like it, seemed to let the bad actors of YouTube off the hook. Roose, like Tristan Harris (whom we'll discuss in later chapters), blamed the technology and the platform. As we'll soon discuss, YouTube's black box architecture is partly to blame, but in this case, the system is gamed by a network of creators who launder radical ideologies into mainstream feeds through the illusion of intellectual debate. In Becca Lewis's extensive report for Data and Society, Lewis writes:

> An assortment of scholars, media pundits, and internet celebrities are using YouTube to promote a range of political positions, from mainstream

82   *Critical Internet Literacies*

versions of libertarianism and conservatism, all the way to overt white nationalism. While many of their views differ significantly, they all share a fundamental contempt for progressive politics – specifically for contemporary social justice movements. For this reason, I consider their collective position "reactionary," as it is defined by its opposition to visions of social progress. United in this standpoint, these YouTubers frequently collaborate with and appear with others across ideological lines. Together, they have created a fully functioning media system that I call the Alternative Influence Network (AIN).[78]

It's sometimes too easy to blame the algorithm rather than the platform or the network. The vast array of far-right creators made critiquing their genre difficult – it was far easier to blame YouTube's machine than the culture that surrounded it or the difficulties that Caleb Cain faced that made these spaces attractive for users like himself.

Lewis's work continues to stand out as a corrective for these simplistic answers. The alternative influencer network is the utopian dream of early scholars like Jenkins that proposed a community of support to uplift thoughts and civic ideologies into the mainstream. In retrospect, we can see that the libertarian mindset that established much of the web's structure and content made this political uplift obvious. The pickup artists of the early 2000s to the trolls on 4chan to the "new atheists" of early YouTube weren't outliers, they were the structure itself – and they were doing well. It took several years for YouTube to adjust their trust and safety and establish what harms many white supremacists were doing to young viewers. Unfortunately, much of YouTube's actions were reactionary as well and inspired new platforms like Rumble, Odysee, and Elon Musk's desire to host video on X. The creator economy was in for its biggest shift yet in 2020.

TikTok Invents a New Creator

The rise of TikTok is both part of the evolution of the creator economy and the audience's desire for new modalities of storytelling and media consumption. TikTok is a vertical-first medium, aiding the vlogger in ways that were unimaginable years ago. In fact, back in 2012, there were outright calls to ban creators from making vertical content, including cute tongue-in-cheek specials like the "Glove and Boots" puppet PSA titled *Vertical Video Syndrome*.[79] The vlogger always had to contend with the extra space on the screen and felt the background must be occupied by visual cues. TikTok and by extension, Instagram Reels focus on the subject in its 9x16 format. In addition, TikTok's structure is perfect for creators as it comes with onboard, easy-to-use tools for video editing. With the addition

The Creator Economy and the Hyper-Niche 83

of CapCut, also owned by ByteDance, TikTok's parent company, editing that used to take hours on a desktop can now be done with thumbs on a phone screen.

TikTok is both the remote control and the television. Thumb flicks shift the content from one piece to the next, inundating the consumer with an endless scroll of media. Standing out in that regard is tough because all content becomes passive in this environment. However, unlike YouTube, TikTok *does* exist as an algorithmic culture. In 2019, Jia Tolentino writes for the *New Yorker*:

> TikTok is a social network that has nothing to do with one's social network. It doesn't ask you to tell it who you know – in the future according to ByteDance, "large-scale AI models" will determine our "personalized information flows," as the web site for the company's research lab declares.[80]

Algorithms are written by humans, and therefore, the bias of the humans gets embedded in the code; this includes racial and gender bias. New influencers rapidly appeared on TikTok, many of whom are younger women who "gamed" the algorithm – intentionally or not.

As Kyle Chayka writes in his 2024 book *Filterworld*:

> The TikTok influencer Charli D'Amelio became famous in 2019 for her dance videos on the platform. But one of the moves she popularized and was often credited with, called the Renegade, was actually created earlier by Jalaiah Harmon, a Black teenager from Georgia. The Renegade was a series of front-facing movements perfect for the TikTok screen, with swinging punches and hip shakes – not too difficult a sequence, but also tough to memorize and thus rewarding to re-perform.

As a creator factory and memetic space, TikTok is a space for expression that feels truly new. There are new visual codes that the creators leaned into that differ from YouTube, drawing media language into a derivative state away from traditional media entirely. It's not just about repeating a style, it's about advancing upon the aesthetic, creating something derivative, but still tied to its original. While YouTube would reference the content, TikTok references the structure.

New creators are aware of their platform nativity – a TikTok video is clearly a TikTok video by its video grammar. In this grammar, creators aware of layering, pointing at the negative space *while* they are recording. If you were to see a TikTok creator recording in a mall, for example, they may be pointing upward at nothing, but they are aware of a future graphic they would be adding later. Further, TikTok grammar includes CapCut transitions, making it easy to jumpcut across temporal moments, changing clothes in an instant or shifting locations. One of the most interesting aspects of TikTok grammar is the shift in jumpcut style: originally exposed, cut after cut, TikTok grammar takes advantage of the "punch-in," cutting closer or further during a jumpcut, as if using closeups as text. Italics, bold, and serious affect may be achieved mid-sentence with a well-timed digital punch-in.

Most new creators also use subtitles in their videos, allowing the AI to transcribe their voice, followed by a textual edit. TikTok knows that "time spent" on the app is valuable and many consumers watch silently, possibly under desks or behind seat cushions in the house. Subtitles are now part of video grammar. This is an optimistic turn of events considering an interest in accessibility and multimodal production, but we should be critical of the system that moderates this text algorithmically, and at scale. The text on the screen is part of the clip and TikTok's moderation system reads it, often delisting videos that border on its version of harm and many users have converted their text using "algospeak," a way of miswriting that dodges content moderation. (This is covered more specifically in Chapter 7.)

Figure 3.3 A TikTok user pointing upward at an onscreen caption that exists on the app, but not when recording.

The Creator Economy and the Hyper-Niche   85

In all, it's important to understand that creators like Alix Earle, Charlie D'Amelio, and Jacob Sartorius are TikTok fluent. Their content isn't part of the algorithm – it *is* the algorithm. As YouTube normalizes over time based on community interest, TikTok absorbs and reproduces trends, working side by side with the marketers, leaning into commodification first, creativity second. What rises to the top is likely what is most transferrable in a memetic sense: easily repeatable, remixable, and able to connect to its referential origins. TikTok's time limit is also a creative part of its success and marketers can feel more comfortable with digital collaborations than YouTube as it feels more like a traditional media commercial, but in the style of influencer content. As of the writing of this book, a bill has been signed to ban TikTok from the US with fears that its Chinese owner is using US data nefariously. On the other hand, TikTok may be a threat due to its different algorithm, one that is not dictated fully by Silicon Valley's ideology.

The TikTokification of Everyday Life

In early February 2020, memes started appearing in Italy about a virus that wasn't going away. As a form of coping, these memes poked fun at the coronavirus rather than its severity and seriousness. Covid-19 would enter the US weeks later and in March 2020, the stay-at-home period began. Rapidly, people (aside from the "essential workers") were expected to shift their careers indoors and online, students were expected to turn on their web cameras and let their teachers into their bedrooms via digital Zoom windows, and the webinar and virtual event market exploded. Everyone became a creator very rapidly. It was the stay-at-home period and the following explosion of niche creators and brand deals that concretized our creator economy.

The first 15 years of YouTube helped us identify YouTube as a place where genres were born and some were perfected. With TikTok's rise in 2019 and 2020, genres took on an entirely new form, adding the suffix Tok to nearly every type of niche. Some of the #Tok content was as simple as transient memes and some, like #BookTok, could help authors sell books and creators become valuable sources of reviews. Internet culture intertwined with the creator economy during the Covid-19 pandemic and became more than an aspirational field for a career, but a space for expression and documentation. Pandemic-related viewing increased, doubling for young people.[81] Influencers and creators atomized, developing content for everything. These hyper-niche pieces of content were dubbed #cores or "Everyday Life" content. Core content is derived from Tumblr and presumes its own aesthetics while Everyday Life is pretty much exactly what it sounds like but comes with its own visual and scripted grammar.

86   *Critical Internet Literacies*

One of the stickiest aesthetics of the stay-at-home era was called "cottagecore," a style of content that mimicked fairy tales and living alone in the woods. For the first time in a long time, FOMO was reduced while anxiety was at all-time high. Cottagecore, and other genres like Get Ready With Me, rose to prominence as ways of coping with the shifts in culture and these hyper-niche genres were easy access points for new creators. As Rebecca Jennings writes in *Vox*:

> cottagecore is just one of an ever-expanding universe of hyper-specific aesthetics proliferating online: There is meadowcore (cottagecore but just the meadows), frogcore (cottagecore but just the frogs), goblincore (cottagecore but with mud and foraged mushrooms and gender-neutral clothing), and dozens of others even the most online young people have probably never heard of.[82]

Cores were so niche that they created their own fashion aesthetics that were designed to attract fast fashion brands.

From a critical perspective, the externalities of the cores may include an abuse of the fast fashion industry, pushing companies like Zara, Forever 21, and Brandy Melville to make clothing that relies on trends. The fast fashion industry is already a trillion-dollar industry and with TikTok's turn toward a more commercial type of site, there is an expectation that audiences would want to participate in the trends as well. As we'll cover in Chapter 7, a rise in shopping at Sephora by young girls is a result of a participatory media environment that encourages people not only to try the new styles but show them off. Fast fashion now relies on social media creators to participate in their clothing trends, and through the rise of even cheaper fast fashion enterprises like Shein, creators should be concerned with the incredible waste and damage fast fashion has on the environment. With inexpensive clothing, easy-to-use techniques, and accessible mobile editing tools, the genres of modern creator economy, Get Ready With Me and Everyday Life, are continuing to rise in popularity.

Everyday Life content has been around for as long as video cameras, but in the TikTok era, this content requires a low amount of media skills. Add the quick evolution of TikTok grammar from Vine, Musically, Snapchat, and you have a modernized visual language that is easy to replicate. The most accessible genre is Get Ready With Me, or GRWM. A mix of makeup artistry or Outfit Of The Day (OOTD) tutorial-like videos while the creator speaks about a given topic. This format requires lighting, a cell phone on a stand, and framing; the editing is linear as makeup goes on in order and so does the story. The marketing opportunity is obvious as brands are aware of the opportunity to put their makeup products front and center. Second, young girls and young women may feel encouraged to participate

The Creator Economy and the Hyper-Niche 87

in the genre as well. In many ways, GRWM uses the same self-effacing technique early vloggers used, but in this case it's visual. It shows the most vulnerable side of the creator to the audience as they make themselves more confident on screen.

There are grammatical rules for GRWM and Everyday Life content. It isn't just about applying makeup; it's about sharing a story or talking about a subject *while* putting on makeup. The bareness removes any performative vulnerabilities and makes them visible. Everyday Life content may contain GRWM in its formatting. Transitions can be quicker in Everyday Life content and some creators literally jump upward on camera, switching clothing on the edit. Further, there is typically a shot of feet walking with either a tilt upward to the destination or a direct cut to the location. While Get Ready With Me is the viewer watching the subject, Everyday Life is from the perspective of the creator. We see the world through the creator's eyes, only recognizing them when we see them in a mirror or stabilizing their camera to show off their outfit. Regardless of the views, the purpose, or the desire to post this type of content online, there is labor involved, specifically labor that goes uncompensated for the majority of creators.

Influencer Creep

We've reached a point where even the least likely creators can join in these genres. With the rise of bad actors expressing "authority," bad faith "debaters" attracting views, and disinformation and misinformation flowing from exciting orators on digital screens, the actual experts like journalists, academics, and scientists are joining the platforms. As Brooke Erin Duffy writes in *Salon*:

> For those gainfully employed, the quest for social media visibility likely has a different impetus, namely claim-staking in our expert domains. Both misinformation and disinformation are rampant online, and declining trust in public institutions is both a symptom and consequence of this din. Expert-influencers – particularly in the realms of medicine, science, and health – are thus important arbiters within decentralized knowledge networks... But crucially, academic researchers and scientists who "put themselves out there" are – much like influencers – ready-made targets for criticism, hate, and harassment.[83]

Duffy notes that Twitter, once a bastion of communication for scholars and journalists, has become a zone of antagonism following Musk's takeover. The precarity and danger for women, people of color, and LGBTQ+ folks increase along with visibility in these spaces.

88 *Critical Internet Literacies*

In 2020, molecular biologist and educator Dr. Raven Baxter used Tik-Tok to remix Megan Thee Stallions "Body," remixing it with the words to explain how antibodies operate. Baxter, who goes by Dr. Raven the Science Maven, titled the track the "Antibodyody Antibody Song," replacing the Megan Thee Stallion's lyrics with "Antibodies, IgM, IgA, IgM, IgE, IgG, IgE" to the beat of the music while pointing out the symbols.[84] Baxter went viral, even gaining applause from Megan Thee Stallion herself. As she completed her graduate studies, Baxter leaned into the creator space, making sure she was sharing factual information about science while also attracting brands. She's done several ads with companies that aren't just science based. On the other hand, as a Black scientist, Dr. Baxter has faced incredible amounts of hatred on Elon Musk's X and has persevered with persistence and care.

Sophie Bishop argues that careers like artist, academic, writer, and journalist rely on the art, pedagogy, scholarship, writing, and research rather than visualizing themselves as a creator, but as the neoliberalization marketplace extends its pressure, these careers are ripe for "influencer creep." Bishop writes:

> If the phrase "mission creep" describes how a campaign's objectives gradually expand until they entail unanticipated and boundless commitment, we might likewise call the expansion of micro-celebrity practice "influencer creep," both for how influencing creeps into more forms of work and for how it creeps further into the lives of workers. The mark of influencer creep is the on-edge feeling that you have not done enough for social media platforms: that you can be more on trend, more authentic, more responsive – always more. It lodges in the back of your mind: film more, post more, respond more, share more. And as with mission creep, there is no apparent way out.[85]

Once you start your creator brand, it becomes quite difficult to extricate yourself from the enterprise. In other words, the labor of the creator economy joins the labor of the work already underway: you make art and you create videos; you write and you create content; you report and you explain it on TikTok.

One of the most prominent examples is journalist Taylor Lorenz. Not only was Lorenz a tech journalist at the *Washington Post*, but she also runs a podcast, several meme channels, and a YouTube channel with explainer videos. Lorenz is fully aware of her role as creator in respect to her journalism career, but now must create media in multiple ways. For Lorenz, this is a boon to her reporting as she has first-hand immersive insights into the precarity and labor of the creator economy she reports on. On the other hand, being part of that digital community opens her up to bad faith criticism that otherwise may have been redirected or ignored. There is an urge to react and engage with users if you are the expert in your field and you may have the knowledge and context to correct the discourse, but you must keep in mind that this form of labor *is* labor and is usually in addition to the labor of your career. Keep an objective distance and be aware that creating online media in the creator economy is an act of courage and resilience and comes with rewards as much as drawbacks.

Changing Minds Through the Creator Economy

This chapter concludes with optimism. While the creator economy is built upon a history of inequity, making its present existence exploitive and occasionally problematic, there are strong examples of positivity. For example, there are YouTubers in Northeast India creating content that helps lower the racism they face in their country. India is YouTube's largest user market at nearly half a billion users, and by extension, contains millions more creators than anywhere else. India, like most countries, suffers from inequalities and racial disparities, especially within its economic classes and regional disparities. According to the *Times of India*, the people of Northeast India, made up of eight states, are often discriminated against "because they don't look Indian enough" and they are usually ignored by mainstream media and Bollywood.[86] This lack of attention results in the perpetuation of harms to these people, many of which are part of Indigenous tribes. YouTube can change all that, and Apollos Kent, who runs "Kents Vlog" on YouTube, wants to show the rest of India and the world what the Naga people eat and how they live.

Apollos Kent is a YouTube creator using the genre "mukbang" to share his culture. Mukbang, a video genre that originated in South Korea from the words "eating" and "broadcast," is another easy access point for creators – if you are willing to eat food on camera. Mukbang is an incredibly popular genre on YouTube and creators fulfill an interesting role online, not only acting a strange version of a food review, but a way to provide "satiation" of eating and "sharing food with other people."[87] Mukbang creators usually just eat, occasionally talking to the camera about some subject, similar to a GRWM or MUA video. Many people actually enjoy watching people eat and put mukbang videos on while they are eating, simulating a community experience. While mukbang may sound strange, creator culture is understanding your audience's desire to feel connection, and food is one of the most important ways of sharing culture and community. Apollos Kent tells Tora Agarwala of *Rest of World* that he participates in mukbang because he wants to "showcase a unique food culture, often stereotyped as 'smelly' or 'stinky.'"[88,89]

90 *Critical Internet Literacies*

"[Kent] cooks the snails on a campfire with indigenous ingredients including ghost peppers and mustard greens. Then, he eats the dish with noisy slurps, licking his fingers with relish, and grunting in appreciation," Agarwala writes. Kent's channel has nearly 1 million followers and his video "Catch snail cook with maize and eat in naga style" has nearly 4 million views.[90] In India, food has been used to discriminate against Northeast Indians and according to Agarwala, "Landlords in the bigger Indian cities often do not rent out homes to people from the region because of the 'stinky' food they cook." Agarwala interviewed several other mukbang producers, all of whom were proud to use the genre to introduce people to the local Indigenous cuisine including meals like honkerü marü, a chutney dish with fermented mustard leaves, garlic, chilies, and tomatoes. The creators make the food and then eat using the video grammar of the style. Kent explains that his biggest issue isn't the video production, but the signal access to upload content. Some of the other creators travel miles to charge their devices.

Argawala's piece concludes with the reality creators face on YouTube: the trolls and the commenters. Fighting racism and discrimination through YouTube comes with reactionary critics. Regardless, Kent continues producing content and now has over 270 videos and the channel and his collected views have paid him enough to buy a refrigerator, a bike, and a car. Kent is a farmer but access to YouTube and his audience can turn his hobby into extra income. He's not living a life "so fast and so full" he won't have time to think about it and he's not going to quit the day job, but Kent is part of the creator economy. He has become accustomed to his labor on top of his labor, but if he was going to cook anyway, why not use his content to break down barriers and fight discrimination as well.

Notes

1 MrBeast [@MrBeast]. Tweet. *Twitter*, November 4, 2023. https://twitter.com/MrBeast/status/1720840900283163032.
2 *I Built 100 Wells In Africa*, 2023. https://www.youtube.com/watch?v=mwKJfNYwvm8.
3 Bertoni, Steven. "Top Creators 2023." *Forbes*, September 26, 2023. https://www.forbes.com/sites/stevenbertoni/2023/09/26/top-creators-2023/.
4 Biino, Marta. "Former Staffers of MrBeast Explain What It's like to Work for the Top YouTuber, from Crashing Trains to Go-Karting in Japan." *Business Insider*. Accessed June 27, 2024. https://www.businessinsider.com/whats-it-like-to-work-for-mrbeast-biggest-youtuber-world-2023-11.
5 Luscombe, Belinda. "In the Belly of MrBeast." *Time*, February 15, 2024. https://time.com/collection/time100-leadership-series/6693255/mrbeast-interview/.
6 Lorenz, Taylor. "The 'Beastification of YouTube' May Be Coming to an End." *Washington Post*, March 31, 2024. https://www.washingtonpost.com/technology/2024/03/30/video-editing-mrbeast-retention/.
7 *Ages 1 – 100 Decide Who Wins $250,000*, 2024. https://www.youtube.com/watch?v=l-nMKJ5J3Uc.

The Creator Economy and the Hyper-Niche   91

8 *Anything You Can Fit In The Circle I'll Pay For*, 2020. https://www.youtube.com/watch?v=yXWw0_UfSFg.

9 *Survive 100 Days In Circle, Win $500,000*, 2022. https://www.youtube.com/watch?v=gHzuabZUd6c.

10 Donaldson usually edits the commercials out after the initial run and some ads are only visible on MrBeast reaction channels. You can see the ad on xQc's video at the 16:51 mark. *Survive 100 Days In Circle, Win $500,000 | xQc Reacts to MrBeast*, 2022. https://youtu.be/OIsmWfNwFZk?si=xwD5-FdRj7i COGmU&t=1005.

11 *Scumbag Dad Takes on MrBeast, xQc & SSSniperWolf*, 2023. https://www.youtube.com/watch?v=hIg4voQE8Aw.

12 Read, Max. "How MrBeast Became the Willy Wonka of YouTube ." *New York Times Magazine*, June 12, 2023. https://www.nytimes.com/2023/06/12/magazine/mrbeast-youtube.html?utm_source=pocket_shared.

13 Broderick, Ryan. "MrBeast Took Money from a Koch-Linked Organization for a YouTube Video (Exclusive)." *Fast Company*, June 7, 2024. https://www.fastcompany.com/91135719/mrbeast-charles-koch-youtube.

14 Jackson, Gita. "Mr. Beast's Squid Game Ripoff Is Exactly the Kind of Video YouTube Rewards." *Vice*, November 29, 2021. https://www.vice.com/en/article/v7dd7j/mr-beasts-squid-game-ripoff-is-exactly-the-kind-of-video-youtube-rewards.

15 Jackson, Gita. "Tina Snow Aegyo on X: 'the "Creator Economy" Is about Reacting, Not Creation Https://T.Co/yIU4zKbgnr' / X." *X* (formerly *Twitter*), November 29, 2021. https://twitter.com/xoxogossipgita/status/14653 72534531108866.

16 Luscombe, Belinda. "In the Belly of MrBeast." *Time*, February 15, 2024. https://time.com/collection/time100-leadership-series/6693255/mrbeast-interview/.

17 Morrone, Megan. "How MrBeast Keeps Winning Fans – and Burger and Chocolate Sales." *Fast Company*, March 2, 2023. https://www.fastcompany.com/90850306/mrbeast-youtube-tiktok-fans-burger-chocolate-sales.

18 "The Creator Economy Could Approach Half-a-Trillion Dollars by 2027." *Goldman Sachs*, April 26, 2024. https://www.goldmansachs.com/intelligence/pages/the-creator-economy-could-approach-half-a-trillion-dollars-by-2027.html.

19 Galloway, Hamilton, and Alice Gambarin. "The State of the Creator Economy – Assessing the Economic, Cultural, and Educational Impact of YouTube in the US in 2022," May 16, 2023. https://www.oxfordeconomics.com/resource/youtube-us/.

20 https://www.nielsen.com/data-center/the-gauge/.

21 Weprin, Alex. "YouTube's Secret Weapon to Win the TV Streaming Wars: Its Top Creators." *Hollywood Reporter*, May 10, 2024. https://www.hollywoodreporter.com/business/business-news/youtubes-secret-weapon-top-creators-1235894945/.

22 *I Tried Houdini's Deadliest Trick*, 2024. https://www.youtube.com/watch?v=0UdXsm9gJ-s.

23 Weprin, Alex. "YouTube's Secret Weapon to Win the TV Streaming Wars: Its Top Creators." *Hollywood Reporter* (blog), May 10, 2024. https://www.hollywoodreporter.com/business/business-news/youtubes-secret-weapon-top-creators-1235894945/.

24 Mayer, Beth Ann. "So, Your Kid Wants to Be an Influencer? Before You Roll Your Eyes – Read This." *Parents*, October 10, 2023. https://www.parents.com/gen-z-wants-to-be-social-media-influencers-8349212.

25 "2022 Creator Report by Linktree." Accessed March 20, 2024. https://linktr.ee/creator-report/.

92 *Critical Internet Literacies*

26 https://www.census.gov/topics/employment/industry-occupation/guidance/indexes.html.

27 Harwell, Drew, and Taylor Lorenz. "Millions Work as Content Creators. In Official Records, They Barely Exist." *Washington Post*, October 26, 2023. https://www.washingtonpost.com/technology/2023/10/26/creator-economy-influencers-youtubers-social-media/.

28 Grothaus, Michael. "Marques Brownlee Just Eviscerated the Rabbit R1. Here's Why Apple Should Pay Attention." *Fast Company*, May 2, 2024. https://www.fastcompany.com/91116542/apple-ios-18-marques-brownlee-rabbit-r1-features-promiseware.

29 Koerner, Brendan I. "I Went Undercover as a Secret OnlyFans Chatter. It Wasn't Pretty." *Wired*, May 15, 2024. https://www.wired.com/story/i-went-undercover-secret-onlyfans-chatter-wasnt-pretty/.

30 Bertoni, Steven. "Top Creators 2023." *Forbes*. Accessed May 21, 2024. https://www.forbes.com/sites/stevenbertoni/2023/09/26/top-creators-2023/.

31 Jarvis, Jeff. *The Gutenberg Parenthesis: The Age of Print and Its Lessons for the Age of the Internet*. New York, NY: Bloomsbury Academic, 2023.

32 Srnicek, Nick. *Platform Capitalism*. Theory Redux. Cambridge, UK; Malden, MA: Polity, 2017. p. 38.

33 McGrady, Ryan, Kevin Zheng, Rebecca Curran, Jason Baumgartner, and Ethan Zuckerman. "Dialing for Videos: A Random Sample of YouTube." *Journal of Quantitative Description: Digital Media* 3 (December 20, 2023). https://doi.org/10.51685/jqd.2023.022.

34 From the authors' paper: "The most promising random sampling technique up to now is the 'Random Prefix Sampling' approach by Zhou, et al. (2011). In a paper which sets out to estimate the size of YouTube, the authors take advantage of an unusual feature (or, more likely, a bug) in the YouTube search software. Every YouTube video is assigned a unique 11-character identifier which is visible in the url after 'youtube.com/watch?v='. Zhou, et al. found that when you search for the string 'watch?v=xy...z' where 'xy...z' is the first part of a valid YouTube ID (prefix) that does not contain a dash ('-'), the search engine will return results beginning with that prefix followed by a dash." p. 8.

35 Kafka, Peter. "YouTube Could Be Worth $400 Billion – That's More than Disney and Comcast Combined. We Should Be Paying More Attention." *Business Insider*. Accessed April 29, 2024. https://www.businessinsider.com/youtube-valuation-mrbeast-how-much-worth-2024-3.

36 McGrady, Ryan. "What We Discovered on 'Deep YouTube.'" *The Atlantic* (blog), January 26, 2024. https://www.theatlantic.com/technology/archive/2024/01/how-many-videos-youtube-research/677250/.

37 As a note, calling Josh Harris eccentric is an understatement – he was fond of donning clown-like makeup and calling himself "Luvvy" (based on the "Lovey" character from *Gilligan's Island*) and saying wildly inappropriate things, even to investors. The documentary shows that even rich, white men can only be *so* eccentric. (Even Elon Musk, in his rightward turn, does not compare.)

38 "The Dot-Com Kids," 1999.

39 "The Dot-Com Kids." *CBSNews.com*, February 15, 2000. https://www.cbsnews.com/news/the-dot-com-kids/.

40 Keets, Heather. "AOL Launches NetNoir." *EW.com*, June 16, 1995. https://ew.com/article/1995/06/16/aol-launches-netnoir/.

41 McIlwain, Charlton. *Black Software: The Internet and Racial Justice, from the AfroNet to Black Lives Matter*. New York, NY: Oxford University Press, 2020. pp. 132 and 136.

The Creator Economy and the Hyper-Niche   93

42 "YouTube Cofounder: 'Video Idea.'" *Internal Tech Emails*, January 3, 2023. https://www.techemails.com/p/jawed-karim-to-chad-hurley-and-steve-chen.

43 *Me at the Zoo*, 2005. https://www.youtube.com/watch?v=jNQXAC9IVRw.

44 "YouTube – Broadcast Yourself.," November 1, 2005. Archived website featuring the iPod Nano giveaway in the upper right of the website. http://web.archive.org/web/20051101094936/http://www.youtube.com/.

45 Grossman, Lev. "You – Yes, You – Are TIME's Person of the Year." *Time*, December 25, 2006. https://content.time.com/time/magazine/article/0,9171,1570810,00.html.

46 https://www.4tvs.com/Journey/Pages/journal.html.

47 Veldhuijzen van Zanten, Boris. "There Were 17,000 YouTubes Before YouTube." *The Next Web*, October 28, 2013. https://thenextweb.com/news/17000-youtubes-youtube.

48 Hoffberger, Chase. "Escaping the Trolls: Franchesca Ramsey's 4-Year YouTube Struggle." *The Daily Dot*, March 6, 2013. https://www.dailydot.com/upstream/youtube-troll-franchesca-ramsey-itrubslotion/.

49 *Shit White Girls Say...to Black Girls*, 2012. https://www.youtube.com/watch?v=ylPUzxpIBe0.

50 Burgess, Jean, and Joshua Green. *YouTube: Online Video and Participatory Culture*. Digital Media and Society Series. Cambridge; Malden, MA: Polity, 2009. p. 6.

51 Fiske, John. *Television Culture*. 2nd [rev.] ed. Routledge Classics. London New York: Routledge, 2011.

52 Beck, Julie. "Why Do So Many People on YouTube Sound the Same?" *The Atlantic* (blog), December 7, 2015. https://www.theatlantic.com/technology/archive/2015/12/the-linguistics-of-youtube-voice/418962/.

53 Ford, Paul. "The American Room." *The Message* (blog), July 14, 2016. https://medium.com/message/the-american-room-3fce9b2b98c5.

54 Rosenbloom, Stephanie. "The Beta Male's Charms." *New York Times*, February 8, 2008, sec. Fashion. https://www.nytimes.com/2008/02/08/style/08iht-07girlfriends.9858053.html.

55 Christian, Aymar Jean. *Open TV: Innovation beyond Hollywood and the Rise of Web Television*. Postmillennial Pop. New York: New York University Press, 2018. pp. 116 and 117.

56 Rojek, Chris. *Presumed Intimacy: Para-Social Relationships in Media, Society and Celebrity Culture*. Cambridge, UK; Malden, MA: Polity Press, 2016.

57 Jones, C. T. "Fans Built Her an Internet Empire. Now They're Tearing It Down." *Rolling Stone* (blog), June 21, 2023. https://www.rollingstone.com/culture/culture-features/colleen-ballinger-miranda-sings-youtube-fans-allegations-1234774947/.

58 *Staples Center Chants "TYLER" at One Direction Concert*, 2013. https://www.youtube.com/watch?v=MO8bblWAhqI.

59 Cao, Steffi. "How 2014 Changed the Internet Forever." *The Ringer*, May 1, 2024. https://www.theringer.com/tech/2024/5/1/24144418/modern-internet-2014-anniversary.

60 Cohen, Joshua. "Obama Meets With YouTube Advisors On How To Reach Online Audiences." *Tubefilter* , March 3, 2014. https://www.tubefilter.com/2014/03/02/obama-meets-with-youtube-advisors-on-how-to-reach-online-audiences/.

61 *President Barack Obama: Between Two Ferns with Zach Galifianakis*, 2014. https://www.youtube.com/watch?v=UnW3xkHxIEQ.

94 *Critical Internet Literacies*

62 Blake, Aaron. "'Between Two Ferns' Video Leads to 40 Percent More Visits to HealthCare.Gov." *Washington Post*, November 26, 2021. https://www.washingtonpost.com/news/post-politics/wp/2014/03/12/between-two-ferns-video-leads-to-40-percent-more-visits-to-healthcare-gov/.

63 Ault, Susanne. "Survey: YouTube Stars More Popular Than Mainstream Celebs Among U.S. Teens." *Variety* (blog), August 5, 2014. https://variety.com/2014/digital/news/survey-youtube-stars-more-popular-than-mainstream-celebs-among-u-s-teens-1201275245/.

64 Vollmer, Christopher, Sebastian Blum, and Kristina Bennin. *The Rise of Multichannel Networks: Critical Capabilities for the New Digital Video Ecosystem.* PricewaterhouseCoopers Strategyand, 2014. https://www.pwc.com/ee/et/publications/pub/strategyand_the-rise-of-multichannel-networks.pdf.

65 Barnes, Brooks. "Disney Buys Maker Studios, Video Supplier for YouTube." *New York Times*, March 25, 2014, sec. Business. https://www.nytimes.com/2014/03/25/business/media/disney-buys-maker-studios-video-supplier-for-youtube.html.

66 *DO WHAT YOU CAN'T*, 2017. https://www.youtube.com/watch?v=jG7dSXcfVqE.

67 *Bike Lanes by Casey Neistat*, 2011. https://www.youtube.com/watch?v=bzE-IMaegzQ.

68 *Black Market Takes Over the iPhone 6 Lines*, 2014. https://www.youtube.com/watch?v=Ef_BznBwktw.

69 *Make It Count*, 2012. https://www.youtube.com/watch?v=WxfZkMm3wcg.

70 Einstein, Mara. *Black Ops Advertising: Native Ads, Content Marketing, and the Covert World of the Digital Sell.* New York, London: OR Books, 2016.

71 "Samsung: Do What You Can't by Leo Burnett." *The Drum*, https://www.thedrum.com/creative-works/project/great-guns-samsung-do-what-you-cant.

72 Herrman, John. "YouTube's Monster: PewDiePie and His Populist Revolt." *New York Times*, February 16, 2017, sec. Magazine. https://www.nytimes.com/2017/02/16/magazine/youtubes-monster-pewdiepie-and-his-populist-revolt.html.

73 Osterweil, Vicky. "Like and Subscribe." *Real Life*, February 12, 2018. https://reallifemag.com/like-and-subscribe/.

74 Itkowitz, Colby. "Who Is Josh Feuerstein, the Man behind the Starbucks Red Cup Frenzy?" *Washington Post*, October 27, 2021. https://www.washingtonpost.com/news/acts-of-faith/wp/2015/11/10/who-is-josh-feuerstein-the-man-behind-the-starbucks-red-cup-frenzy/.

75 Gordon, Lewis R. *Fear of Black Consciousness.* 1st ed. New York: Farrar, Straus and Giroux, 2022. p. 59.

76 Sellner is banned from numerous countries due to his extreme bigotry. See: https://www.aljazeera.com/news/2024/3/19/far-right-austrian-figure-martin-sellner-banned-from-entering-germany.

77 Roose, Kevin. "The Making of a YouTube Radical." *New York Times*, June 8, 2019, sec. Technology. https://www.nytimes.com/interactive/2019/06/08/technology/youtube-radical.html, https://www.nytimes.com/interactive/2019/06/08/technology/youtube-radical.html.

78 Lewis, Becca. "Alternative Influence." *Data & Society*. Data & Society Research Institute, September 18, 2018. https://datasociety.net/library/alternative-influence/.

79 *Vertical Video Syndrome – A PSA (Glove and Boots)*. https://www.youtube.com/watch?v=dechvhb0Meo&t=52s.

80 Tolentino, Jia. "How TikTok Holds Our Attention." *New Yorker*, September 23, 2019. https://www.newyorker.com/magazine/2019/09/30/how-tiktok-holds-our-attention.

81 Hedderson, Monique M., Traci A. Bekelman, Mingyi Li, Emily A. Knapp, Meredith Palmore, Yanan Dong, Amy J. Elliott, et al. "Trends in Screen Time Use Among Children During the COVID-19 Pandemic, July 2019 Through August 2021." *JAMA Network Open* 6, no. 2 (February 1, 2023): e2256157. https://doi.org/10.1001/jamanetworkopen.2022.56157.

82 Jennings, Rebecca. "Cottagecore, Taylor Swift, and Our Endless Desire to Be Soothed." *Vox*, August 3, 2020. https://www.vox.com/the-goods/2020/8/3/21349640/cottagecore-taylor-swift-folklore-lesbian-clothes-animal-crossing.

83 Duffy, Brooke Erin. "Influencer Culture Is Everywhere – Even in Academia." Salon, April 30, 2022. https://www.salon.com/2022/04/30/influencer-culture-is-everywhere-even-in-academia/.

84 *Antibodyody Antibody Song – Raven the Science Maven*, 2020. https://www.youtube.com/watch?v=KBpQg6JMxSc.

85 Bishop, Sophie. "Influencer Creep." *Real Life*. Accessed October 25, 2023. https://reallifemag.com/influencer-creep/.

86 Sharma, Archit. "Why Northeast India Face Racism in Its Own Country?" *Times of India*, May 26, 2020. https://timesofindia.indiatimes.com/readersblog/wakeup-india/why-northeast-india-face-racism-in-its-own-country-20390/.

87 Sanskriti, Sanskriti, Ishita Guglani, Shiv Joshi, and Ashish Anjankar. "The Spectrum of Motivations Behind Watching Mukbang Videos and Its Health Effects on Its Viewers: A Review." *Cureus*, August 30, 2023. https://doi.org/10.7759/cureus.44392.

88 Agarwala, Tora. "Mukbang Creators in Northeast India Fight Stereotypes with Food." *Rest of World*, July 11, 2024. https://restofworld.org/2024/northeast-india-mukbang/.

89 Rest of World is an incredible resource for learning about tech around the globe, especially learning about diverse creators in their creator economy tag: https://restofworld.org/series/creator-economy/.

90 https://www.youtube.com/watch?v=25g273Xwdtk.

4   Memes and Visual Communication

Where's Your Head At?

In the summer 2023, a series of memes appeared online that made jokes about women getting lobotomized alongside memes about how much men allegedly think about the Roman Empire. "i don't want to be a girlboss anymore, i want to take pictures of the cows while my husband drives me to my lobotomy," Twitter user pictoria vark posted in June 2023 – the tweet went viral.[1] On the other subject, Instagram user gaiusflavius posted on Reels, "Ladies, many of you do not realise how often men think about the Roman Empire. Ask your husband/boyfriend/father/brother you will be surprised by their answers!"[2] gaiusflavius's post set off a viral challenge that peaked on TikTok a few weeks later. Both these memes were easy to participate in and inspired remixing and sharing, the minimum requirements for digital objects to be considered memes. Users remixed the lobotomy memes into Pinterest or Etsy aesthetics; one shirt reads "Live, Laugh, Lobotomy." The Roman Empire meme took the form of women asking their husband/boyfriend/father/brother how often they thought of the subject, many answering with the casual "every day."

Most people believe memes are simply funny, shareable images and videos and fail to recognize they are reductionist media, embedded with a host of meanings coded in their construction and deployment. In the case of these memes, they contain a series of layered references, most of which users do not need to know to participate. In general, and at scale, memes may also act as a cultural barometer, enabling trend forecasters, strategists, theorists, and sociologists a glance at the overall "mood" on social media. On the other hand, memes like these are temporal and ephemeral, representing a moment and acting as dated archival material rather than long-term cultural artifacts. These particular memes are examples of pessimistic or cynical trends and double as methods of coping in response to overwhelming feelings from off-platform experiences; neither are overtly dangerous on the surface. It may seem concerning that any mention of

DOI: 10.4324/9781003483885-4

getting lobotomized may be humorous, but these are used in an ironic way. When used in memes, irony is not the typical definition of signifying the opposite of the intended message, but rather an expression more akin to a sarcastic or sardonic use.

Do women *really* want to get a lobotomy? Do men *really* think of the Roman Empire *every day*? Memes are intricately and importantly woven into culture, especially in communication environments and dynamic interactive sites like social media and message boards. Memes that the general public interact with usually flow from the depths of forums or subreddits, rise into mainstream internet culture, become a trend, get overused, and fade away. Occasionally they reach a volume that exceeds their containment and become analyzed and discussed in mainstream news cycles. Most mainstream coverage neglects to inform the public of the multiple meanings that derive from the memes, and this inspires our necessity to increase our meme literacies to properly read memes. Since memes exist as media (visual or audio), we too often treat them like media to be consumed. However, they are unlike other media as their recognizable referential qualities and fortune cookie-like traits allow people to share complex emotions or complex feelings (most visible in "me when" or "me:" memes). Importantly, memes like the lobotomy or Roman Empire memes are distinct because they also carry additional meanings beyond their specific references and mood-based trends.

In September 2023, EJ Dickson of *Rolling Stone* asked Mike Duncan, host of "The History of Rome" podcast, why men were particularly interested in the Roman Empire meme; Duncan responds: "I think a lot of it probably can come back to a Roman history becoming equivalent to military history, and military history is definitely something that is always going to be more of interest to men than women, just on a practical level."[3] While this is a satisfactory explanation, Dickson delves further and wonders if there may hidden meanings inside the trend acknowledging that women don't typically think of historical empires. Duncan expands:

I think it probably comes down to a bit of the representation matters thing. As men, we can always look past and see men who were poor, men who were middle-aged, men who were smart, men who were dumb, men who were emperors. Every available option is available to us if we're doing historical fantasizing. And if you want to get into it, you probably were reading about those great people, because they're the ones who left records. And there's the ones that we know about. And so you get into a mindset. And you can imagine yourself in that role, like, "If I wanted to, yeah, I could definitely sit down and imagine what would I do if I was a Roman emperor," which is impossible for a woman to do.

98 *Critical Internet Literacies*

Historically, the narratives of women who existed in ancient history don't have as robust histories as men have. Traditional history is coded in patriarchal hegemony, relying on texts and narratives from those who had access to discover them (men), tell their stories (men), and develop long "great *man* of history" narratives. To think of the Roman Empire is a fantasy of memory and romantic storytelling and extremely few people may imagine it properly.

To read the Roman Empire meme critically, we must acknowledge the misogyny embedded in the meme as well as the whitewashing of history. Likely, nearly all participants in this meme have little awareness of these additional traits and why they may be included. From a critical perspective, the Roman Empire meme uplifts far-right ideologies directly into the mainstream social media environment. Mike Duncan recognized this as well, calling men who imagine themselves a hero of Empire to be living in "Fantasyland" as the great majority of Roman citizens were just regular people who lived banal lives under the thumb of many of these "great men of history."

Second, reading this type of meme may remind us that the cultural memory of Ancient Rome is coded within a contemporary retelling. The most obvious example is the misunderstood aesthetics of white columns, white marble statues, and classical architecture that the far right has included in their ideology. These traits are false. Ancient Rome was colorful and gaudy, crowded and dirty, and barely any stone was left unpainted; Romans seemed to love reds and browns and yellows. When people's husbands/boyfriends/fathers/brothers answered the meme's prompt, some may have imagined a false history. In *Harper's Bazaar*, Rosa Sanchez goes a step further in her coverage of the meme (in which I am quoted), illuminating the way racist and misogynistic groups like the Proud Boys and neo-Nazi groups idolize ancient empires, fixated on the "larger-than-life mythological figures like Hercules and Theseus, who exude strength and blonde power, then, are seen as the models of an ideal leader to an ideal society. War, muscles, Sparta!"[4] Sanchez recognizes that the people answering the question are not likely to support extremist ideals, but this meme "targeting your boyfriend is helping keep the patriarchy alive."

There should be even more concern regarding lobotomy memes. The meme evolved from new aesthetics derived from the cores of TikTok, specifically that of the "coquette" and "bimbo" genres that lean into irony and "nihilistic feminism." Sophie Wilson writes of the meme in *Dazed Digital* that the meme's aesthetic is downstream from the "heroin chic" look of the 1990s where women presented themselves as disconnected or disassociating. The meme relies on what TikTok users called "lobotomy chic:"

> The dead-eyed lobotomy chic look, in which the subject puts on a blank stare and disaffected pout, has become a go-to Insta pose for everyone

Memes and Visual Communication 99

from Billie Eilish to lobotomy chic posters girls [*Euphoria* actor] Chloe Cherry and [model and influencer] Gabriette.[5] The pose is often accompanied by messy minimal make-up, preppy clothes and ironic Catholic symbolism all captured in close-up selfies or using digital cameras with the flash on.[6]

In an era of DIY makeup artistry and Get Ready With Me trends that go beyond Outfit Of The Day (OOTD) and into thematic getups, lobotomy chic was a new and popular meme to replicate.

In her *Washington Post* op-ed, Caroline Reilly provides some background:

It's hard to pinpoint exactly why lobotomy chic came *en vogue*, but in a lot of ways, it makes sense. Women are exhausted – constantly ricocheting between ideals of living foisted on us and then sold as our own desires. In the mid-2010s, Girlboss feminism was preaching liberation through capitalism – beating men at their own game by playing according to their rules.[7]

Like the Roman Empire meme, the lobotomy meme seems to be based in overt cultural shifts in the 2020s. As the internet sometimes acts as a display of reactionary philosophies, the concept of lobotomization is connected to the rise of misogynist trends like the tradwife, itself a reaction to women's empowerment and angrily derived from anti-#MeToo activists. Going even deeper reveals the privilege of using this meme: like the concept of "touching grass," many memes are coded in an aesthetic that disregards its history.

Sophie Wilson continues, "Online depictions of empty-headed housewives and disaffected pouts largely erase this part of the history and ignores how lobotomies were weaponized against LGBTQ+ people and people of color as a tool to violently enact homophobic and racist ideologies." In their reductionist state, memes end up shallowing out meaning and context and reduce the ability to discuss the effects of the subject on culture. Reilly agrees and acknowledges that "smearing Vaseline over the lens of history" is not unique to the lobotomy meme, but it does "divorce lobotomy chic as a trend from the horror of its reality." Reilly explains:

Put simply, this is not just about making light of the past, about being insensitive to the generations that came before us – but about having such a myopic view of society that you fail to see the ways in which the legacy of these horrors lives on. While the specific practice of spearing a woman's brain for being disabled, opinionated or anxious is no longer done, the use of medicine as a weapon for the subjugation of women persists.

100 *Critical Internet Literacies*

Lobotomization of women began nearly a century ago, and while cultural memory only lasts so long, the desensitization of a serious issue is clearly within the power of the meme. Unless the systems themselves are altered, the expression of this type of coping mechanism will exist.

The benefit of increasing our knowledge of these two examples is exactly the purpose of meme literacies. In their reductionist state, memes provide us the opportunity to deconstruct, expand our knowledge, and learn more about culture. Increasing our meme literacies also opens the door for curiosity and interrogation of other memes. In addition, we must practice meme literacies as many memes contain well-disguised (and often attractive) messages designed specifically to open the portal of rabbit holes that may initialize radicalization. To combat this possibility, the more we learn to discuss memes maturely, the more we must build resilience.

This chapter examines a handful of case studies that can be applied in classrooms and in lectures. Teaching and exploring memes happen to be a risky endeavor and each Google search on a projector is a gamble of career-ending moments, potentially captured by students' cell phones and shared online – it is best to rehearse meme education before class. The examples used in this chapter are well-practiced and explained, but in no way should any public search go unvetted or be extemporaneously presented. Remember, as internet culture researchers, scholars, and journalists dig into the meaning of memes, those who know how to encode messages get better at encryption. It is not cat and mouse as there is no chase and meme literacy does not have the goal of coming to a definitive "understanding" of all memes; this is unlikely to ever happen. The goal, like that of understanding our modern creator economy or digital cultures, is to create a toolset to use for reading future examples.

We Live in a Derivative World

Before 1976, scholars did not have concise term for what we now call memes. Instead, we used terms like "tropes" or "visual metaphors." From early print through modern visual communication, sharable and remixable cultural artifacts existed, but lacked the terminology. As many know, it was biologist Richard Dawkins who coined the modern term "meme" to represent these things, relating them to organisms and biology. Memes, to Dawkins, were a unit of cultural information, like biological genes, carrying information and ideas capable of replication and evolution, transferred by people. What many don't know is that Dawkins' 1976 *The Selfish Gene* is not solely about this, and the section regarding memes – especially in retrospect – is quite minimal. Though Dawkins receives the credit, we must also move beyond his definition for two reasons. One, his version of meme is too broad for the specific type of internet-based or internet-derived meme

Memes and Visual Communication   101

that we interact with consistently in the 2020s. Second, while TikTok Challenges more resemble Dawkins' definition, he compared his term with cultural biology, hinting at memes' fitness and survival – much like natural selection; in the digital world, this definition lacks accuracy and thoughtfulness to digital cultures. Today, Dawkins' worldview is situated strongly in biological dualism, and he has leaned into the ideologies shared by the heterodox intellectual dark web and new atheists who espouse anti-trans rhetoric and a share a close-minded viewpoint on non-binary individuals.

This is the last mention of Dawkins in this chapter, and we'll use more modern definitions of the term going forward. To make thing simple, we'll utilize Limor Shifman's definition of digital meme as our baseline: "(a) a group of digital items sharing common characteristics of content, form, and/or stance, which (b) were created with awareness of each other, and (c) were circulated, imitated, and/or transformed via the Internet by many users."[8] Shifman's definition is now a decade old, but is still accurate and general enough to encapsulate the memes that have emerged in digital spaces since the early bulletin board services started sharing them, however, it mainly applies to memes of the 2010s and 2020s when more people had access to visual tools like meme generators, photoshop, and social media. In this chapter, we'll also be paying close attention to a meme's metatextual nuance and referential layers.

"The meme is always more than a particular instance because it has a double character. To function as a meme, media must express an organizing syntax. The meme-instance is also, always, a member of a meme-series" Scott Wark argued on his research blog in 2015.[9] In Wark's view, memes evolve in co-evolutionary ways not distinct from other memes. In other words, the meanings of emojis may change in the same way meme meanings may change. Early digital memes were often fairly straightforward, needing very little extrapolation and were WSYIWYG ("What you see is what you get"). For example, if you received an image of a rabbit with a pancake on its head, that was all you were seeing, no additional subtext. Layering was added by the context of the sender and receiver and less embedded in the image itself.

As the internet evolved into a more visual space, many memes were being created as early reaction images – being deployed as a reaction to posts and the context of that specific reaction gave the image meaning. Many of these early memes were observational and used the internet to add humor and jokes to everyday reality. For example, you could simply add a caption to an anthropomorphized household object to create a meme when your sense of pareidolia creates recognition to the inanimate object. For example, many people have a small clothing hook in their house with two up-curved hooks and off-centered screw holes. If you wanted to anthropomorphize the hook, you could imagine it being a small, strange-looking

102 *Critical Internet Literacies*

Figure 4.1 An early digital meme from the late aughts showing an anthropomorphized coat hook reimagined into a feisty drunk octopus.

octopus. A caption like, "Drunk octopus wants to fight!" causes the viewer to see the likeness through pareidolia and imagine a small drunk octopus rather than a hook.

It is important to note that much of this chapter will be focusing on text descriptions of memes rather than sharing their images. The reason is twofold: first, nearly all memes contain images that require permission to use in commercial settings or in published texts, and second, describing memes helps support the argument laid out in Chapter 7 encouraging accessibility and explanation. Not everyone can "see" a meme and presenting memes without alt-text or specific descriptions excludes people. While some may think the explanation of a meme "ruins" it or takes the fun away, that is a weak argument as memes can be referred to through their visual attributes. The sense of pareidolia is a visual sense, but we should recognize the responsibility of description anyway.

Pareidolia is the ability to anthropomorphize inanimate objects so we may see faces or likeness to other living beings. It's better to mistake something for being a predator and run away than not recognize it and get preyed upon. In the digital world, pareidolia helps us with the referential

Memes and Visual Communication 103

layers of a meme and connects these references instantaneously. Another biological trait may be apophenia, the ability to perceive meaningful connections between things that are likely unrelated. Like the way you think of a movie or quote in relation to an experience, you can simultaneously think two things at once. However, when we apply apophenia, we must recognize its roots in the study of schizophrenia. Schizophrenia itself has become a dark meme inside of far-right spaces and incel forums online.

Getting back to the derivative nature of images online: early memes spawned variations consistent with a strong format and formula while encoded with a message-based grammar. These codes helped meme makers and meme sharers understand the emotions that underpinned the images themselves. For example, early photoshop memes built in the early "haiku" style or "image macro" style – as in text/image/text – each used their respective image avatar to signify the grammar. Gene Wilder's "Condescending Wonka" (taken from a still from 1971 film *Willy Wonka and the Chocolate* Factory), for example, required remixers to use sarcasm and condescension in the message. (Top text: "Oh you just graduated?"/ Wilder grinning / Bottom text: "You must know everything.") The text was written in Impact font, a grammatical requirement of early macro memes. Not only was Impact font available on Mac or PC, but it was also one of the standard web fonts. The font was usually always presented with a several point black stroke (border) around the text. These graphical cues also enabled meme makers to signify their medium in contrast to other messaging mediums.

After multiple years of meme generators and derivatives of the image macro memes, memes began to evolve their language and grammar. Both the Doge and Pepe the Frog memes popularized internet memes outside the structural template. One could not have known at the time of the influence memes would have on culture and politics, acting as tools for multilayered rhetoric and in-group dogwhistling. When a man dressed as Pepe the Frog rushed up the steps of the US Capitol on January 6, 2021, it was apparent that memes could be weaponized beyond propagandistic purposes and motivate action. In a very short period, memes evolved from WYSIWYG image jokes to grammatical image macros to political weaponry and subterfuge. Memes are a method of communication with built-in memory and referential nuance. Like the geological layers in the strata that enable archaeologists to read backward through time through fixed temporal data points, memes retain elements of the *culture* that developed the visual aesthetic. The further derivations benefit from the reader's knowledge of the reference but continue to operate without connection to the original meanings.

Memes are cultural surplus. Memes are decadent. Most memes are artifacts rather than canonical cultural material. They are built to represent

104   *Critical Internet Literacies*

an era of digital culture rather than act as long-term cultural value. W David Marx argues that memes are cheap, fast, and disposable, losing their cultural value rapidly and while in the aughts, memes were the medium of internet culture. Now, we are overwhelmed by content through many channels. Marx writes:

> aughts memes turned out to be funny the way inside jokes at summer camp are funny: You had to be there. They make no sense outside of their initial context. And it doesn't help that many were accidental successes, rather than conscious works of art made with craft and care.[10]

On the other hand, today's memes, challenges, trends, and content would not exist without our earliest examples. Some matter, some don't, but our awareness of the cultural moment helps us read the present-day expressions of memetic tendencies.

Today's memes are so layered and nuanced that we must read *through* the meme, as an archaeologist would excavate the layers of strata, we must do so digitally, which means exploring horizontally as well as vertically. What is a method of reading *through* a meme? How may we develop frameworks to convert memes into language and utility? As our first approach, we'll start with a small, yellow dog named Kabosu and her lasting impact on the internet and history.

Usable Meme Literacies: The Doge Meme

On May 24, 2024, the beloved internet famous dog Kabosu passed away, loved wholeheartedly by her human, Atsuko Sato. Kabosu was 18 years old, a long life for a dog. The yellow Shiba Inu dog was world famous and it's possible that most people who have seen her do not know her real name – they know her as "Doge." Kabosu's side-eyeing glance from a photo taken in 2010 in Atsuko's home became the icon on millions of memes, a Nascar racecar, and inspired derivative memes like "Swole Doge" (who usually accompanies "Cheems," who is another Shiba named Balltze). She is also memorialized in statue form in her hometown in the Chiba prefecture in Japan. Her international fame can be sourced to the internet's ceaseless cultural expression and a series of interesting moments in internet history that enabled the meme to emerge.

The Doge meme is our first case study as it is one of the "safest" memes to search for, rarely revealing coded messages that border on harm. When you search the term "doge" and click images, it is one of the few memes that doesn't result in memes with questionable messaging and possible hate symbology. The search term alone is proof of Doge's impact; on Google the search reveals primarily variations of the dog's head in numerous poses and images of DogeCoin, the cryptocurrency boosted by cheerleader Elon

Memes and Visual Communication   105

Musk (who is referred to as "the Dogefather" by the crypto community). If you continue to scroll the search results, you'll likely only find images of the yellow dog in its many iterations and remixes. However, what makes the Doge meme fascinating is the fact that the yellow dog *is not* the Doge. That term belongs to a group of aristocrats that managed the finances of the Republic of Venice from 726–1797 CE.

For over one thousand years, the Doge ruled and operated from the Ducal Palace – known as the Doge Palace – built in 1340 CE in Piazza San Marco in Venice, Italy. The elected magistrates were part of the aristocracy and served for life as part of the Republic of Venice. Their power was immense and each year, they would hold a special ceremony in the Grand Canal on Ascension Day, throwing a ring into the waters of the canals to show their dominion over the sea.[11] Each Doge had their own coin with their face stamped on it, like that of the Emperors of Classical Rome. Their coin was known as "ducati," not DogeCoin. In 1501, Doge Leonardo Loredan was painted by Giovanni Bellini in the style of high Renaissance artwork and today the painting hangs in the Palace, now a museum. If you were to tell Doge Loredan in 1503, that someday, the term Doge would represent a small yellow dog rather than hundreds of years of Ducal magistrates, it's likely he'd laugh at you. How is it possible that over one thousand years of history could be overwritten in fewer than 15 years? What enabled this volume of contributions to this specific meme? What makes this meme in particular so influential to meme culture?

Using the Doge meme as a framework offers a tool to analyze other memes as we excavate their embedded meanings. It is crucially important to be aware that no meanings in memes are "hidden," rather they are encoded in creative and witty ways, often shrewdly masked in emotional tactics. To reveal the layered meanings and retrieve a meme's context is an act of meme literacy. Some memes, like those featuring political ideology, contain unreleased kinetic energy, meaning they are designed to inspire civic or direct action (see: "Stop the Steal"). The Doge meme is also an accessible meme with clear origins that can be excavated both temporally and culturally. Without each constitutive element, the meme would not be possible, popular, or even as interesting to remix and share. The Doge meme is a reaction meme, a remix meme, and a crypto mascot.

How a Timeless Meme is Created

In its later years, the Flash-animated webseries *Homestar Runner* switched its style to a puppet show. In 2005, Matt Chapman and team put together a series of puppet-driven shorts titled "Biz Cas Fri" (Business Casual Friday) and on their first episode "Biz Cas Fri 1,"[12] Homestar, in his typical awkward annoying way, interrupts Strong Bad as he tries to finish his "3ʳᵈ

106 *Critical Internet Literacies*

quarter projection analysis spreadsheets" and just as Strong Bad mentions "there's been no sign of –" Homestar enters the screen and says:

> "What, is up, my dog?!"
> "Ugh I am not your dog" Strong Bad responds.
> "Rondleman,[13] you crack me up! That's why you're my D-O-G-E."
> "Your *Doge?* What are you talking about?"

And for the first time in possibly centuries, the word "Doge," pronounced dōhj, was spoken, this time in reference to a slang endearing moniker. One, or possibly hundreds, of viewers at that moment heard the term and immediately embedded it in their memory, situated like an earworm and replacement for the word dog in certain situations much the way Millennials would say "doggo" or "puppo" in the 2010s.

Four years later, in 2009, Japanese kindergarten teacher Atsuko Sato and her husband adopted their Shiba Inu dog Kabosu (meaning Pumpkin in Japanese) and started a blog to keep photos of their new family member. In a post on February 13, 2010, Sato posted a thread titled "What's for dinner tonight?" featuring her husband playing with Kabosu.[14] The third photo in the photoset shows Kabosu happy, arms crossed, and looking sidelong at her human. In a completely different part of the internet, in October 2010, a Reddit user submitted the photo of Kabosu to the subreddit r/Ads with the caption: "LMBO LOOK @ THIS FUKKIN DOGE." This would be the first time the term Doge was mapped to this specific dog. But the meme did not start there. At the time, LolCats and their slight derivatives were the primary modality for meme formats.

Linguist Gretchen McCulloch has argued that LolCats, with their deconstructed textual communication style ("I can haz cheezburger?" "I'm in ur bed sleeping"), are more similar to first-generation internet language, which was based on text speak, written as txtspk.[15] This form of communication was used because of the lack of our modern virtual qwerty keyboards where users were reliant on tapping messages on a number pad. (LOL is 555666555 and emojis were emoticons: :-).) From a linguistic standpoint, we adopted these shortened messages into speech, pronouncing them and using them as language. (We will return to this in further chapters with a discussion on "algospeak.") In our paper for the *Journal of Cultural Politics*, Matt Applegate and I argue that the Doge meme, with its layered genesis, represented the emergence of a new internet language, one both reactive and cumulative to the previous language iterations.[16]

At the same time the term doge was being applied to Kabosu, digital cultures on Tumblr were creating theme accounts, focused on hyper-specific types of content and user expression. Sites like fuckyeahbabyanimals.tumblr.com were exactly as advertised and soon after, sites like fuckyeahdoge.tumblr.com and dailydoge.tumblr.com were general Tumblr blogs that offered

Memes and Visual Communication 107

images of dogs, referring to them as doges. The next layering was the shift in meme grammar, moving away from Impact font and replacing it with Comic Sans to represent a dog's inner monologue rather than the cats' bolder text. This appeared on the site shibaconfessions.tumblr.com where "funny text in comic sans over unrelated pictures of shibas" was the offering.

McCulloch explains the grammar of Doge formed on Tumblr as well, sourcing from a style of collaborative posting using what she calls "doge phrases" where sentences were stacked with adverb qualifiers like "much, very, and such," and so on to turn long phrases into silly speech ("such beauty," "very rose," etc.) and then exciting phrases like "wow," "amaze," and "excite" were added.[17] Finally, *all* these aspects layer into the meme, taking Kabosu's face and adding multicolor Comic Sans text with "doge phrases." The original Doge meme was simply Kabosu with the words "Wow," "What r you doing," "r-a-p-e keep your hands away from me," "concern," and "so scare," leaning into Kabosu's concerned look at the hand approaching her space.

While we may use a media archaeological approach to analyze this type of meme through its layered attributes, recognizing each layer (the text, the grammar, the aesthetic, the images, the temporal moment, and the distribution), using internet literacies would give us far more insight into the impact of memes in both their creation and their widespread use. The Doge meme was a collaborative meme that took several years to turn into the voluminous meme we know today. Born of the internet, it also holds an interesting space that Pepe the Frog cannot due to Pepe's origin as artist Matt Furie's creation. Even though Kabosu was real, the elements are collective.

The impact of Doge led software engineers Billy Markus and Jackson Palmer to create a reactionary cryptocoin to combat the hegemony of Bitcoin (a reactionary currency) as the first "meme coin."[18] More importantly, the Doge meme was remixable without any buried codes or harmful speech, and anyone could create one so long as they abided by the grammar. After the creation of millions of Doge memes, very little evidence of the Doges of Venice appears in a search for the term Doge. Now you must qualify the search with "Venetian Doge" or "Venice Doge" to reveal the original and even in those results, you'll find Kabosu's side-eyed glance. In terms of digital meme history, Doge unlocked the format at the same time more people had access to photo manipulation tools and were using memes to communicate. The memes of the next few years would change history.

Reading Metatext: Dead Plants, Ugly Shoes, Odd Flags, and Armed Militias

Memes, in their referential, nuanced, reactionary, and layered state, contain text that either references other memes or cultural signifiers that require the reader to either immediately understand the text and share them

108 *Critical Internet Literacies*

intentionally or miss the signifiers and share them uncritically. The former is often used as a propaganda tactic and the latter is due to a lack of internet literacies. We are not immune to propaganda, but we are especially vulnerable to coded messages in the form of memes. To read metatext, we're going to start with two different memes encoded in similar ways. Metatext is often nuanced and requires multiple ways of "reading" the material through a variety of contextual clues. Whereas we may read text linearly, metatext requires us to read text through other modalities, like reading aloud or reading in reverse. Let's look at two examples of memes created with metatextual references.

First, picture an image of dying house plants on a shelf. There is a text overlay in Impact font that simply states, "Water Those??" as bottom text (Figure 4.2). In another, picture an American Flag, similar to the "thin blue line" reactionary pro-police flag, with black and white stripes but instead of a blue line in the center, there is a Hawaiian floral pattern, where the stars should be is an image of an igloo (Figure 4.3). Both are memes created as metatext for significantly different reasons, each requiring internet literacies to decipher. The first, the one showing dead plants, means **shoes**. The second, with the Hawaiian print and igloo on a flag, means **armed militia**.

We need the same skills to decipher both memes and both have off-platform use and notoriety. First, the dead plants meme asking the reader

Figure 4.2 A layered meme where the dead plants stand in for shoes because the call to action "Water Those?" really means "What are those?"

to water them gives a clue by incorporating the question marks. The text is homophonic and meant to be read out loud, especially stressing the second word: "What are those?" This meme is a layered meme in reference to a Vine video recorded by Brandon Moore, known as Young Busco, when he encountered a police officer in Berkeley, California. In the six-second video, we hear Moore as he trains his camera on the officer's face and says: "Officer I have one question for you: 'WHAT ARE THOOOOSE??!'" as his camera tilts rapidly down and focuses on his shoes.[19] The phrase became an audio meme, primarily used by teenagers to make fun of shoes that were deemed uncool. The meme became so prevalent that it appeared in Ryan Coogler's 2018 *Black Panther* Marvel Cinematic Universe film. When T'Challa walks in wearing sandals, his sister Shuri remarks "What are those??!" with wide eyes, stressing the word "those" as the camera cuts to Chadwick Boseman's sandals. (T'Challa, unaware of the joke, responds "those are my t'chanclas.") The joke was an added gift to people who spent enough time on the internet to understand the reference, an act commonly used in shows like *Family Guy*, but not often used in big budget blockbuster films.

On the other hand, the flag meme uses the same meme trickery to hide from content moderation systems, operate under the radar of the public, and to proudly display their internet bona fides. The flag is multilayered and multi-referential and designed as a counter-sigil to other meme-based organizations. First, the flag with the thin line is based on the counter-Black Lives Matter "thin blue line" flag created in reaction to the Black Lives Matter movement. The flag itself was created by a man named Andrew Jacob while he was in college. Inspired by his defense of the police force after the police killings of Eric Garner, Tamir Rice, and Michael Brown, Jacob developed a flag and brand based on the symbology police wear when an officer is killed. While Jacob told the Marshall Project his intent was not reactionary, a Blue Lives Matter movement was growing along with the rise of Trump and his support of police and extrajudicial power.[20]

According the The Marshall Project, the term thin blue line was popularized in the 1950s by William H Parker, the chief of the Los Angeles Police Department, who was known to be unambiguously racist. For years, the image of the thin blue line was on bumper stickers and patches, but Andrew Jacob, who is white, converted it into the flag symbol that is now both ubiquitous and remixable. The flag itself is now a meme that enables any cause to pick a color and replace the line in the middle of the flag. Why the Hawaiian pattern and the igloo? These are both homophonic memes based on a meme. There is an armed extremist militia movement known as the Boogaloos that uses both these icons. The origin is quite esoteric as it refers to the sequel of the 1984 film *Breakin'* which was about American

110 *Critical Internet Literacies*

breakdancing. Its sequel, *Breakin' 2: Electric Boogaloo*, was released seven months later and critically panned. It became a referential in-joke about the idea of creating sequels. The Boogaloo movement derives its name from their anticipation of a second civil war, a sequel desired by accelerationist or radicalized white supremacists who organize on social media.

According to investigative journalists Robert Evans and Jason Wilson of Bellingcat, the Boogaloo Movement, that uses the terms "Boogs" or "Boogaloo Boys" or "Boogaloo Bois," uplift bigoted hate speech from 4chan, specifically /k/ (4chan's channel dedicated to weapons), into Facebook groups.[21] The groups lean into gun rights rather than hate speech, bypassing moderation. However, the Boogs have used their meme techniques to disguise themselves: rather than "Boogaloo" you may say "Big Luau" or "Big Igloo," both homophonic memes designed to encode their meaning. This then goes further as the Boogaloo adherents dress in Hawaiian shirts to show their solidarity with one another. This militia is also represented fictionally in Alex Garland's 2024 *Civil War*. In other words, the uplift of the meme(s) to mainstream is part of a meme's popular trajectory.

While both these memes use similar tactics, they are incongruent in their power and role in society. Dead plants and shoes are a display of in-group jokes and metatextual references, but their end point is humor or poking fun. On the other hand, Hawaiian shirt print on a flag is encoded with racism, white supremacy, 4chan radicalization, misplaced victimhood, and a desire to enact violence. The Boogaloo Boys continue to operate with honor to their internet roots, working to share their ideology under the radar of the public with the keen knowledge of the collective lack of internet

Figure 4.3 The Flag of the Boogaloo Boys featuring both the "Big Igloo" and the "Big Luau."

Memes and Visual Communication 111

literacies. This secondary model, built upon the layering discovered in the Doge meme, is used prolifically in online spaces, especially in the "manosphere" and white supremacist message boards.

Meme Codification: From Meaning to Performance, the "Karen" Meme

On the morning of May 25, 2020, Christian Cooper was out birdwatching in Central Park in an area known as The Ramble when he noticed a woman and her dog nearby – the dog was off-leash though the area of the park required leashes. Christian Cooper asked the woman, whose name is Amy Cooper (no relation), to leash the dog and when she didn't comply, he attempted to give the dog a treat to reduce any possible agitation toward him or the birds. Amy Cooper took out her cell phone and threatened to call the police. Christian Cooper took his out as well and started recording her. "Please, call the cops," we hear on Christian's recording. Amy Cooper responds, "I'm gonna tell them there's an African American man threatening my life."[22] Christian Cooper uploaded his video to Facebook where it went wildly viral, gaining millions of views on the site and of its reposts on Twitter. By that afternoon, Amy Cooper had lost her job and surrendered her dog. She also gained something she likely didn't want, the meme moniker "Karen."

The Karen meme is an unfortunate role played mostly by white women who knowingly or unknowingly perform an act of privilege and subtle racism while on camera. The meme is most recognizable by the stereotypical haircut, made famous by Kate Gosselin of the reality series *John and Kate Plus 8*. The hairstyle is usually blond, with a high rise in the back and swooping bangs that angle down beyond the chin. Some may know this haircut as the "May I Speak to the Manager" hairstyle for the same reasons as above. Aside from Amy Cooper, known as the "Central Park Karen," the summer of 2020 introduced a variety of Karens who were caught on camera expressing rage, racism, and in some cases, threats of violence. How this meme operates gives us another example of how much the overlap of internet culture affects our everyday lives, attitudes, and reactionary behavior. The Karen meme peaked in the early months of the stay-at-home period of the pandemic while the use of outdoor spaces became shared environments for people pent up in their apartments and houses, shifting norms of behavior in an uncertain time while images of police brutality against Black people were dominating news cycles. As Dr. André Brock Jr. explained in *Time Magazine* at the time:

One of the things that has worked throughout American history is finding a way to project whiteness in need of defense or protection. For

112 *Critical Internet Literacies*

men, it's a fight; for women, it's calling men to help on their behalf or demonstrating that they are so frail that they cannot handle the weight. So in this moment, where we've been trapped in our house for six weeks with nothing to do but feel, [so] when you see these videos, you have nothing else to do but watch them and see people's reactions to them... a grievance for white women and white people, but also an anger by people that even if they are white, can see the injustice of the situation.[23]

Being called a Karen is paradoxical as it is considered "offensive" but also earned by being "offensive." On the other hand, the moniker is now occasionally weaponized as a retort thrown at women who are share opinions or critique of things deserving of critique.

How does this metatext work? Why Karen? The layers to this meme are more potent than that of Doge and align more similarly to that of the Boogaloo flag. Some memes contain energy stored in their meaning. (A point we'll expand upon further in the following chapter.) The Karen memes are signifiers of a relationship to societal norms and expectations, but only appear when actions are performed. Unlike IRL memes like "planking" or "owling," the Karen memes are an exhibition and to be labeled a Karen enters the subject into the meme space which typically results in public awareness, admonishment, and stickiness. It's further leveled up by its reactionary meta properties – labeled usually on white women in response to an unwarranted amount of aggression toward dark-skinned people.

So why Karen? The women labeled Karens are not likely to even be named that. According to data from the Social Security Administration, the name Karen peaked in the mid-1960s. The pejorative Karen peaked in the early 2020s – labeled on women far younger than those birth years of popularity. Interestingly, the meme also comes from an earworm from 2005, the same year the term "doge" re-entered the lexicon. During a bit by comedian Dane Cook in a stand-up special, he joked that "every group has a 'Karen,' and she's always a bag of douche." A simple one-off name picked by Dane Cook has even deeper roots than the name, but his moniker is what becomes the meme. According to researcher and host of NPR's "Code Switch" podcast, Karen Grisby Bates explains that historically there was a reference to "unreasonable white women" during the antebellum period and Jim Crow periods of the United States. The term used then was "Miss Ann."[24]

Memes are not just of their present moment or limited by their display on a specific person. They are codifications of reductionist concepts that the community agrees work best for the transference of the idea. In the case of the Karen meme and the Boogaloo flag, these memes are encoded to uplift the concept and hegemony of white supremacy out in the open. They are visuals for a performance of Western white power as it acts out against perceived oppression. Memes like these are now the norm by comparison to the easy, shareable, format-based image macro memes of the late aughts. The incursion of the Doge meme empowered meme makers to open the structure, encode metatext, and bury meaning several layers deep, many containing stored energy, and this can be seen in the memes that resulted in the violence at the US Capitol on January 6, 2021 or in "manifesto" memes that inspire mass violence. Memes in the 2020s are distinctly more referential, acknowledging the growth of internet fluency gained after the stay-at-home period of the pandemic and the globalization of trends through TikTok and Instagram. On the other hand, today's memes are adjusted to in-group messaging, no longer requiring viral uplift to maintain popularity. Sometimes, the more niche the better.

Decoding or Debunking Pepe the Frog's Meme Magick

"We actually elected a meme as president" one of the many anonymous users on 4chan's /pol/ posted next to the image of Pepe the Frog the evening of Tuesday, November 8, 2016. While many journalists believed they would be celebrating the collapse of the alt-right that evening, the 4chan contingent was celebrating their victory in converting their narrow, angry trolling version of internet culture into an avatar of avarice that would now be president of the United States.[25] A mainstream curiosity was piqued as to how the internet could have aided in the election of Donald Trump and focused mainly on the fact that Trump's campaign not only courted some of the more openly bigoted denizens of the web, but used them to rally an electorate. Surveys would later show that the online trolls were not enough to sway the vote, but it didn't stop them from taking credit.

As shown in the exhaustive 2020 documentary *Feels Good Man* (which we'll discuss further in Chapter 6), the role the Pepe the Frog meme played in the election was akin to "meme magick" – the magic with the "k" at the end meaning a spiritual practice of rituals or occult-like beliefs. Pepe was thought to be a sigil, loaded with metaphysical properties of collective occult spirituality, and many believed their use of Pepe aligned with the election of the US president. In short, many users in the forums felt they had an ability to harness Pepe the Frog's meme powers as a collective to push an "unelectable" reality star into the presidency. Pepe, like Doge, is a combination meme. First appearing in Matt Furie's comic series "Boys Club" about a handful of anthropomorphic stoner animal roommates, Pepe was simply one of the characters. Furie would post many of the frames and pages from his book on MySpace, and in 2005 he posted the now infamous panel of Pepe using the toilet while pulling his pants all the way to the ground. When asked later by his roommate Landwolf why he goes to the bathroom like that, he responded: "Feels good man."

114 *Critical Internet Literacies*

Furie, as shown in *Feels Good Man*, had no idea what the internet would do with that phrase and over the next several years, "feels good man" was repurposed as a mantra in the weightlifting sections of the early aughts internet. (The weightlifting communities were adjacent to the pickup artistry communities and represented early versions of the manosphere.) In the early 2010s, Pepe become popular though an odd version of meme scarcity, similar to baseball card collecting, as young people entering the digital space fought to claim rights to internet-born content and keep it online. Scarcity in this sense meant making variations of Pepe that were too inappropriate to share widely, keeping them as archival material rather than as memetic tools. But Pepe was also a perfect meme for the very online. As Morry Kolman writes in *Bitcoin Magazine*:

> Pepe soon became a fixture in these communities, his variations and visage becoming commonplace. Found a dollar on the street? Feels good man. Didn't get the job? Feels bad man. He was the perfect reaction image; a genre of meme that lives and dies on its ability to accurately reflect the feelings of the user posting it. Not only was he simple and authentic, but the two constituent parts of Pepe as a meme – his face and his catchphrase – could always individually stand in for the whole.[26]

The goal of the meme community that supported Pepe was to replicate, but not distribute, the image. The meme *belonged* online. While Pepe was founded in the pages of comics, it belonged to the domain of "NEETs." The socioeconomic class-based term refers to usually young men who are either disenfranchised or disconnected from society. It means "Not in education, employment, or training" and this group saw themselves as the opposite to "normies," referring to people in society who felt the system was working for them comfortably. This class ownership of Pepe was counter to his growing popularity. As he was altered, he became more mainstream and as Kolman further argues, "Pepe's normification is his commodification." As Pepe was posted on mainstream social media, he lost his power of scarcity. Due to Pepe's wider spread use, the deeply online community reacted by altering Pepe in a variety of racist, antisemitic, and hate-filled ways, so abhorrent they would be flagged on social media sites and unable to be broadcast in media. These tactics, used in previous generations by guerilla activists and civil rights defendants, also allowed anonymous users to maintain their invisibility through unpublishable content.

Further, Pepe benefited from a series of coincidences that convinced users that the image was "magical" or held occult-like powers. People who used Pepe were often part of the World of Warcraft community where instead of "LOL" the term "Kek" was used as it was the Korean

Memes and Visual Communication   115

onomatopoeia for laughing. Coincidentally, there is an ancient Egyptian god known as Kek which happens to be a frog. While these alignments are simply part of meme genesis, Pepe fans believed they were a sign that they could use Pepe to manifest reality. When Donald Trump retweeted his likeness in the form of Pepe the Frog in 2016, it gave credence to the communities that not only have the darkest parts of the web had made it to the campaign of the president, but meme magick was possible. We must be more rational about this approach and understand its myopic reality. In Ryan Broderick's 2018 *Buzzfeed* piece, "This is How We Radicalized the World," he notes that Trump was a singular representative of a global rightward shift. While many reports had been focusing directly on the impact of internet culture on the election, one could step back and recognize the structural issues that contributed to Trump's rise. Broderick writes:

> The way the world is using their phones is almost completely dominated by a few Silicon Valley companies. The abuse that is happening is due to their inability to manage that responsibility. All of this has become so normalized in the three years since it first began to manifest that we just assume now that platforms like Facebook, YouTube, WhatsApp, and Twitter will exacerbate political and social instability. We expect they will be abused by ultranationalist trolls. We know they will be exploited by data firms. We wait for them to help launch the careers of populist leaders.[27]

Populism's rise globally is a boon to social media companies and to media in general. It's good for ratings and engagement, but populism's true value is in the coherence of communities in an unregulated space. While it could be argued the Pepe the Frog contributed to Trump's election, Pepe really had more value as a secondary avatar, one still active today in the form of users who prioritize trolling over discourse and disenfranchised young men expressing their woes. Pepe the Frog contains no more magick than that of any occult practice, but its singular identity helps cohere ideologies. In a sense, that is magical because we don't often give enough credit to organic communities as their soft power of influence grows, but in the case of Pepe, the story is still ongoing.

The Feels Guy: The Everlasting Wojak

A lasting effect of Pepe the Frog's expression in the meme space is in the meme's representation of emotional affect. Morry Kolman explained that the image or the phrase "feels good man" stand in for each other, but in simpler communication styles, the web's most online users needed

116   Critical Internet Literacies

something far more visual – and less attached to someone's intellectual property – to represent their emotions. In 2010, a new character was introduced similar to Pepe in comic form named "Wojak." Published on a German imageboard like 4chan by artist Christian Grodecki, Wojak was usually accompanied by the phrase "I know that feel bro" and his bald, beady-eyed likeness was usually seen in an embrace with a similar Wojak. According to Francesco Iazzi in *NSS Magazine*, Wojak's expression in his embrace reveals a "certain veiled bitterness" that is "one of the purest expressions of social awkwardness and the disillusionment of millennials online."[28]

The Feels Guy has been renamed, reformed, restyled, and reused in possibly millions of scenarios. You may recognize him online as the "Doomer," which is just the Wojak with a beanie, a cigarette, and a hoodie. Doomer Wojak is just one of the dozens of variations of the meme and represents the avatar of an ageing audience. At one point, many of the users of the Doomer guy were young shitposters on 4chan, but as they grew older, they adopted a more mature version of their persona. Doomer is representational of younger, more endearing users, followed by text like "Has too many memes," "Listens to sad music because other music is generic," or "Likes comics and anime but won't admit [it]." As users grew, so did Wojak; Doomer now dons facial hair and saggy eyes with more contours in its face. Now, the original Doomer is called the "Zoomer," a moniker for Gen Z teens adopting the persona. There is a female-presenting version as well, known as "Doomer girl," which is just simply Wojak with softer features, short black hair, and a choker necklace.

The most disturbing derivative of Wojak is the NPC, a version of the meme with (somehow) fewer features, a pointed nose, and usually colored completely grey, and used most often as a derogatory image by those on the far right. NPC, meaning "non-playable character," refers to the extra characters in video games that display little or no agency in their computerized worlds. In 2016, the meme appeared on the 4chan video game /v/ board where posters asked the existential question of whether they may be an NPC. It soon morphed into a slur when applied to people who used the same political catch phrases consistently, aimed mostly at progressives or the left. However, the NPC meme burst into mainstream discussion when Kevin Roose wrote a *New York Times* piece about it in 2018 following Twitter's takedown of bot accounts using the NPC avatar.[29] Roose took the bait of the 4chan trolls who had gamed Twitter in hopes that the NPC would become more visible, attracting more disaffected people down its rabbit hole. Roose's lack of internet literacies covered the meme from its surface meaning, but failed to recognize its codes, simply laundering some of the far right's ideologies onto the *New York Times* and its readers.

Julia Alexander of *The Verge* helped clear up the confusion in a long-form piece explaining the NPC's issues and critiquing Roose's uplift. Alexander writes:

> Reporting on hyper-niche memes, even when they're attached to more newsworthy events, inevitably carries a cost in terms of amplification. To report necessarily means giving new symbols to wider audiences, which gives bad actors more power in a self-proclaimed fight against censorship. The paradox reporters are often faced with is finding a responsible way to report on harmful memes spreading without amplifying hate.[30]

Alexander relates the NPC meme to Pepe, recognizing its power as an avatar of hate speech but contends that the coverage misses the point of memes like Pepe, Wojak, or the NPC. She writes that the NPC meme was covered because of Twitter's actions rather than *why* 4chan trolls would compare "liberals to sub-humanoid beings." The NPC meme is a visual reaction to progressive anger and acts more like a blanket takedown than a good faith way of understanding another person's point of view. Like the disaffected Wojak, the NPC was a label to place on *the other*, allowing the poster to feel that they had some agency and free will while the other did not.

The NPC meme is still used, but no longer fully coded as far right. It more likely represents the lack of agency in a given situation. Wojak, Doomer Girl, and Doomer/Zoomer are often used in endearing settings, compared to their opposite: the Chad, a strong-chinned, bearded, blond-haired version of the Wojak. These memes are now representatives of mood, acting as universal internet characters that are recognizable to internet audiences. All use of these memes must be read in the context of their *intent*, which is far harder to analyze than you may think. Regardless, in a world of chaos, the Wojak and its variations are signs that people are trying to make sense of it all, one meme at a time.

From 4chanification to Fashwave: Rebranding Memes

Trump's election had a unique outcome on the world of memes, and although most focus on Pepe the Frog, other 4chan iconography became more visible. The public had become aware of Pepe the Frog and many blamed the internet's communities for using Pepe as a hate symbol. As this book continues to argue, the lack of internet literacies mixed with public awareness causes a reactionary shift in terms of content moderation and public reception. The misunderstanding of internet culture, or the lack of serious interpretations of it before Trump's election, did not prepare

118 *Critical Internet Literacies*

average media consumers for the reality they had been already living in for several years. Further, the success of Donald Trump's campaign and his willingness to court the online far right succeeded in "mainstreaming" darker ideologies. Populist leaders around the world followed suit. In Italy, far-right provocateurs and politicians like Matteo Salvini of the fascist-sympathizing Lega Party leaned on meme makers to help recruit younger voters into the ideology. In Brazil, Jair Bolsonaro's "Bolsominions" were (extreme) far-right followers that merged the identity of meme culture with their outward stance by mixing the yellow Minions from the *Despicable Me* film franchise with their leader's likeness.

Memes and content streaming up into the mainstream had a secondary effect on social media: engagement. Far-right content plays an interesting role in the economy of social media platforms. For one, it energizes the base and believers, allowing them to engage and follow content typically cordoned to subcultures. Second, those opposed to the content – and specifically Donald Trump – developed their own reactionary movement known as the #Resistance, doing similar recruitment operations that the far right had developed earlier. The more provocative content benefits the platforms and the shareholders and there was a fair amount of leeway in content moderation when it came to content that achieved higher engagement. New hate-fueled meme accounts grew in popularity, empowered by the visibility of the filter-impaired US president. These accounts reposted the least harmful tweets from the darker parts of Twitter and Telegram and created their own memes that espoused "America First" concepts like guns, Christian Nationalism, and misogyny.

In 2019, Taylor Lorenz described this trend in *The Atlantic*. Lorenz interviews several young men who became more politically engaged following Trump's election and came across popular Instagram meme pages like @the_typical_liberal and far-right activist Rogan Handley's @dc_draino, two pages that openly support Trump and Trumpism. At the time of Lorenz's writing, both pages were private, hiding from reactive content moderators – today they are both public and Rogan O'Handley is often seen in Trump's social circles. Instagram's explore page and algorithm were once known for their knack of pushing users down rabbit holes and Lorenz describes her experience on the site:

> Following just a handful of these accounts can quickly send users spiraling down a path toward even more extremist views and conspiracies, guided by Instagram's own recommendation algorithm. On March 17, I clicked Follow on @the_typical_liberal. My account lit up with follow requests from pages with handles alluding to QAnon, and the app immediately prompted me to follow far-right figures such as Milo Yiannopoulos, Laura Loomer, Alex Jones, and Candace Owens, as well as

Memes and Visual Communication 119

a slew of far-right meme pages such as @unclesamsmisguidedchildren and @the.new.federation. Following these pages resulted in suggestions for pages dedicated to promoting QAnon, chemtrails, Pizzagate, and anti-vaccination rhetoric."[31]

The further mainstreaming of Pepe also resulted in the Anti-Defamation League declaring Pepe a hate symbol, much to Matt Furie's chagrin. Furie later won a lawsuit against Alex Jones for misusing Pepe's likeness and as a result, memers created Pepe variants that devolved from the Furie-like avatar.

While some variations of Pepe had made their way to Hong Kong in the form of a resistance campaign against oppression, other variations ventured deeper into the darkness. One variation, which we'll go further into next chapter, is the "groyper" variation, a fatter version of Pepe with arms crossed and glaring; the groyper Pepe is used primarily by the "Groyper Army." Following the white nationalist march in Charlottesville, Virginia, groypers cohered behind Nick Fuentes, a young podcaster who not only espouses white nationalist beliefs and Christian conservativism, but extreme misogyny, racism, antisemitism, and Holocaust denial. Fuentes styles his hair short on the side and bushy on the top and wears suits and ties. He insists that the rhetoric he uses on his podcast is ironic (though this is to avoid moderation). He once advised a caller to his podcast to respond to his wife with, "a vicious and forceful backhanded slap with your knuckles right across her face." He then hastens to add, "Just a joke... I would never lay a hand on a woman, unless she had it coming."[32]

Groypers emerge in public wearing oversize foam Make America Great Again hats and complain that many in the far right aren't far-right *enough*. The term groyper is likely connected to an antisemitic trope but is rarely ever defined with certainty to continue to obfuscate any specific constraints to their movement. The term, like many terms from the internet, is also designed to seem so silly that the news has a difficult time reporting on the subject. Saying "groyper" on the news to an unaware public may result in unserious discussions and laughter from journalists who should be taking the subject much more seriously. Groypers also use tactics to uplift ideologies into the mainstream, all while hiding behind their moniker. According to an extensive report by the Institute for Research & Education on Human Rights, Nick Fuentes and Patrick Casey (the leader of another racist group called The American Identity Movement) started what they called the "Groyper Wars," and attempt to replace Trump with an even more nationalist candidate to hold their values.[33]

While social media sites finally began clamping down on far-right imagery, new aesthetics also began to emerge online. Users aligned with Fuentes's America First ideologies started getting in the ear of politicians

120 *Critical Internet Literacies*

like Arizona's Paul Gosar and Georgia's Marjorie Taylor Greene. These politicians used memes in their political processes, often retweeting fan material encoded with far-right messaging to their followers. While some politicians continue to "play dumb" with the meaning of the messages, it still moves far-right propaganda into the mainstream. On the other hand, many in this space feel deeply threatened by the possibility of mainstreaming their views and consider that tactic a problem to their movements.

* * *

Following the release of The Facebook Papers in 2021, Meta products readjusted their algorithm to allegedly protect users, but the damage had already been done. Memes evolved once again and were often found encoded with Christian Nationalist imagery, masculinity, "traditional aesthetics," and "traditional values." Pages like @worth__fighting_for and @trad_west_ have a collective half-a-million followers and lean directly into the "fashwave" aesthetic. Though the original aesthetic was far more obvious with hate symbols, the new pages act as though they are motivational content for vulnerable, younger users. For example, on @trad_west_, the pinned memes display white supremacist and masculine messaging, stating "the world you were born into is gone, replaced by degeneracy." The meme asks users to "Start with yourself" and "Reclaim your destiny." The images embedded in these memes show the 9/11 terror attacks followed by images of corporate media, McDonalds, and fairly clear images of Chinese leadership as well as featuring a statue of Jesus with glowing red eyes.

The foundation of fashwave is vaporwave, an earlier aesthetic based on nostalgia, built by fans of the synthwave (hear: modern synthesizer with techno beats) music genre who used visual memes to express what they loved about it. Designed by extremely online computer programmers, web coders, and gamers who listened to the electronic music loaded with sounds and atmospheres from the 1980s and early 1990s, the genre was deeply satirical, both making fun of the nostalgia and also expressing genuine love of the media of the time. The images they developed, many of which accompanied recordings of the music, placed indistinct figures against backgrounds of wavy, psychedelic neon colors that looked like the pixelated backgrounds of 16-bit video games. Fashwave added new characters, some of whom wore red, white, and black swastika armbands.

Fashwave often piques the interest of the uninitiated through its aesthetics while bonding those who are in the know. It grants each member of the insider community permission to access fascism in modern aesthetics. New participants in this developing culture dig themselves into it more deeply, exploring the ideas behind the symbols. Fashwave is different from previous memetic trends in the way it infiltrates in quietly insidious ways.

In March of 2021, for example, Tom Hanks's son Chet helped make the fashwave memes mainstream. In a tone-deaf attempt to make a joke about rapper Megan Thee Stallion's 2019 hit "Hot Girl Summer," the younger Hanks declared that 2021 would be "White Boy Summer." In short order his joke was careening around the internet. In response Chet Hanks was deluged with allegations that he was a racist dogwhistling to white supremacists. It quickly turned into a full-blown white-supremacist meme that received wide distribution on the Telegram chat app remixed in fashwave aesthetics.

In their extensive breakdown of the meme, Bellingcat's Garrison Davis and Robert Evans explain the meme's traits:

> On Instagram, a number of White Boy Summer memes featuring Nazi motifs were observed coexisting next to more general White Boy Summer content depicting conservative political commentators and other popular figures who have a more mainstream profile. The fact these two types of content can be found in the same spaces suggests the term has the potential to draw in more moderate right-wing users who can then be exposed to radical and extremist propaganda. The more extreme White Boy Summer, or WBS, memes often include the same sort of radical imagery first seen in 8chan posts and videos geared towards inspiring terrorist attacks in imitation of the Christchurch shooting. In 2019, shootings in El Paso, Texas, Poway, California and Halle, Germany were all birthed from this community.[34]

The power of the White Boy Summer meme can be seen in the way it circumvented the platform's ability to block hate speech. Nick Fuentes adopted the slogan and went on a "White Boy Summer Road Trip" in 2021. The phrase was pasted onto images of Tucker Carlson and Florida Governor Ron DeSantis. These images are often altered to include the wraparound sunglasses favored by Nick Fuentes. As Andrew Anglin, founder of fascist neo-Nazi website The Daily Stormer, has said, "The core of marketing is aesthetic. We need to look appealing," he wrote. "We have to be hip and we have to be sexy."[35]

Some of the "traditional" aesthetics are even loaded with overt misogyny focusing on women's appearance – specifically young pregnant women and women wearing dresses or traditional cultural clothing. A short scroll through the @worth__fighting_for page reveals an endless barrage of both coded and blatant white supremacist content. These memes differ from their original roots by using a different font style and templates. The font is similar to Impact, but rather than a stroke, it is highlighted in black; nearly all text is in capital letters. The memes often reuse popular meme iconography and icons like Wojak, Chad, Stacy, and troll faces. There is an

122 *Critical Internet Literacies*

even further romanticization of Western European imagery, focused on the architecture and medieval towns, filled with engagement captions designed to ask whether the US has lost its way. Even a small amount of scrutiny on any of these memes can detect their inability to correctly understand the context of what they are saying.

These are memes made specifically for the least literate and hidden in plain sight. Instagram, afraid of being labeled a "liberal" platform, enables the hosting of these pages because they continue to toe the line of appropriate content, never truly inciting any harm off-platform. These are memes that host an ideology, not a motivation, therefore these memes could easily be considered "Christian fan pages." It is up to us to push back against the bigoted premise baked into the imagery and in the next chapter, we'll delve further into the tactics used by this genre to push hatred into the mainstream.

On Cope, Meme Weaponization, and Dark Brandon

The rise of populism and the rightward shift in the 2010s was somewhat reactionary to the "hope and change" mentality of the aughts. The 2008 financial collapse sent ripples across the economy on a global scale and resulted in a wave of cynicism that best manifested in digital spaces. Therefore, it is no surprise that reporting on elections in the 2010s pointed to the effect memes had on the movements. For example, in May 2017, far-right populist candidate Marine Le Pen ran against French president Emmanuel Macron and used memes, especially the strategies from the US far right, to boost her following. Members of the subreddit /r/TheDonald, created a strategy guide for French online populists and shitposters to participate, focusing their issues on immigrants and economy.[36] The digital tactics did not translate to electoral wins and Macron was re-elected.

What is the point of these memes? What purpose do they serve if they act as digital tools? In many ways, online political memes reproduce a form of coping with societal changes and the meme's messaging create in-group knowledge that "someone else is out there" with the same intentions. As users grow older, their civic tactics shift as well, and in the US, low-level memes were created in reaction to populist memes in #Resistance channels and Facebook pages. These memes are usually just provocative tweets, screen captured, recaptioned, and shared, showing up in the most liberal of Facebook pages. Facebook and Meta products obviously gained from the reactionary memes as more participation was occurring within the boundaries of their products rather than on Reddit. As Reddit began to crack down on hate speech coming from sites like /r/TheDonald, Meta properties only gained from their new center of liberal coping memes that peaked during the Trump presidency.

Memes and Visual Communication   123

On the other hand, as #Resistance memes became mainstream and more common, a reaction on the right developed their own, more coded memes to adjust their energy. Trump's continuous messaging that he was the victim aligned with the internet's ideological belief system, propagated by NEETs and those who feel they have been "censored" or excised from family events due to their possibly bigoted speech. The message of victimhood is the most useful, as it aligns with the concept of coping and supporting the underdog throughout a difficult time. For example, following President Trump's first impeachment in 2020, he posted a tweet featuring an image of himself that stated: "In reality, they're not after me, they're after you. I'm just in the way," positing that he was an avatar of his followers percieved woes.[37]

Following Trump's defeat by Joe Biden, meme makers used memes at an accelerated rate to cope with their loss and deal with their emotions. In late December 2020, a variation of the "I'm just in the way" phrase became visualized as a meme and a call to action. One of the memes created by a member on a pro-Trump forum featuring an image of Donald Trump holding a shield over a small, childlike anthropomorphic Pepe the Frog, burning arrows sticking out of the shield and into Trump. Pepe was safe. The caption read: "He has had our back. Do you have his? 1/6/2021 Washington, D.C."[38] As we know now, many of those memes contained an intense amount of stored kinetic energy that inspired supporters to storm the US Capitol on January 6. Both the #Resistance memes and victimhood Trump memes, as well as global memes espousing similar feelings of loss, could easily be considered part of the genre of coping memes.

* * *

When Joseph Biden became US president in 2021, he promised a quieter presidency than his predecessor. However, by this point, we understood memes could have impacts that increase danger in the case of mass shootings, incel terrorism, and an insurrection. Biden is no stranger to being a meme and was visible in a variety of images during the Obama presidency. Biden was seen with ice cream, around a Corvette, with a mullet, and so on, but he was not an organic meme creator. In contrast to Trump, Biden's gaffes were reported as errors rather than ridiculous quips to be remixed online. However, the memetic energy that helped fuel the insurrection could not be matched by the Democratic leader. In turn, a new anti-Biden meme emerged by accident during a Nascar race on October 2, 2021 when driver Brandon Brown was interviewed by an NBC Sports reporter following his first place finish. In the background, the crowd starts the chant "Fuck Joe Biden!" The phrase was used quite often at Nascar events, and according the to AP, NBC and Nascar attempt to hide the crowd's noise but it was far too loud.[39] The reporter, hearing the chant, explained to the

124   *Critical Internet Literacies*

TV audiences that he heard "Let's Go Brandon!" rather than the expletive filled – and FCC banned – phrase.

Soon after, the one-to-one meme became a memetic handshake among Trump-supporting Republicans aiming to please their angry base. As one of the easiest, simple memes, Let's Go Brandon contains no nuance or subtext; the meme is a phrase replacement. The nuance of Let's Go Brandon is in its delivery. While it is acceptable to say "fuck," and both the word and phrase are protected by the First Amendment, there is an additional performance in expressing "appropriate" language and conservative values using the meme's word replacement. More importantly, the meme is a perfect slogan for merchandise and at least two physical stores named Let's Go Brandon opened in the United States. These stores sold pro-Trump paraphernalia and Let's Go Brandon T-shirts, bumper stickers, decals, and face masks. Acting like low-culture propaganda, Let's Go Brandon is the opposite of the fashwave aesthetic, but it also carries harmful energy. Many supporters used the phrase to post in public places like Starbucks or message boards and the meme played a secondary role in training basic direct and civic action. Even in the case of trolling, the act of civic participation is still civic participation.

As a meme, Let's Go Brandon is limited in its remixability and suggests an ends rather than a means, however, the meme did evolve. The meme name "Brandon" was repurposed by both the far left and far right to make fun of Joe Biden and acknowledge the coded f-word in its deployment. A section of the far-right meme space known as Dark MAGA, which used fascistic imagery, neo-Nazi symbology, and white supremacist coding (like the same group that amplified "White Boy Summer") remixed the idea to make fun of Joe Biden as "Dark Brandon." The images, reminiscent of anime imagery, featured Joe Biden as an ironic supervillain, willing to harm the civilians he leads. They gave him glowing eyes, like those used in meme imagery, meaning charging up, and soon, Dark Brandon was adopted by more creative users who remixed Biden's image to make fun of Biden supporters. The tactic backfired – sort of. Biden fans found the imagery exciting and "cool" and Democrats began using the meme in support of Biden as it presented him as far more exciting than he appears.

The use of Dark Brandon upset many on the far right as it significantly depowered the game that was being played. Following several Biden policy wins including the Inflation Reduction Act, politicians like Senator Chris Murphy posted images of Dark Brandon. To approach this critically, one must consider that this meme, like others, are reactionary – Dark Brandon technically belongs to the far right and using the meme means playing on the far right's playing field. As Aja Romano of *Vox* explains:

To some degree, this is all just a return volley. The Democrats who started to run with "Dark Brandon" clearly hoped to ape the style of

Memes and Visual Communication   125

the edgy "Dark MAGA" memes, combining their aesthetic with depictions of Biden as a take-no-prisoners badass leader. MAGA supporters used their own over-the-top memes to reframe Trump's perceived bumbling incompetence as a giant disguise, a foil for the competent strongman that lay beneath. Now Biden supporters are repeating the magic, framing Biden's perceived bumbling incompetence as a mask for a tough, masculine warrior who gets things done. Turnabout, fair play, etc.[40]

To create or use memes in this reactionary format means the Biden campaign is playing on field not only dominated by the far right, but also *designed* by the far right. It may not be prudent to play the game at all to consider any chance of winning in this genre of media.

In May 2024, Biden's team posted a job opening for a "Partner Manager, Content and Meme Pages" to the Biden/Harris re-election campaign page.[41] While the position calls for a meme page operator, nowhere in the description does it call for the candidate to be a meme creator, rather someone who "will initiate and manage day-to-day operations in engaging the internet's top content and meme pages." This assumes that the Biden campaign is aware of the role internet creators play in the connection to a younger audience, but perhaps some definition of the role may be necessary due to the shift in memes in the 2020s. The era of the "Meme War" is over and weaponization is now much more apparent and in the open. As edgy Christian Nationalist memes have been replaced by the "tradwife" movement and "stay at home girlfriend" influencers, memes have become embedded, normalized, and even celebrated in culture. Now, the term meme may require an updated definition.

Reading Memes in the 2020s

"My vibe right now is sorta eclectic boho cottage core maximalist disco low carb trad cath indie sleeze cactus core femcel rustic Midwest emo Chloe Sevigny BPD Starbucks dorm anime mean girl West coast Kennedy Assassination" reads a meme posted to @namaste.at.home.dad's Instagram meme page. We can spend time deciphering this meme and all its terms and its irony, but it would serve no more purpose than to explain that the memes of the 2020s rely on users to fully understand the references and the "vibe" that the meme is presenting. In this case, these words are printed in TikTok caption font above an image of a young woman making her bed with white sheets and a pink pillow. The meaning of this meme is a satire on the hyper-niche and the TikTokification of everyday life where users feel they must find a label for every minute emotion they

126   Critical Internet Literacies

may be feeling. In the 2020s, many memes no longer resemble any of their historical precedents, relying solely on the community to engage if they feel the "same" as the poster.

Memes of the 2020s are still layered, nuanced, and referential, but the power is now with meme makers who have achieved a space of curatorial expertise and community awareness and are more willing to be known publicly as memers. According to meme researcher and founder of the Meme Studies Research Network,[42] Idil Galip, as outlined in her *Internet Histories* article:

> Today, it is possible to follow the work of meme makers who create their own cohesive artistic and authorial styles, like we would the oeuvre of painters, writers, or musicians. Internet meme creators can break through online anonymity and cultural obscurity by using a variety of digital platforms, such as Instagram, Patreon, Twitter, Facebook, Discord, and YouTube. Meme creators are inextricably linked to the mercurial trends of digital culture as they act as scribes and shapers of public discourse.[43]

Meme creators now combine earlier meme characters with present-day aesthetics that emerge on TikTok or Instagram Reels. In addition, most meme creators work collaboratively, sharing ideas, using direct message backchannels, or reposting other accounts' memes. The concept of cope is now embedded and understanding these memes only works if you are following the meme curator who fits your niche interest. Nearly all meme pages and meme makers are fully aware of the role they play within the structure of social media. In fact, at the height of the stay-at-home period, Instagram hosted a Global Meme Summit on Zoom and invited Mark Zuckerberg to thank the meme pages for their participation – and extremely low-cost labor.

Memes are changing, moving beyond their structuralism towards a standard method of communication, varying in nearly infinite aesthetics, their creators embedding *their own* references into them. Shifman's definition is limited to its time and now the definition is fractured. In the first *Critical Meme Reader*, Chloë Arkenbout, Jack Wilson, and Daniël De Zeeuw argue:

> the meme screws with time, and in this it is pompously and parodically postmodern... the meme also screws with narrative, or what could be called the gentrification of time... and memes are also tricksters, as they make us believe we control them while it's actually the other way around.[44]

Memes and Visual Communication   127

Galip compares memes to the grotesque era of art history in her article "The 'Grotesque' in Instagram Memes." She writes that like the Renaissance accident of rediscovering Nero's Domus Aurea when the art inside was considered "grotto-like" with frivolous and uncanny aesthetics, memes are similar in both their aesthetic flamboyance and carnival-like feel, but also reliant on precarious labor and creators to make these memes.

The new memes of the 2020s are hyper-specific, leaning into expression. Many memes that could be found on accounts like @namaste.as.home.dad's account, run by Joelle Bouchard, are an array of memes outside of a consistent aesthetic, mixing fonts, colors, earlier meme references, and occasionally require the caption to tell the full story. Galip writes, "The disruption of the viewer's expectations in grotesque memes defamiliarizes the viral meme format, introducing a different vision of the meme." It is this definition that fits best within the post-post-post-modern era of the internet meme (just a few decades old). Now, the idea of the shitpost, originally designed to derail conversation or shock a visitor, is the standard model of communication. Irony over seriousness *is* the game. To be a memer today is no longer the realm of "memelords" like @thefatjewish or @fuckjerry, but can be anyone, or any niche. Even journalists like Taylor Lorenz have started meme pages; Lorenz uses them as both a hobby and a sort of ethnographic experiment to understand digital workflows.

But anyone can now curate a meme page through the reverse process of their camera roll. Screengrab your favorites, post the ones you want your audience to see, or create memes with any aesthetic. The more hyper-niche the better. For example, @northwest_mcm_wholesale is a meme account that originated to make fun of Portland's most unique citizens, Oregon area hipster trends, and their alleged infatuation with mid-century modern furniture. The account continues to do so, but now leans into making fun of economic inequalities, virtue signaling by corporations, and critiques performative consumption and overpriced food. These memes are an amalgam of formats, styles, and aesthetics, relying on the fan base to fully understand the content. The meme manager, possibly named Herman Wakefield, considers himself a shitposter and shares his original memes with other meme pages that curate similar jokes.

In that sense, it is the manager and the memer who contain the knowledge of new meme literacies. The pace and the demand of the audience is so high that now many meme pages act as secondary sources of income. Meme pages may offer advertising embedded within memes themselves or as plugs. For example, the wholesome meme channel @kalesalad posts branded memes in partnership with internet-savvy brands like Hinge directly to their page. Many companies now connect to meme creators with partnerships to circumvent the Federal Trade Commission's demand that

128 *Critical Internet Literacies*

"#ad" be placed on the post. Now, memers may just call themselves a "partner." Further, many meme pages use their Stories feature to post advertisement and brand promotions relying on their relevance to the meme community. This hyper-niche promotional tactic is lucrative for the meme maker, and they often set their own price scales.

Reading today's memes utilizes the same meme literacies of the past, but we now need an updated definition. While Limor Shifman's definition continues to hold up, many memes today are created as an endpoint, meant to be shared, not remixed. Today, researcher Giovanni Schiazzi is working on a way to update the definition of a meme and this research is ongoing. Schiazzi's goal is to both further define the modern meme, but also develop a model to train machines to better detect, categorize, and archive memes at scale. As memes are global, sharing the culture of their site-specific audiences, memes are cultural artifacts. With hundreds of thousands of niche memes created every hour, we are threatened by the possibility of their loss and degradation over time, especially if a channel is banned or taken offline. We now know that memes are a mood barometer, and therefore an archive would benefit researchers, scholars, historians, and internet art historians. Memes are now part of our visual language and our meme literacies help us "read" the reality around us by looking "through" its meanings, deciphering its connections to life around us.

Notes

1 pictoria vark [@pictoriavark]. "I Don't Want to Be a Girlboss Anymore, i Want to Take Pictures of the Cows While My Husband Drives Me to My Lobotomy." Tweet. *Twitter*, June 29, 2021. https://twitter.com/pictoriavark/status/1409703068631846921.
2 gaiusflavius. "Gaius Flavius 🏺🏛 on Instagram: 'How Often Do You Think about the Ancient Rome? 🏛🏺 #ancientrome #roma #romanempire #Rome #antiquity #history.'" *Instagram*, September 19, 2023. https://www.instagram.com/reel/CwIZgAKNbnQ/.
3 Dickson, EJ. "Why Are So Many Men Obsessed With the Roman Empire?" *Rolling Stone* (blog), September 16, 2023. https://www.rollingstone.com/culture/culture-features/men-obsessed-roman-empire-explained-tiktok-1234826340/.
4 Sanchez, Rosa. "Well, Here's What We Think of the Roman Empire." *Harper's BAZAAR*, September 19, 2023. https://www.harpersbazaar.com/culture/features/a45211117/roman-empire-tiktok-trend-patriarchy-history-explained/.
5 https://www.instagram.com/gabbriette/.
6 Wilson, Sophie. "Why Are We so Obsessed with Lobotomies?" *Dazed*, September 12, 2023. https://www.dazeddigital.com/beauty/article/60782/1/why-are-we-so-obsessed-lobotomies-rise-ironic-nihilistic-feminism.
7 Reilly, Caroline. "Opinion | The Lobotomy-Chic Trend Has an Ugly History." *Washington Post*, August 3, 2023. https://www.washingtonpost.com/opinions/2023/08/03/lobotomy-chic-tiktok-social-media-tennessee-williams/.
8 Shifman, Limor. *Memes in Digital Culture*. MIT Press Essential Knowledge. Cambridge, Massachusetts: The MIT Press, 2014.

Memes and Visual Communication 129

9 Wark, Scott. "The Meme in Excess of Its Instance." *Excessive Research* (blog), September 30, 2015. https://transmedialeblog.wordpress.com/2015/09/30/scott-wark-the-meme-in-excess-of-its-instance/.

10 Marx, David W. "No Canon for Old Memes." *Culture: An Owner's Manual* (blog), February 13, 2024. https://culture.ghost.io/no-canon-for-old-memes/.

11 https://en.unesco.org/silkroad/silk-road-themes/festivals/marriage-venice-sea.

12 *Biz Cas Fri 1*, 2009. https://www.youtube.com/watch?v=tLSgRzCAtXA.

13 "Rondleman" is one of the many made up names Homestar gave to Strong Bad.

14 kabosu112. "今夜のご飯は何ですか？." かぼすちゃんとおさんぽ。. Accessed May 28, 2024. https://kabosu112.exblog.jp/9944144/.

15 McCulloch, Gretchen. "Will We All Speak Emoji Language in a Couple Years?" *Mental Floss*, April 9, 2015. https://www.mentalfloss.com/article/62584/will-we-all-speak-emoji-language-couple-years.

16 Applegate, Matt, and Jamie Cohen. "Communicating Graphically." *Cultural Politics* 13, no. 1 (March 1, 2017): 81–100. https://doi.org/10.1215/1743 2197-3755204.

17 McCulloch, Gretchen. "A Linguist Explains the Grammar of Doge. Wow." *The Toast*, February 6, 2014. https://the-toast.net/2014/02/06/linguist-explains-grammar-doge-wow/.

18 Salzman, Avi. "Dogecoin Started as a Joke. Now It's Too Important to Laugh Off." *barrons*. Accessed May 29, 2024. https://www.barrons.com/articles/dogecoin-started-as-a-joke-now-its-too-important-to-laugh-off-51620229273.

19 *What Are Those Original*, 2015. https://www.youtube.com/watch?v=HNtz 05bhI1k.

20 Chammah, Maurice, and Cary Aspinwall. "The Short, Fraught History of the 'Thin Blue Line' American Flag." *The Marshall Project*, June 8, 2020. https://www.themarshallproject.org/2020/06/08/the-short-fraught-history-of-the-thin-blue-line-american-flag.

21 Evans, Robert, and Jason Wilson. "The Boogaloo Movement Is Not What You Think." *bellingcat*, May 27, 2020. https://www.bellingcat.com/news/2020/05/27/the-boogaloo-movement-is-not-what-you-think/.

22 Aguilera, Jasmine. "White Woman Who Called Police on a Black Man at Central Park Apologizes, Says 'I'm Not a Racist.'" *Time*, May 26, 2020. https://time.com/5842442/amy-cooper-dog-central-park/.

23 Lang, Cady. "How the Karen Meme Confronts History of White Womanhood." *Time*, June 25, 2020. https://time.com/5857023/karen-meme-history-meaning/.

24 Goldblatt, Henry. "A Brief History of 'Karen.'" *New York Times*, July 31, 2020, sec. Style. https://www.nytimes.com/2020/07/31/style/karen-name-meme-history.html.

25 Ohlheiser, Abby. "Analysis | 'We Actually Elected a Meme as President': How 4chan Celebrated Trump's Victory." *Washington Post*, October 26, 2021. https://www.washingtonpost.com/news/the-intersect/wp/2016/11/09/we-actually-elected-a-meme-as-president-how-4chan-celebrated-trumps-victory/.

26 Kolman, Morry. "Pepe." *Bitcoin Magazine – Bitcoin News, Articles and Expert Insights*, August 4, 2022. https://bitcoinmagazine.com/culture/pepe.

27 Broderick, Ryan. "This Is How We Radicalized The World." *BuzzFeed News*, October 29, 2018. https://www.buzzfeednews.com/article/ryanhatesthis/brazil-jair-bolsonaro-facebook-elections.

28 Iazzi, Francesco. "How Wojak Became the Meme of the Moment." *nss magazine*, March 29, 2020. https://www.nssmag.com/en/article/21372.

130 *Critical Internet Literacies*

29 Roose, Kevin. "What Is NPC, the Pro-Trump Internet's New Favorite Insult?" *New York Times*, October 16, 2018, sec. U.S. https://www.nytimes.com/2018/10/16/us/politics/npc-twitter-ban.html.
30 Alexander, Julia. "The NPC Meme Went Viral When the Media Gave It Oxygen." *The Verge*, October 23, 2018. https://www.theverge.com/2018/10/23/17991274/npc-meme-4chan-press-coverage-viral.
31 Lorenz, Taylor. "Instagram Is Full of Conspiracy Theories and Extremism." *The Atlantic* (blog), March 21, 2019. https://www.theatlantic.com/technology/archive/2019/03/instagram-is-the-internets-new-home-for-hate/585382/.
32 Tom Dreisbach [@TomDreisbach]. "Last Night, Far-Right Extremist Nick Fuentes Went on a Lengthy, Violent and Misogynist Rant. A Viewer Asked How to Respond to His Wife 'Getting out of Line.' Fuentes, Who Has Received Support from Congressman Paul Gosar, Responded: 'Why Don't You Smack Her across the Face?' Https://T.Co/pdcVzYWeXS." Tweet. *Twitter*, April 23, 2021. https://twitter.com/TomDreisbach/status/1385656609351692290.
33 Institute for Research and Education on Human Rights. "From Alt-Right to Groyper (PDF) ★ Institute for Research and Education on Human Rights." Accessed June 3, 2024. https://irehr.org/reports/alt-right-to-groyper-pdf/.
34 Davis, Garrison, and Robert Evans. "White Boy Summer, Nazi Memes and the Mainstreaming of White Supremacist Violence." *bellingcat*, July 1, 2021. https://www.bellingcat.com/news/2021/07/01/white-boy-summer-nazi-memes-and-the-mainstreaming-of-white-supremacist-violence/.
35 Moore, Booth. "White Polo Shirts of White Supremacists, Neo Nazis Take Center Stage." *Hollywood Reporter*, August 14, 2017. https://www.hollywoodreporter.com/news/general-news/white-nationalist-uniform-polo-shirts-takes-center-stage-charlottsville-1029184/.
36 Clark, Peter Allen. "The Alt-Right's Worldwide Weaponization of Memes." *Mashable*, May 5, 2017. https://mashable.com/article/alt-right-memes-france-world.
37 Tweet removed after a *New York Times* copyright complaint. https://www.reuters.com/article/idUSKBN243060/.
38 See the meme in the center of my piece "On Copium Memes and Media Martyrdom." *Medium*, January 4, 2021. https://newanddigital.medium.com/on-copium-memes-and-media-martyrdom-ac2c69d3e4a8.
39 Long, Colleen. "How 'Let's Go Brandon' Became Code for Insulting Joe Biden." *AP News*, October 30, 2021. https://apnews.com/article/lets-go-brandon-what-does-it-mean-republicans-joe-biden-ab13db2120679284 55a3dba07756a160.
40 Romano, Aja. "The 'Dark Brandon' Meme – and Why the Biden Campaign Has Embraced It – Explained." *Vox*, August 11, 2022. https://www.vox.com/culture/23300286/biden-dark-brandon-meme-maga-why-confusing-explained.
41 https://jobs.lever.co/BFP/87722c1a-e593–4c2e-a630–50671dea033f.
42 https://memestudiesrn.wordpress.com/.
43 Galip, Idil. "Methodological and Epistemological Challenges in Meme Research and *Meme Studies*." *Internet Histories*, June 9, 2024, 1–19. https://doi.org/10.1080/24701475.2024.2359846.
44 Arkenbout, Chloë, Jack Wilson, and Daniel de Zeeuw, eds. *Critical Meme Reader: Global Mutations of the Viral Image*. INC Reader 15. Amsterdam: Institute of Network Cultures, 2021.

5 The Online to Mainstream Media Pipeline

Detecting and Decoding Uplifted Content

In our hypermediated present, the off-chance danger of getting radicalized is no longer confined to the internet's information flows. Rabbit holes of conspiracies, reactionary ideologies, and harmful beliefs may now appear outside their formative sources, emerging in news reports about novel curiosities of the digital world or delivered through friends who "heard it on TV." The majority of stories about internet phenomena are cute and engaging (see: Target yodeling kid or that other kid that loves corn), but there are dangers that take aim at a public who generally lack the internet literacies to steel themselves from engaging with the material in a critical or skeptical manner. Over the last several years, there has been a normalization of extremist and harmful ideologies on the internet due to the long, and unfortunate, so-called "4chanification of the internet."[1] From Elon Musk's rightward turn after his acquisition of Twitter to Christopher Rufo's out-in-the-open public relations smear campaigns against critical race theory and college presidents like Harvard's Claudine Gay to more aggressively coded campaigns containing toxic masculinity, anti-trans rhetoric, and antisemitic messaging, the mainstream media occasionally provides a place to launder and uplift harmful speech.

This chapter focuses on several case studies of mainstream media (even alternative mainstreams) laundering internet-based, encoded content directly to uncritical audiences. These examples represent an outgrowth of marketplaces that merge both the creator economy's worst assets (like grifting, merch, and manipulative media) and the memetic flows of reductionist concepts that veil harmful origins. In general, these examples are "good" for platforms and media industries as they generate reaction, engagement, ongoing discourse, even if misguided. How may we detect such moments as they're uplifted into the eyes of the general audience, especially when available reporting on internet-born encoded media often fails to provide context and background on their subject matter. For example,

DOI: 10.4324/9781003483885-5

132 *Critical Internet Literacies*

our first study looks at NBC News and *USA Today*'s reporting on Estee Williams, a "tradwife" influencer who creates an unbelievable amount of content espousing "traditional values" and regressive women's rights. Williams' goal is twofold: first, she wants more followers as her role in the creator economy requires scale; second, she represents the meme of "Western aesthetics," coded with misogyny, Christian Nationalism, and in some cases, her content codes the darker and more insidious parts of 4chan culture.

We'll also focus on how much of these harm-intent internet-born pieces are even able to surface into the mainstream when they're allegedly harmful. In both the "OK" hand gesture and the "Save the Children" movements, we can see a direct line of trolling from 4chan and even worse, QAnon. These uplifts are tactical, well-rehearsed, and repeatable, honing the method each time further. In rare occasions, bad actors are unable to launder their material, but only when there is enough awareness of their contextual underpinnings and a willingness to promote skepticism among the audience without veering into partisan or biased reporting. Even then, general consumer culture may still be affected by influencer tactics or on-line grifts. Two examples are the pre-teens who mobbed Sephora stores looking for Retinol and young men acting out in class at the behest of "masculinity" hustlers. We sometimes come across these examples by pure accident, especially when they forcibly leap into mainstream consciousness like that of "meme stocks" – which are less meme than stock but use internet tactics which operate on the "just joking" paradox of "plausible deniability."

Applying a modicum of media literacy is helpful to these instances, but there is always a difficulty when content is driven by memes or the creator economy because irony and subtext are inherently hard to read and explain to others. As with the other chapters, the overall goal is to create a method or a model for an ability to have discussions about these dynamic shifts. These tactics have been intertwined for so long we sometimes cannot see them. Not only do we have to help our friends, family, and colleagues become better at their internet literacies, but we must do so to protect the most vulnerable: the targets of the coded undertones like people of color, women, immigrants, and the transgender community. Digital citizenship and civic rights are emboldened by internet literacies, and if we do it right, we can shift the discussions to more positive cases.

Hoaxes, Challenges, and Viral Moments on TV

"Shout out tonight – Honestly, please stop twerking. It's not attractive, it's not cute, and your underwear is showing," CNN's Erin Burnett explains

The Online to Mainstream Media Pipeline   133

on her evening program in September 2013. For the kicker of her show, Burnett presented, uncritically, a video of a young woman who was "trying to make a sexy video for her boyfriend" by twerking and shaking her butt for the camera. The video ends dramatically when the girl's roommate walks in, pushing her into a coffee table (conveniently covered in candles and alcohol), and she catches on fire and screams. Erin Burnett explains that twerking Caitlin is fine and hopes she "learned her lesson."[2] Understandably, this video is the entertaining ending on Burnett's program and the kicker is supposed to be a lightheaded bit on news shows that alleviates the mood at the end of serious programming. In this case, Burnett was displaying anger about the idea of twerking itself, insinuating video uploader Caitlin Heller deserved what was coming.

The wildly viral video was uploaded days earlier amid a moral panic about twerking following the 2013 MTV Video Music Awards in August that year where Miley Cyrus twerked on stage in front of Robin Thicke's crotch. The clip of Cyrus's twerking went viral both online and on dozens of news channels who were trying to explain to parents the dangers of the dance – which, depending on the news source, claimed it was overly sexual or appropriated from Black culture or distasteful and bad for children to witness.[3] Amid this panic, Caitlin Heller's video was uploaded to YouTube, immediately convincing people twerking was *also* dangerous. However, the video had some interesting inconsistencies that some skeptical viewers pointed out. For one, the timing is just *too perfect*, ending just in the middle of the fire. Second, did we see Caitlin *prepare* for the fall? Just a few days after Burnett's segment, Jimmy Kimmel set out to find the answers, inviting Heller onto his show.

Kimmel interviews the young twerker through her webcam before walking across the stage to join her on camera in her "room" which is hidden behind curtains on Kimmel's set. There, he asks if he may share the entire video of Heller's accident, replaying the video which now extends beyond the screaming to Jimmy Kimmel, dressed identical to Heller, walking through the door with a fire extinguisher to put the fire out. Heller exclaims "Thanks Jimmy Kimmel!" "All part of the job, ma'am," Kimmel replies – which it is, since he and his team created the video. "To the conspiracy theorists on the internet who thought the video was fake, you were right," Kimmel explains.[4] He then reveals Heller is played by stuntwoman Daphne Avalon and the whole thing was made by Kimmel's team, led by director Brad Morrison who shot and directed the sketch two months earlier as a "fail" video, a popular viral trope at the time. The attention to detail was exquisite: Morrison explains in *Fast Company* that everything from the paint to the baseboards to Heller's pants tag sticking out of her pants was by design.

134 *Critical Internet Literacies*

The Kimmel team simply uploaded the video to YouTube in early September without any promotion whatsoever. Morrison explains:

> The timing was excellent. Miley's performance at the VMAs had everyone talking about twerking, and my video – that looked very real – featured a very convincing twerking fail that ended with a cute girl catching on fire. Who wouldn't want to watch that? And people arguing over whether it was real or not just added fuel to the fire.[5]

This media incursion is one of the best examples of uplift that exists as it shows the amount of work that goes into moving content from online to mainstream spaces. Kimmel's team could not have predicted Cyrus's act at the VMAs when they produced the video, but cultural coincidences are all too common. Morrison's video is professionally made, requiring hours of planning, casting, rehearsing, set-building, timing, and filming, to say little of the mess a fire extinguisher makes for each recording. Making this stunt "look real" wasn't as important as the trend being part of the news cycle, which primed audiences for the associated panic.

From the amateur perspective, media manipulation is possible just as well. As explained in Tyler Funk's 2023 film *Anything for Fame*, TikTok influencer Ava Louise pulled a similar stunt in 2020. Louise (who we'll discuss further in the next chapter) was deeply cynical about media information flows and decided to make herself famous doing a vile stunt. During the height of the pandemic in 2020, a terrible TikTok challenge emerged where people would lick ice cream in a store and put the container back. Louise went a step further when she learned that airline toilets were vectors of the virus transmission. Ava Louise, who was known for doing low-effort, attention-seeking drama content online, intentionally created a viral video by licking an airline toilet seat and posting it on TikTok. She went incredibly viral for her disgusting trick. (She explains in the film she cleaned the toilet first, but there is no way to endorse this stunt.) Her newfound fame taught her how to further manipulate media and she started spreading rumors about an alleged affair between Kanye West and influencer Jeffrey Star and she went viral again.

Both Ava Louise and Jimmy Kimmel employed similar tactics to uplift their online content directly into mainstream spaces and both succeeded in leveraging their content amid panics that caused reaction among parents, people with anxiety, and those with low information literacies. These stunts are reliant on smart production, awareness of the systems, and coincidence. What we may learn is that these are also models to use when talking about other examples that come from darker and more harmful spaces, coded as cute, novel, or unique. Some tactics of uplift take weeks or even months to conceptualize and strategize before deployment, and others become so well built, it creates a participatory media environment for others to play along in a trend-based setting. When the uplift becomes standardized and normalized, the goal is complete and no longer novel, but the harm is already done. We need to keep a critical eye on many of these projects as they will continue throughout the 2020s.

Tradwives: Encoding Multiple Layers of the Darker Internet

"Although she is responsible for cooking and cleaning their Virginia home, Williams doesn't venture outside – not to the gym, to buy cleaning supplies or to meet a girlfriend for coffee – without calling her electrician husband Conner to ask for permission, nor does she leave the house after dark alone," Elise Solé writes on Today.com in March 2023.[6] Solé is writing about the popular 25-year-old TikTok and YouTube influencer Estee Williams who is one of the top influencers of the tradwife movement. "It's 2023 and this is my choice," Williams tells Solé in the interview, pointing out that her subordinate role isn't forced upon her, but rather something she's proud of doing. It isn't until the eighteenth paragraph that Solé mentions its notorious connections to the more harmful parts of the internet: "The Tradwife lifestyle shares borders with the alt-right movement on social media through common hashtags like #FeminismSucks, #ConservativeWomen, #TwoGenders and #DomesticDiscipline. Often these hashtags accompany vintage memes showing housewives smiling while sorting laundry and serving dinner." This is unfortunately followed by an immediate coda: "Not all Tradwives are alt-right or far-right politically, though."

The Today Show, and its constitutive elements, are part of a media ecosystem that serves one of the most lucrative consumer markets in the United States: the adult 25–54 market and the overall 18–49 market. Its role in television is to be the morning show that calmly introduces the country to the news through soft reporting, entertaining interstitials, and in some cases, taking bad actors at face value for the benefit of ratings. In this case, Estee Williams rose to prominence so rapidly, that Today.com was interested in telling the story – and they weren't the only one. *USA Today* also ran a story about Estee Williams a few months later, recognizing the "controversy" carried by this movement, noting it sits in a false sense of nostalgia.[7] However, overall, the article reads like boosterism, noting that "Williams wants to be clear that not all trad wives are far-right extremists." The tradwife movement *is* an extremist movement, though it is disguised as an influencer lifestyle and aesthetic and therefore not solely filled with far-right adherents – though arguably it may be willful ignorance of the movement's roots.

To the defense of Williams, Fox News Digital claims that nearly all coverage of the tradwife movement is negative commentary, and the article

136   *Critical Internet Literacies*

focuses on the reasons one may want to join the movement. Williams explains she became a tradwife following her divorce and after she "traded in her love of weight-focused bodybuilding and form-fitting activewear for lower-impact workouts and flowy dresses leading up to and after her January 2023 wedding."[8] The variants of tradwife content include the "stay at home girlfriend" and to some extent, wellness influencers, holistic mommy bloggers, and religious mom influencers. As we discussed in previous chapters, being an influencer consists of regular and skilled labor. Beyond performing, recording, editing, and uploading, there's administrative labor in marketing and social media management. For Estee Williams to describe it as subservient gratitude to her husband, she disguises the labor well. Williams quickly rose to prominence for a variety of reasons, but mostly because her aesthetics – blond wavy hair, bright white teeth, and clothing that could be picked directly out of a 1950s advertisement for a KitchenAid appliance.

The 2020s have introduced meta-memes and participatory parts of the creator economy through easy to replicate aesthetics. Online aesthetics are malleable, offering more ways of using the meme outside the boundaries of social media. These details illuminate *why* Williams represents the most popular of the tradwives, though there's hundreds of others participating in the movement and many of them perform their lifestyle on social media. Though Williams tells Fox News that she rejects advertising and sponsorships "in favor of sharing her 'purpose and message,'" she is still part of the creator economy, selling an ideal to her followers. This ideal is not only reactionary but is seemingly safe enough to promote on mainstream sites. Even worse, the movement *is* a rabbit hole, one specifically sourced from the far right and designed to engage young, vulnerable viewers in a trap of grotesque patriarchal standards coded in a participatory model.

In the Today.com piece, Solé interviews a social psychologist who reckons that the tradwife movement could be reactionary to the "overall liberalization of American belief systems." Like the thin blue line flag that was developed in reaction to the Black Lives Matter movement, tradwives *could be* a result of people seeking to return society to "a simpler time with fewer individual freedoms." On the other hand, what if we reconsider this movement as a long-term success story of the far right's stance against gay and LGBTQ+ people? What if tradwives could be reread as a model of the results of both the 4chanification of the web and the rebranding of QAnon as it weaves itself into everyday cultural paranoia? While the social psychologist is right, tradwives *are* a reaction to movements that make people uncomfortable, there is a far more insidious reality: the far right has successfully developed a new language to embed patriarchy through encoded harmful messages through a novel disguise.

The Online to Mainstream Media Pipeline   137

Excavating the Roots of the Tradwife Reactionary

The tradwife movement is not new, however, many of its modern aesthetics are derived from TikTok and YouTube trends. Estee Williams' role in the movement's rebirth was likely coded through an updated version of the conservative view on "family matters," exacerbated by the pandemic era's role in deepening the conspiratorial mindsets that succeeded through mass engagement. In Melinda Cooper's 2017 *Family Values: Between Neoliberalism and New Social Conservatism*, she writes that the shifts in society to support the social welfare of minorities pushed conservatives back to family values-oriented lifestyles, reacting to neoliberal policies of progress and profit.[9] In the Trump era, a deep reaction to progressive movements of the Obama era (meaning the introduction of new progressive vocabulary and updated civil rights) resulted in a similar pushback among hard conservatives.

For example, in 2016, the Obama administration's Department of Justice and Department of Education's civil rights divisions offered guidance to schools regarding gender identity and rights for transgender individuals who sought to use bathrooms that represented their gender identity to reduce discrimination and segregation.[10] The letter makes no intention to change laws, but rather encourages schools to follow updated Title IX rules regarding gender identity. In the following years, this resulted in *extreme* backlash, including several "bathroom bills" in US states like North Carolina, Alabama, Oklahoma, and Tennessee that barred transgender people from using bathrooms that differed from their biological sex. These bills were not only discriminatory, but dangerous for an already vulnerable population. In some cases, these bills were struck down, but others changed the language through embedding the ideology in family values and protection of children.

This is where it becomes intertwined with internet culture. In the darkest corners online, 4chan users would often use their forums to post horrific and terrible images of child pornography – not always because they were perverted, but occasionally as disgusting trolling behavior to prove 4chan's digital culture as outside the law and devoid of consequence (as discussed in Chapter 2). In a strange and terrible trope, they have used the term "CP" to represent the "bit" they were playing and make meta-memes like "Mods are asleep, post CP" meaning they would post edgier content to see if they would get reprimanded by the volunteer moderators.[11] CP would be recoded as in-group keywords like cheese pizza, Captain Picard, Captain Planet, and chocolate pudding (to name a few).

In the run-up to the US 2016 election, a hacker known as Guccifer 2.0 released a huge trove of emails from Hillary Clinton's campaign manager John Podesta. In a now infamous story, many of the emails referred to

138 *Critical Internet Literacies*

Podesta's regular visits to Comet Ping Pong, a local Washington DC pizza place. The emails, distributed through WikiLeaks, were scoured through by pro-Trump 4channers, noting the amount of times Podesta referred to "cheese pizza" and they made ironic jokes that Podesta was engaged in child trafficking and child pornography. While obviously a mean joke on the internet, far-right influencers like Brittany Pettibone, Mike Cernovich, and Jack Posobiec spun the jokes into paranoid accusations, leveling claims of widespread pedophilia by the Democratic Party (partly as a result of Anthony Weiner's emails and scandal as well).[12] A the rumor grew, it became a story of satanic symbology mixed with the idea of a secretive cabal trafficking children underneath the restaurant (which has no basement) and spread rapidly across the web. Dubbed #PizzaGate, it nearly ruined the restaurant owners' lives, but even worse, in December, a radicalized man, armed with an assault rifle, walked into the restaurant and fired a round into the ceiling.

The theory spread from there and became the foundational pillar within the ideology that supports QAnon. As we know now, QAnon became the umbrella conspiracy for hundreds of varied conspiratorial thoughts and during the lockdown period became the accelerant for hundreds of new conspiracists to find solace in their paranoid outlooks in the digital ether. The pandemic and the global racial justice movements were difficult to explain holistically and there was a lack of distinct leadership, as a result, influencers stepped in to help people cope with their confusion and distrust. In July 2020, Anna Merlan writes for *Vice* that the "Conspiracy Singularity has Arrived." She writes:

> It's not just QAnon. The strain of living in this particular time, with a dragging, devastating pandemic and a global uprising against police brutality and racial injustice, crashing together at the highest speed, has accelerated something that's been going on for years. Call it the conspiracy singularity: the place where many conspiracy communities are suddenly meeting and merging, a melting pot of unimaginable density. UFO conspiracy theorists and QAnon fans are advocating for drinking a bleach solution promoted by anti-vaxxers.[13]

Even worse, the idea of the pedophilic cabal was about to explode in ways that were completely unhinged but changed the 2020s permanently.

Save the Children

Two specific events resulted in the reactionary shift that defines our paranoid habits of the 2020s. First, there was the curious incident of the low-cost furniture site Wayfair being accused of trafficking children in July

2020, followed by an extremely poor timed and inappropriate ad campaign by Balenciaga in late 2020. The Wayfair saga was one of the first moments where the results of four years of QAnon had managed to burble to the surface of mainstream news. In short, Wayfair was the center of a very internet-centric conspiracy. It was selling furniture with names like Samiyah or Yaritza (similar to the way IKEA names their furniture) and QAnon adherents noticed that some furniture on the site was priced exorbitantly. For example, a storage cabinet named Samiyah was listed for $12,899.99 and to paranoid conspiracists, they believed it was because missing children were sold as part of the set.

Any logic applied to this would immediately debunk the issue, however, it grew into a complete conspiracy requiring debunking by several outlets. The actual story is very internet based. Sites like Wayfair operate with the benefit of web search and SEO is often tricky to maintain for extended lengths of time. When a product, like the Samiyah cabinet, runs out, sites like Wayfair face a reality of either taking the listing down and losing their search traction and discoverability, or changing its price to unbelievable levels so no one will buy it, but it maintains its algorithmic stability.

Figure 5.1 A screengrab from a conspiratorial TikTok video containing the images of both a missing child and a piece of furniture with the same name.

140 *Critical Internet Literacies*

This is literally a case of the internet's hegemony on product sales techniques at scale and the immense reliance on search, but to those with low internet literacies and radicalized by QAnon, this was a scandal. It was derided by most everyone, but that didn't stop the shift to recontextualizing QAnon with a rebrand: #SaveTheChildren. Like a rebirth of the Satanic Panic that accused daycares of satanism, QAnon adherents under the banner of #SaveTheChildren blamed the lockdown and masking for similar reasons.

The difference this time is the rise of the aesthetic foundations of influencer cultures. These influencer-based amplifications resulted in #SaveTheChildren rallies, often taken in good faith by news agencies who reported on them as though they were a serious movement. In that regard, some members of the rally likely had little idea the movement comes from QAnon. As Anna North explained for *Vox*, there was a danger that "#SaveTheChildren could pull more women into the QAnon fold" because many women at the rallies were dressed in stylish, "Instagram-ready" aesthetics.[14] The performative act of saving the children plays directly into the space of internet irony. One cannot be accused of wrongdoing if you are trying to help children. On the other hand, the increased number of calls to the government agencies reporting Wayfair or otherwise used vast amounts of resources, and in many cases hindered actual investigations.

Then it got weirder. In fall 2020, the high-fashion brand Balenciaga ran a controversial ad that featured children, stuffed bears in sexual bondage, and for some reason, a court document about child pornography. It's unclear what choices were made in the production of this campaign, but it is one of the largest examples of the inability to understand how much the internet and everyday life are intertwined. The ad repulsed more than just the QAnon crowd and populist YouTuber June Lapine, better known as ShoeonHead, tweeted her disgust. In Ali Breland's extensive *Mother Jones* article "How Q Became Everything," he writes:

> Her tweet took off, boosted by large right-wing accounts, including the notoriously transphobic LibsofTikTok [run by Chaya Raichik]. Together, these influencers – none of whom maintain explicit links to the Q movement – galvanized masses of people to throw up their arms in disgust. As right-wing influencers like Candace Owens and Andrew Tate seized on the Balenciaga panic and dolled it out to their audiences, it became one of the biggest stories on the internet.[15]

And that brings us back to the tradwife movement. These reactions and events have enabled bad actors to leverage their bigoted views in the model of a new language and vocabulary. Originally threatened by new

The Online to Mainstream Media Pipeline 141

progressive language, vernacular, and acceptance, the reverse happened simultaneously. Breland further explains that no one could have predicted:

> just how far QAnon would go, or that its adherents would eventually help establish a messy new grammar with conjunctions that, in a time of economic and cultural anxiety, combined all of these things: a cabal of liberal elites running a child trafficking ring.

From there, the language shifted to politics, using terms like "gay agenda," "gender ideology," and "grooming." "Public figures who embrace the traditional atomic family – like [Ron] DeSantis, [Chaya] Raichik, and [Chris] Rufo – smoothed out the grammar that Q established into more palatable versions, as people wholly unconnected to QAnon used this echoing rhetoric." In turn, what we have witnessed through the emergence and popularization of something as niche as the tradwives is the success of a new vocabulary to talk about ideologies without raising flags. Terms like "groomer" are bait and designed to repulse in similar ways to the term "groyper" – they result in engagement and normalize the algorithmic content moderation systems. By repeating the term over and over in videos and on social media, it becomes more difficult for social media to moderate the posts, especially when used by people in apparent good faith. The word groomer is just borderline enough to continue needling the perceived victims, and as extremism goes, it will eventually result in the pendulum swinging the other direction.

As the growth of new "girlish" aesthetics like coquette and cottagecore are becoming popular with Gen Z on TikTok and the reactionary memes of fragile masculinity are expanding beyond the manosphere, a gendered response is being performed by cisgender women through the feminine aesthetics of a false nostalgia. Traditionalism and Christian Nationalism have become more normalized in politics and the Christian Nationalist Speaker of the US House of Representatives Mike Johnson called for a "return to 18th Century values." What once seemed extreme and reactionary are now functional ideologies. While the rise and normalization of these ideologies cannot solely be connected to the internet, it is without a doubt that the internet's novelty and participatory enthusiasm helped uplift them into the mainstream.

Some may see a woman preparing meals and wearing aprons as a cute performance, but it is tied deeply to far-right extremist ideas and deepening conspiratorial mindsets. What started as a bit by 4chan trolls metastasized into reality, turning a joke about moderation into a full-blown shift in the way we interact with events around us. Then, all it took was a shift in the way influencers were attracting hyper-niche audiences and the space

142 *Critical Internet Literacies*

for the tradwife genre emerged. Estee Williams may play the role of this pseudo-nostalgic character, but eventually, the audience concretizes into a modern trend. On May 31, 2024, Williams posted a glamour photo of her and her husband on Instagram under a faded American flag. Her caption reads:

> Proud to be an American
> Proud to be a wife
> Proud to have a blue collar husband
> Proud to be a homemaker
> Proud to be a Christian
> Proud to have left college behind
> Proud to stand by Donald Trump
> God bless America[16]

The Just Joking Paradox

How many we consider a media literacy of "joking" or "irony" or "edgy" content online as it influences everyday life through mainstream access? What does it mean when someone is "doing a bit" or producing "satire" while we're sure they are serious, but using a fundamental loophole? Terms like these have completely different meanings in the digital space, acting as a "get out of jail free" card from Monopoly, a mulligan of sorts for bad behavior. Say something horrible and mean? "Just joking!" Express a situation that causes harm? "Just joking!" Typically, "just joking" is used by children to test the boundaries of appropriate behavior and once a child learns the tactic, important conversations are necessary from teachers and parents on how to communicate. According to Media Smarts, a digital media literacy organization from Canada, the goal is to increase empathy and teach ethics to combat this trait.[17] In digital spaces, the lack of ability to read sarcasm or meanness increases the difficulty of communication as most of our communication is through face and eye expressions and gestures. Trolls online also play the game to detect the borders of speech and test the systems in which they participate.

Just joking is a paradox, it is both harm and not harm, dependent fully on context and intent. However, we may argue that the deployment of "just joking" is not a paradox, it is coded with a model of uplift to test the boundaries of the Overton window, pushing the edges out ever so slightly, normalizing the harm until the retort "just joking" is unnecessary. This form of speech is so prevalent online that we need a way to discuss it. For this example, we'll use a memetic gesture to talk about how this process works. In December 2019, just before the Army-Navy game, ESPN's Rece

The Online to Mainstream Media Pipeline 143

Davis addressed the crowd in front of dozens of cadets just before the game. Just over Davis's shoulder, you can see a cadet playing "the circle game," a childish game of "made you look" popularized by the show *Malcolm in the Middle* in 2000. It requires the thumb and forefinger to touch with three fingers extended placed on your hip or somewhere inappropriate. As a childish joke, it is incredible internet fodder on YouTube, TikTok, and of course, 4chan. Its origin begins a year into the Trump administration when 4channers – who felt the mainstream media was becoming more antagonistic to them – began "Operation O-KKK," designed to trick liberal viewers and the mainstream media into thinking there was an awful incursion from the web occurring, designed to upset people whose nerves were still frayed from the Trump election. Their operation, like many before, was a crowd deployed act in hopes of agitating for the "lulz."

Their meta-game went viral and soon after far-right influencers started flashing the symbol to get attention and reactions. But then, in the nature of the environment, some white supremacists adopted it to *actually* signify white supremacy. These far-right influencers believed they too were trolling but were taking the bait from the true pranksters. On the other hand, it worked and soon the gesture was in what Abby Ohlheiser calls the "purgatory of meaning" which additionally causes all people interacting with the symbol to exist in the same purgatory.[18] The symbol started appearing everywhere and raising fears among the audience that the new dogwhistle was empowering hatred. The frequency illusion, also called the Baader-Meinhof Illusion, is a form of confirmation bias that is caused by the introduction to something and the assumption that it is brand new.[19] But it was a joke, or an "op" as 4channers called it, and they celebrated the results of their actions.

As white nationalists like Richard Spencer used the gesture, the more it concretized and codified its meaning. The media was in a frenzy. The lack of internet literacies did not provide the audience with the resilience to properly read the bit and many took the symbol as a terrifying new start to the presence of fascism. The following year, penalties were doled out to perpetrators of the stunt. From the US Coast Guard to police officers in in Alabama to baseball fans, flashing the symbol became taboo and problematic.[20] "Just joking!" the gesture flashers would say, but it really did have multiple meanings. Its final codification as a hate symbol occurred when Brenton Tarrant, who pleaded guilty to 92 charges after the horrific livestreamed mass murder of 51 people in Christchurch, New Zealand, flashed the OK hand symbol at his court hearing.[21] Tarrant's horrific spree was possibly inspired by edgy content online and he created a manifesto that was loaded with extreme memes and references. Tarrant's goal with his manifesto was to hope the mainstream media would publish

144 *Critical Internet Literacies*

it, thereby opening the door for recruitment and radicalization of future violent offenders.

Memetic to Kinetic: Mainstream as a Tool

From mainstream social media platforms (like Meta products) to mainstream news, neo-fascistic movements have learned to use these spaces for effective methods for spreading their views. In 2022, Belgium's populist neo-fascist group Vlaams Belang spent over a million pounds on social media advertising. Their views are full of hatred, and they target LGBTQ+ people and push anti-democracy propaganda. Social media sites gladly took their money.[22] While online spending proves beneficial because groups can test variations of ads and see their success through analytics, using the mainstream media is far more affordable. While populist groups around the world have villainized mainstream media, they rely on their coverage to maintain their presence among the general public. Brenton Tarrant's manifesto was designed to use the mainstream media as an accomplice in further radicalization of vulnerable publics – likely young, disaffected white men.

In the past, memes and online trolling had a reliable method of codification and use. The source of new ideas was usually built in the attention economy of 4chan, relying on the engagement to structuralize neologisms, nicknames, and hate speech. When a term or meme would gain foothold, it would be visualized, often through characterizations of the meme or references to other memes. On occasion, users would use apophenia to connect references across genres and meanings, causing a confusing mishmash of image and terminology. This was intentional as the more "schizophrenic" the meme, the more its meaning was obfuscated. Once popular, the meme or term would emerge in Reddit threads, group chats, or real-time discussion forums like Discord or Telegram. Finally, the persistence of the term would eventually normalize it, causing it to be used ironically by edgy posters (who sometimes refer to themselves as "edgelords") on Instagram and then by sarcastic accounts making fun of the edgy posters. Due to its mainstreaming, the term usually lost power and was considered passe.

In the years after 2020, content moderation systems and human-guided trust and safety measures have made social media a safer place. (Though many, including myself, would argue the damage has already been done and the normalization of previous terms will continue to cause harm.) As a result, meme groups at the extreme fringes, like that of incel forums or extreme gore, have created a new method for uplift, one that requires the attention of media. The new method is far more cyclical, relying on multiple iterations, tests of variations, and result-based processes. As with the former model, the idea, meme, or trope is established in the meme

The Online to Mainstream Media Pipeline   145

factories. Very often they work faster now as the tropes of victimhood, disenfranchisement, martyrdom, or a sense of "marginalization" (in quotes as it does not mean this in reality) have been standardized in these spaces. Terms like "grooming" are then used within in-group messaging and backchannel communication. Once recognized in its repurposed meaning, it can then be memed and spread across multiple platforms, typically starting with the more fringe sites like 4chan and 8chan then up the ranks to Reddit and Discord. Modern memes are far more aesthetic, so a "look" is established as a scapegoat for the attack. For example, drag queens who do children's story hour become the target of the attacks.

On far-right Instagram channels, the memes are tested for a more mainstream audience. For example, on far-right Rogan O'Handley's @ DC_Draino Instagram account, alongside posts supporting Mike Johnson, Tucker Carlson, and Marjorie Taylor Greene, O'Handley posts an anti-Pride meme. The meme is a side-by-side comparison, on the left is a masculine presenting, and likely non-binary person with a beard, wearing sunglasses and a crop top. The person appears to be heavyset. On top of the person, the caption reads: "Celebrated for One Month." On the other side, is Bobby Henline, a US Veteran (and comedian) who served in both the first and second Gulf Wars and was physically scarred on over 40 percent of his body after getting hit by an IED in Iraq. In the image, Henline is in dress uniform, displaying his medals and regalia; his head is bare and you can see his scarring. The caption over Henline reads: "Thanked for One Day." O'Handley's caption reads, "In the end times, they'll say evil is good and good is evil. That sadly sounds a lot like where we're at now," followed by an American flag emoji.[23] The comments section is filled with hateful messages and anti-gay slurs. The meaning of this meme is obvious, but technically does not cross the boundaries of harm – it's all in the metatext.

The meme's aesthetics are traditional, but tolerated by Instagram's moderation standards. What is required is engagement. If the meme does *not* result in kinetic or civic action, it becomes normalized, and the cycle starts all over again. At a certain point, the memes incite action, occasionally leading to violence. In the case of Chaya Raichik's LibsofTikTok account, this happens quite often. LibsofTikTok is an account that scours TikTok for content that aesthetically matches stereotypical harmful depictions of gender-queer, liberal, and progressive users, reposting them for her bigoted audience. Raichik's account relies on the cycle of attention to operate and she has now become a structural part of the anti-LGBTQ+ movement. Taylor Lorenz writes for the *Washington Post* in 2022:

> On March 8 [2022], a Twitter account called Libs of TikTok posted a video of a woman teaching sex education to children in Kentucky, calling the woman in the video a "predator." The next evening, the same

146   *Critical Internet Literacies*

clip was featured on Laura Ingraham's Fox News program, prompting the host to ask, "When did our public schools, any schools, become what are essentially grooming centers for gender identity radicals?"[24]

Raichik founded LibsofTikTok in 2020 during Covid under a different account name; a year later she started her "parody" account LibsofTik-Tok as a way of leaning into the groomer discourse that was proliferating among the far-right calling for teachers who posted their personal videos on TikTok to be fired. According to Lorenz, Raichik's big break happened when Joe Rogan spoke about her account on his wildly popular podcast (discussed shortly) and Raichik was instantly influential.

She leaned into conspiracy theories and aligned herself with anti-trans legislation, especially in Florida, and found her content uplifted into the mainstream by Tucker Carlson and Jesse Waters of Fox News. A Media Matters investigation found that Ron DeSantis's press secretary Christina Pushaw was in contact with Raichik often and claimed the LibsofTikTok account "truly opened her eyes."[25] Here we have a concrete example of an influencer affecting the legislation of a US state. Unfortunately, it gets even worse. LibsofTikTok became so influential, the account has inspired various forms of stochastic terrorism. In a long-form piece for *USA Today*, Will Carless writes "When Libs of TikTok Tweets, threats increasingly follow." Carless adds that Raichik often tweets exact details of events like drag story hour or accuses hospitals of hosting children's Pride events. In one tweet in June 2022, Raichik posted: "A children's hospital in Nebraska is co-hosting a children's pride event. They advertise there will be a booth where attendees can make an appointment for 'gender affirming care' such as puberty blockers." (The tweet, now deleted, mentions the specific hospital.) From there, hundreds of calls flooded the hospital and many bomb threats were called in.[26]

LibsofTikTok now has 3.6 million followers on Elon Musk's X as of this writing and her influence is immense. She skirts the content moderators by never insisting on any violence or instigating, but rather insinuating that *something must be done*. Raichik explains that she just "reposts" content, but Carless found this to be untrue:

> One [post] in October, for example, featured an Instagram video of a New York music teacher, joyfully waving a Progress Pride flag while the message "Happy National Coming Out Day – Black, Gay and Thriving" appears at the bottom of the screen. "An actual elementary school teacher in NY," reads Raichik's comment on the video.

To be clear, these videos aren't shared with Raichik, she makes it her job to find them and repost them, making sarcastic comments that rile up her fanbase. It's a tactic that operates on a fine line. Following the results of

The Online to Mainstream Media Pipeline   147

the January 6 insurrection, people are more wary of direct instigations – Raichik knows how to make sure she's seen as just joking when she posts. Now public, Raichek finds herself invited to speak at the yearly Conservative Political Action Conference, also known as CPAC, with clear evidence that online influence migrates directly to the mainstream.

Joe Rogan: The New Mainstream Uplift

The Joe Rogan Experience is downloaded and streamed by over 11 million people per episode.[27] By comparison, *The Five*, Fox News's most watched television program, averages 2.9 million viewers per episode. Rogan maintains a hold on a coveted consumer demographic: his audience is primarily men, skewing younger in the 18–34 demographic, and he reaches men up to their late 50s. His popularity continues to increase, and he recently signed another exclusive contract with Spotify for an alleged $250 million dollars. When Joe Rogan tells stories, he's aiming to entertain his audience, not critically interrogate his sources, but it is fair to assume that many of his listeners take his word for truth. The shift in trust in mainstream media has also altered Rogan's perception among his audience: he's both popular and legitimate to his rabid fan base. According to a Gallup poll, confidence in media is low, matching 2016's 32 percent trust level.[28] Rogan revels in his role outside the realm of an official journalist which relieves him from the responsibility of veracity.[29] But that power, like Jimmy Donaldson's, comes with the knowledge that Rogan is competing directly with traditional media models.

At the endpoint of the "streaming wars" where we've become subject to multiple subscriptions to on-demand entertainment, tracking audience consumption is told through the metrics, and by those standards, *The Joe Rogan Experience* is a mainstream talk show. Joe Rogan, who plays the everyman "just asking questions," is the avatar of the contrarian, heterodox fan of internet content. On the other hand, the audience of traditional media often has disdain for Rogan's followers, who *The Atlantic* journalist Devin Gordon calls the "middle-bro audience that the cultural elite hold in particular contempt" which causes most of Rogan's critics to be unable to "grasp the breadth and depth of the community he has built, and they act as though trying is pointless."[30]

Aja Romano writes about Rogan's role in media in *Vox*:

> Like the internet itself, Rogan and whatever dangerous misinformation, conspiracy theories, jerky bigotry, or offensive views he wants to serve up today are all unstoppable and essentially answerable to no one. He has all of the audience, money, attention, and prestige of a traditional gatekeeper, but with barely any real pressure to assume responsibility for repeatedly making high-profile mistakes on the job.[31]

148   *Critical Internet Literacies*

Rogan has amplified bad actors, comedians, pseudo scientists, conspiracists, fringe theorists, and politicians. He lets them talk, barely pushing back, often asking his producer Jamie Vernon to Google some things, sometimes disregarding the truth when Jamie debunks him. Unfortunately, Rogan himself comes across news stories and uplifts them, regardless of their reality. In one sad example, Joe Rogan and Chaya Raichik both shared a conspiracy theory about litter boxes in classrooms. Speaking to his guest, former US representative Tulsi Gabbard, Rogan shared a story about a school that let "furry" children use litter boxes. Furries are a fandom subculture of people that wear large, anthropomorphic fur suits. They are often baselessly accused of perverted acts and are used as fodder for reactionaries.

After Rogan amplified the conspiracy theory, it became a flashpoint issue among far-right politicians like Colorado's Lauren Boebert. According to an exhaustive investigation by NBC News, over 20 conservative candidates repeated Rogan's claim and his clip became viral media. The story, like that of the "slap a teacher" challenge hoax, was spread widely on Facebook groups. In the investigation, NBC News reporters interviewed people who were part of the furry fandom as well as furry convention coordinators – no one had ever seen a litter box meant to be used by a human at any event. The story is much more depressing: NBC News found exactly one school in the US with a litter box. Its intended use is in case of a lengthy lockdown due to gun violence where young people may have to relieve themselves without leaving the classroom.[32] Months later, on his podcast, Rogan admitted the litter box rumor was unfounded; the damage was already done.[33]

Joe Rogan and Gamified Antisemitism

Aside from the issues facing LGBTQ+ people, Rogan occasionally promotes antisemitic tropes or jokes from the internet. In early 2024, Rogan uplifted a strange story to his audience about an event in Brooklyn, New York; the story emerged from viral tweets. Speaking to his guest, comedian Jim Norton, Rogan tells a tale about a real, albeit confusing, story about Jewish people tunneling in New York City. While Rogan admits to having no idea what's going on, he immediately shares a story that had gone viral on Elon Musk's X over the last several days about a man who claimed to have heard the digging for several months under his apartment. Rogan explains:

> Um, I don't know exactly what's happening. All I know is very short clips that I found on the internet. But the funniest thing is this one guy on Twitter that was saying a while back, uh, I live on a ground floor apartment and I hear Jews underneath me.[34]

Rogan doesn't share the source of the story, nor any more details, but assumes his audience is aware of the viral posts. Rogan then shared the story about a hapless tenant named "Richard Strocher" who allegedly lived above a roughshod tunnel excavation in Crown Heights, Brooklyn, NY. Strocher had posted that he had proof he was right about hearing "yiddish under the floor" and his tweets had gone viral as they predated the national news reporting about the strange event in the Orthodox Jewish Community in Crown Heights. The tweets fit into the engagement bait sector of X as they show corroboration to an actual, if odd, niche, and hyperlocal, event. It's very unlikely that the majority of Rogan's listeners would have learned about the incident had Rogan not told the story.

Three days before Rogan told Jim Norton about the man who cried tunnels, Richard Strocher posted "some of you owe me an apology" captioning an embedded image of an alleged earlier tweet. He posted this at 12:49am on January 9, 2024. Strocher then replied to himself in a thread 10 minutes later with "I AM NOT CRAZY" in all caps. His all-caps post was made to substantiate his claim that he heard "yiddish under the floor" of his NY apartment in November and December of 2023. Strocher's only evidence of his plight was screenshots of posts he allegedly made on November 7 and December 11. In Strocher's "original" post from November 7, it stated "There are Jews living under my apartment. I hear them its like they are digging or something. For the record: I live at ground level and we do NOT have a basement!!!"[35]

Figure 5.2 A tweet from the groyper "Richard Strocher" that used gamified antisemitism to trick people into following a groyper account.

150   *Critical Internet Literacies*

However, because Strocher used screenshots rather than embedding his original tweets, the post received an X Community Note (a system designed to be some sort of crowdsourced fact-checking tool) that claimed Stocher's original tweets did not exist. Strocher replied that he "had to delete" his original post because he was accused of being "schizophrenic and antisemitic" and demanded that @CommunityNotes apologize. By the time Joe Rogan brought the post up on his show, Strocher's tweet had over 2.5 million views, and although metrics are questionable on X, this is still a very viral post.

On Elon Musk's X, as it differs from its previous iteration known as Twitter, the algorithm is deeply affected by engagement rather than veracity, authority, or breaking news. Strocher's post worked well after several boosts from prominent accounts hours after the national news broke the story of an apparent clash between the NYPD and members of the Chabad Lubavitch Synagogue at 770 Eastern Parkway in Crown Heights, Brooklyn on January 8. To be clear, Rogan wasn't the only one to spread the viral news story, but he is the most popular. By January 11, Strocher's tale had become content fodder on TikTok and several accounts created commentary of the bewildering incident to share with hundreds of thousands of fans. However, if users spent a few extra seconds to analyze the post, we could hope that most would simply realize it isn't a good idea to take information at face value from a man whose name is an immature and crude spin on masturbation.

There is no Richard Strocher. And it likely doesn't matter to Joe Rogan who has spread a variety of mistruths in the past. But in this case, Richard Strocher is likely a groyper, using well-established techniques to lift antisemitism into the mainstream. Like Jimmy Kimmel's viral twerk hoax, this hoax was pre-structured by groypers who focused intently on events in Jewish communities, especially following the October 7 Hamas attack on Israel. The evening of the event that Strocher used to leverage his viral tweets, only a local news outlet and The Daily Caller (which was founded by Tucker Carlson) reported the event. It's likely Strocher, or the groyper operating the dummy account, timed the post to make the lie seem real. Just as there is no Richard Strocher, there are no apartments above the Chabad Lubavitch Synagogue. Rogan and the unwitting TikTok users had participated in what could only be described as "gamified antisemitism" built upon insidious tactics designed by the groyper movement. Aside from instantly debunking the claim simply based on the fact Strocher's name is obviously a joke, there are other ways to debunk this claim before it made it to TikTok or Joe Rogan.

* * *

The Online to Mainstream Media Pipeline   151

First, when you look at Strocher's embedded image of his own tweet, you can see the "Follow" button clearly. Why would Richard Strocher have images of his account as though he weren't following it? Second, the X data (as of the writing of this book) on the bottom of the screenshot doesn't match. On one, it shows Reposts and Likes, on the other it shows Reposts, Quotes, Likes, and a Bookmark. To those who have ever used a tweet generator, it immediately feels as though these posts were created hastily and made specifically for this post.[36] To verify the authenticity of Strocher's post, one may click on his account and learn his background. His bio read at the time: "FOX News, The Blaze – Host of The Richard Strocher Show on #Rumble - LIVE: Mon-Fri 9 PM ET – Sommelier, Carpenter, and Research Junkie #BelieveStrocher" (the #BelieveStrocher was added after the viral tweet). Strocher is not verified, which means the account is not paying for the attention or making money from advertising. (The words Fox News and The Blaze mean nothing.) He seems to make his own online show on the far-right video site Rumble but provides no link. What we know is that Richard Strocher is a self-described "patriot" and consistently posts his support of the groyper movement and Donald Trump, and posts incredibly distasteful and racist memes. After his viral tweet, his following increased to over ten thousand.

To give those who fell for Strocher's tweet's credit, the internet's ubiquity sometimes leads to extraordinary coincidences. In 2011, a Twitter user accidentally live-blogged the raid and subsequent assassination of Osama Bin Laden[37] and in early 2021, a fitness instructor in Myanmar captured the first moments of a military coup in the background of her exercise video.[38] These serendipitous moments are extremely rare, but they do exist. But in this case, Strocher's tactics were gamed similarly to Kimmel's accidental timing of Miley Cyrus's actions at the VMAs. This time, the real story had happened and Strocher used it to his advantage. On mid-afternoon, on January 8, the New York Police Department was called to the Chabad Lubavitch synagogue at 770 Eastern Parkway in Crown Heights, which is the world headquarters of the Chabad Lubavitch movement as well as The Institute for Spreading the Teachings of Moshiach (meaning Messiah). The saga began weeks before the NYPD were called in which probably got the attention of the groypers, who dedicate a fair amount of time to their antisemitism.

The story unfolded when a group of "young renegades" from a more extremist branch of the Chabad Lubavitch movement broke through the walls of the synagogue after digging a 50-foot, illegal tunnel and refused to leave. The renegade students hoped to create a place to study closer to where the Moshiach had allegedly bathed before his death in 1992.

152   *Critical Internet Literacies*

By that evening, chaos ensued in what the *New York Post* described as a "riot" and when the students refused to leave, the elders of the synagogue threatened to fill in the tunnels with cement. The videos from the event, recorded by several people, show confusion, yelling, and destructive chaos.

Rogan has never retracted his story and it's likely that very few of Rogan's listeners are subscribed to Taylor Lorenz's Instagram channel where she debunked the event on her Reels video similar to the work done here. Rogan, for all his fame and ability to connect to the masses, does not have an editor, nor a team of fact checkers. Rogan's content is consumed far more than any mainstream content and relies on the audience to have the skepticism to see through Rogan's "just a guy asking questions" heterodoxy. This is likely not the case for the majority of audiences and while this may seem like a bland example, the media manipulation by groypers is ongoing and we need to be aware that viral events like this may be gamified hatred, not coincidental, novel moments online. Sometimes hatred is disguised so well, it sounds real.

Why it Matters: Media Manipulation as a Tactic

"We launched the Claudine Gay plagiarism story from the Right. The next step is to smuggle it into the media apparatus of the Left, legitimizing the narrative to center-left actors who have the power to topple her. Then squeeze."[39] The tweet, posted by Republican strategist Christopher Rufo, explained quite clearly how he would deploy his strategy to remove the president of Harvard University following her testimony on Capitol Hill regarding the pro-Palestinian protests. Rufo is better known for his open attacks against critical race theory, a legal argument taught in law schools, though he claimed it was part of an overall shift in education among liberal colleges. He went as far as to claim it was part of "cultural Marxism" – a coded antisemitic term against liberal professors and academics. From years of watching 4chan uplift attacks to mainstream media and culture, Rufo has learned that *it works*.

Without going into the precise details (as it's been covered extensively in many mainstream news outlets), Rufo amplifies online grievances as direct attacks against his victims, then follows it up by playing the victim when journalists and reporters find his attacks shallow and bigoted. According to Moira Weigel in *The New Republic*, before Chris Rufo's uplift of the issue in 2019, very few people even spoke about critical race theory. Weigel explains that Rufo has the patience to enable his "incoherent attacks" to take hold.[40] Rufo's techniques are possible due to his deep knowledge, and deep cynicism, of the media systems themselves. As a result, politicians like Florida Governor Ron DeSantis have given Rufo power, naming him

The Online to Mainstream Media Pipeline   153

directly to the Board of Trustees of the New College of Florida. Written directly in his bio, DeSantis's note states:

> In recent years, Rufo has led the fight against critical race theory in American institutions. Rufo's research and activism inspired a presidential order and legislation in fifteen states, where he has worked closely with conservative governors and lawmakers to craft successful public policy.[41]

Rufo's tactics are drawn directly from internet trolling, so well coded into common culture, his tactics seem political and standard rather than from the standpoint of bigotry. Rufo, like Tucker Carlson, is very aware of the extremely online far right and their populist powers when they act collectively. Speaking directly to *them* rather than the public is his tactic, but the media has little idea of the uplift strategy deployed by the people he activates. Many reporters take Rufo at his word, assuming a good faith argument though it is very clear this is a man who acts in bad faith nearly all the time. For example, following Claudine Gay's resignation in early January 2024, NPR reported the resignation and the plagiarism charges without mentioning Rufo's involvement a single time.[42] That same day, *Politico* ran a piece interviewing Rufo, never once asking about his tactics and simply referring to him as a "conservative activist" who was in a "celebratory mood" following Gay's announcement.[43] These are both irresponsible in their coverage and accidently permit the online to mainstream pipeline to subsist and grow.

These tactics need to be incorporated into media literacy education and journalism programs. Rufo's patience is his trick, knowing he can move the needle little by little, directly in the open, then claim he didn't hide anything. It's immodest at best, hateful at worst. It also doesn't always work. In April 2024, former chief executive of the Wikimedia Foundation, Katherine Mahar, was named the new chief executive of NPR. In protest, NPR senior business editor Uri Berliner wrote an opinion piece in former *New York Times*'s reporter Bari Weiss's *The Free Press* newsletter. Berliner claimed that NPR "coalesced" around progressive worldviews. While not fully a controversial statement, Christopher Rufo dug through Mahar's tweets and found criticism of Donald Trump in her past. While this retort and attack may have been secluded to the internet, the *New York Times* devoted an entire article to Rufo's concerns and laundered his ideas directly to the public uncritically and without acknowledging his continual bad faith attacks.

This time, NPR stood by Mahar and disregarded Rufo's attempt. As NBC News's Brandy Zadrozny posted on Threads:

> Watch what's going on with NPR CEO, Katherine Maher. A big moment where Chris Rufo's schtick seems to be failing. He tried [to] ride

154 *Critical Internet Literacies*

the wave of far-right anger over that fact-wanting "whistleblower" article in Bari Weiss's rag but even with another assist from the NYTimes, NPR gave a full-throated "Nope" and stood by Maher. In the days since he's been spitting fantastical claims into the wind, including that Maher is CIA, censoring the internet and toppling governments (actually he's saying that!).[44]

Zadrozny mentioned that Rufo, flailing for the news to grip this story, claimed Mahar was a US state agent. He got this from a single tweet by Slim Amamou, a Tunisian activist, posted in 2014.[45] As Zadrozny then mentions, while several reactionaries were pushing Rufo's new attack, "media and the researchers, educators, and leaders targeted, don't have to play the game this guy made up." Resolve and a critical approach to internet literacies empowers us to see through bad faith attacks and identify future attempts.

Uplift Will Soon Be Unnecessary

As this book argues, we are always online, therefore we are witnessing the normalization of these tactics in real time. We cannot undo what has been done but we must be aware that platforms crave the attention and require the extremes to continue to scale. In further chapters, we'll discuss other examples of more subtle uplift, disguised through normalization like young girls (8–11 years old) mobbing Sephora shops looking for retinol or young men "mewing" in class. These girls were inspired to shop for anti-aging creams by influencers, unaware that many influencers are endorsed by the brand. Mewing, developed by British orthodontist Dr. Mike Mew and his son, where you clench your teeth and push your tongue to the roof of the mouth to develop a stronger jaw, is completely bunk science but promoted by masculinity influencers to help young men with softer jawlines.

These online to mainstream media incursions are extremely harmful and require parents to tune into the more esoteric content online. While retinol is useless for pre-teens, the behavior displayed in Sephora stores is sometimes questionable. Many people reacted by requesting Sephora ban children from the stores, which never happened. Even if retinol doesn't work on young girls, the sales help the store profit. On the other hand, mewing, which goes through a craze every so often, has found new popularity and is used by young people in classrooms to avoid answering questions. Teens simply point at their mouth when called up, telling the teacher subtly they are mewing. The roots are far more harmful and we'll discuss this in Chapter 8.

Confusing trends lead to reactions and moral panics and nearly all benefit social media platforms. Platforms profit from panics and public pushes

The Online to Mainstream Media Pipeline   155

for regulations as they lower competition and shift the responsibility away from critical approaches to governmental oversight. In the case of atomized media, this only helps those who have learned to encode harmful messages into their content. As influencers continue to be normalized and useful in the mainstream context and advertising becomes far more subtle, so does the propaganda and perpetuation of bigoted or patriarchal ideologies of the extreme fringe. Pressure should be applied to the advertisers who support these flows and parents should not lean into easy solutions. Learning the tactics of the internet's most talented is not exclusive to academic texts like this one, it is a skill learned by listening, applying care, and patience.

Notes

1 Broderick, Ryan. "The 4chan-Ification of the Web." *Garbage Day*, May 3, 2024. https://www.garbageday.email/p/4chanification-web.
2 *See Fake Twerk Dance End in Fire*, 2013. CNN. https://www.youtube.com/watch?v=1P5SKnqwdr0.
3 Freeman, Hadley. "Miley Cyrus's Twerking Routine Was Cultural Appropriation at Its Worst." *The Guardian*, August 27, 2013, sec. Opinion. https://www.theguardian.com/commentisfree/2013/aug/27/miley-cyrus-twerking-cultural-appropriation.
4 *Jimmy Kimmel Reveals "Worst Twerk Fail EVER – Girl Catches Fire" Prank*, 2013. https://www.youtube.com/watch?v=HSJMoH7tnvw.
5 Fera, Rae Ann. "Director Brad Morrison Reveals How He and Jimmy Kimmel Made The Best Twerk Fail Video. Ever." *Fast Company*, September 11, 2013. https://www.fastcompany.com/3017194/director-brad-morrison-reveals-how-he-and-jimmy-kimmel-made-the-best-twerk-fail-video-ever.
6 Solé, Elise. "Cooking, Cleaning and Controversy: How the 'tradwife' Movement Went Viral." *TODAY.com*, March 7, 2023. https://www.today.com/parents/family/traditional-wives-tradwives-controversy-tiktok-rcna67253.
7 Triggs, Ariana, Claire Hardwick, and David Oliver. "What Is a 'Trad Wife'? These Controversial Women Are Drawing Attention – and Opinions." *USA Today*. Accessed June 7, 2024. https://www.usatoday.com/story/life/health-wellness/2023/07/14/trad-wife-meaning-controversy/70407456007/.
8 Moore, Cortney. "'Tradwives' Push Back against Critics Who Say Their Viral Homemaking Lifestyle Is 'Alarming' and 'Creepy.'" *Fox News*, February 8, 2023. https://www.foxnews.com/lifestyle/tradwives-push-back-critics-who-say-viral-homemaking-lifestyle-alarming-creepy.
9 Mabie, Melinda Cooper, Ben. "Family Matters." *Viewpoint Magazine*, March 19, 2018. https://viewpointmag.com/2018/03/19/family-matters/.
10 "Dear Colleague Letter on Transgender Students." *Department of Justice, Department of Education*, May 13, 2016. https://www.justice.gov/opa/file/850986/dl.
11 "Post CP." *Know Your Meme*. July 11, 2013. https://knowyourmeme.com/memes/post-cp.
12 Fisher, Marc, John Woodrow Cox, and Peter Hermann. "Pizzagate: From Rumor, to Hashtag, to Gunfire in D.C." *Washington Post*, April 12, 2023. https://www.washingtonpost.com/local/pizzagate-from-rumor-to-hashtag-to-gunfire-in-dc/2016/12/06/4c7def50-bbd4–11e6–94ac-3d324840106c_story.html.

156 Critical Internet Literacies

13 Merlan, Anna. "The Conspiracy Singularity Has Arrived." *Vice* (blog), July 17, 2020. https://www.vice.com/en/article/v7gz53/the-conspiracy-singularity-has-arrived.

14 North, Anna. "#SaveTheChildren Is Pulling American Moms into QAnon." *Vox*, September 18, 2020. https://www.vox.com/21436671/save-our-children-hashtag-qanon-pizzagate.

15 Breland, Ali. "How Q Became Everything." *Mother Jones*, June 3, 2024. https://www.motherjones.com/politics/2024/06/how-q-became-everything-big-feature-wayfair-balenciaga/.

16 "Estee Williams (@esteecwilliams) · Instagram Photos and Videos," May 31, 2024. https://www.instagram.com/p/C7oneR5OeYK/.

17 "Just a Joke? Printable Activity Sheet." *MediaSmarts*. Accessed June 10, 2024. https://mediasmarts.ca/teacher-resources/just-joke-printable-activity-sheet.

18 Ohlheiser, Abby. "Analysis|How the 'Okay' Hand Sign Keeps Tricking Us into Looking." *Washington Post*, December 20, 2019. https://www.washingtonpost.com/technology/2019/12/16/how-okay-hand-sign-keeps-tricking-us-into-looking/.

19 Zwicky, Arnold. "Language Log: Just between Dr. Language and I." *Langauge Log* (blog), August 7, 2005. http://itre.cis.upenn.edu/~myl/languagelog/archives/002386.html.

20 Swales, Vanessa. "When the O.K. Sign Is No Longer O.K." *New York Times*, December 15, 2019, sec. U.S. https://www.nytimes.com/2019/12/15/us/ok-sign-white-power.html.

21 Falconer, Rebecca. "Mosque Attacks Suspect Gives 'White Power' Sign in Christchurch Court." *Axios*, March 16, 2019. https://www.axios.com/2019/03/16/christchuch-attacks-brenton-tarrant-1552716245.

22 Ahmad, Nafees. "The Truth About Neo-Fascism on Social Media." *Fair Observer* (blog), December 20, 2023. https://www.fairobserver.com/world-news/the-truth-about-neo-fascism-on-social-media/.

23 "Rogan O'Handley (@dc_draino) · Instagram Photos and Videos." June 10, 2024. https://www.instagram.com/p/C8AdL5fBfuA/.

24 Lorenz, Taylor. "Meet the Woman behind Libs of TikTok, Secretly Fueling the Right's Outrage Machine." *Washington Post*, December 7, 2022. https://www.washingtonpost.com/technology/2022/04/19/libs-of-tiktok-right-wing-media/.

25 Gogarty, Kayla. "Anti-LGBTQ Twitter Account 'Libs of TikTok' Seemingly Inspired Attacks from Florida Governor's Press Secretary." *Media Matters for America*, April 14, 2022. https://www.mediamatters.org/twitter/anti-lgbtq-twitter-account-libs-tiktok-seemingly-inspired-attacks-florida-governors-press.

26 Carless, Will. "When Libs of TikTok Tweets, Threats Increasingly Follow." *USA Today*. Accessed June 11, 2024. https://www.usatoday.com/story/news/investigations/2023/11/02/libs-of-tiktok-tweets-death-bomb-threats/71409213007/.

27 Popli, Nik. "Spotify's Joe Rogan Controversy Isn't Over Yet." *Time*, February 11, 2022. https://time.com/6147548/spotify-joe-rogan-controversy-isnt-over/.

28 Brenan, Megan. "Media Confidence in U.S. Matches 2016 Record Low." *Gallup.com*, October 19, 2023. https://news.gallup.com/poll/512861/media-confidence-matches-2016-record-low.aspx.

29 See also Jon Stewart lambasting Jim Cramer following the 2008 Financial crises. Stewart claimed he was able to charge Cramer with accusations that journalists cannot because he is a comedian.

The Online to Mainstream Media Pipeline   157

30 Gordon, Devin. "Why Is Joe Rogan So Popular?" *The Atlantic* (blog), August 19, 2019. https://www.theatlantic.com/entertainment/archive/2019/08/my-joe-rogan-experience/594802/.

31 Romano, Aja. "How Do You Solve a Problem like Joe Rogan?" *Vox*, February 23, 2022. https://www.vox.com/culture/22945864/joe-rogan-politics-spotify-controversy.

32 Kingkade, Tyler, Ben Goggin, Ben Collins, and Brandy Zadrozny. "Cat Litter Box Myths Are Suddenly a Culture War Flashpoint. Here's How That Happened." *NBC News*, October 14, 2022. https://www.nbcnews.com/tech/misinformation/urban-myth-litter-boxes-schools-became-gop-talking-point-rcna51439.

33 Reyes, Ronny. "Joe Rogan Admits the Story He Told Tulsi Gabbard about 'Litter Box in Girls' Bathroom' Was a Lie." *Daily Mail*, November 3, 2022. https://www.dailymail.co.uk/news/article-11386793/Joe-Rogan-admits-story-school-installing-litter-box-girls-bathroom-lie.html#comments.

34 "Joe Rogan Experience #2086 – Jim Norton." https://ogjre.com.

35 Richard Strocher X [@RichardStrocher]. "Some of You Owe Me an Apology Https://T.Co/OzG20SKNka." Tweet. *Twitter*, January 9, 2024. https://twitter.com/RichardStrocher/status/1744597287568019805.

36 Example of a Tweet Generator: https://www.tweetgen.com/create/tweet.html.

37 "I Liveblogged Osama Raid without Knowing It." *NBC News*, May 2, 2011. https://www.nbcnews.com/id/wbna42855474.

38 "Myanmar Coup: Fitness Instructor Unwittingly Films Video as Takeover Unfolds." *BBC News*, February 2, 2021. https://www.bbc.com/news/world-asia-55901774.

39 Christopher F. Rufo [@realchrisrufo]. *Twitter*, December 19, 2023. https://twitter.com/realchrisrufo/status/1737209215738069232.

40 Weigel, Moira. "Christopher Rufo's Troubling Path to Power." *The New Republic*, November 27, 2023. https://newrepublic.com/article/176809/christopher-rufos-troubling-path-power.

41 "Governor Ron DeSantis Appoints Six to the New College of Florida Board of Trustees." Accessed June 13, 2024. https://www.flgov.com/2023/01/06/governor-ron-desantis-appoints-six-to-the-new-college-of-florida-board-of-trustees/.

42 Romo, Vanessa, and Ayana Archie. "Claudine Gay's Resignation Highlights the Trouble with Regulating Academic Writing." *NPR*, January 3, 2024, sec. Education. https://www.npr.org/2024/01/03/1222588885/harvard-president-claudine-gay-resigns-plagiarism.

43 Ward, Ian. "We Sat Down With the Conservative Mastermind Behind Claudine Gay's Ouster." *POLITICO*, January 3, 2024. https://www.politico.com/news/magazine/2024/01/03/christopher-rufo-claudine-gay-harvard-resignation-00133618.

44 https://www.threads.net/@brandyzadrozny/post/C6tVkoluXoC.

45 Slim Amamou is also one of the people who boosted the video and aftermath of Muhammad Bouazizi's self-immolation in Tunisia in 2010, helping spark what would be known as The Arab Spring.

6 The "Social Dilemma" Dilemma
Critiquing Awareness Media

The Sky is Falling Dilemma

In September 1956, the *New York Times* television critic Jack Gould wrote that Elvis Presley's appearance on the *Ed Sullivan Show* disturbed adult viewers as they were worried about their children seeing such an act of "striptease behavior." He writes, "At least some parents are puzzled or confused by Presley's almost hypnotic power; others are concerned; perhaps most are a shade disgusted and content to permit the Presley fad to play itself out," remarking how parents have developed a panic over the appearance. By the end, Gould is sympathetic to the teens, saying they already have all the problems they need, without the parents' anxiety pressed on them.[1] In the early 1990s, US Senators held hearings on the impact of video game violence and their effect on society, worrying that the fighting game *Mortal Kombat* could encourage real-world violence. In 1999, the Columbine High School Massacre continued the moral panic around video games. The extreme violence was unprecedented and horrific but had little to do with video games. The issue returned in 2019 when Representative Kevin McCarthy blamed video games for the mass shooting in El Paso, Texas.[2]

Moral panics are hype-based, widespread fears that are often irrational. They spread via mainstream media and are amplified on Facebook pages, social media, and through politicians looking for more attention. People believe in panics because they glom onto our feeling that there is a threat to our value system or our communities.[3] Typically a moral panic is an extremely simplified wave of excitement about something perceived to be bringing societal collapse. Soon, "experts" emerge to supply the public with someone or something to blame rather than propose reasonable solutions or follow through with compassionate care. Moral panics are a reactionary industry propped up by reactionaries who, at best, may attempt a good faith effort to explain the situation, and at worst, be grifters who work for ratings, views, and clicks. As we know, the last two decades focus

DOI: 10.4324/9781003483885-6

The "Social Dilemma" Dilemma: Critiquing Awareness Media   159

has been on the panics surrounding our use of the internet, its constitutive technologies, smart phones, and social media. These are most definitely not going away and as a result, we are introduced to the whistleblowers, ethicists, and tech moralists who espouse claims that society is devolving and disintegrating. The internet and social media are more difficult than Elvis and *Mortal Kombat* to analyze, but "doomerist" approaches and moral panics do far more harm than good.

The modern tech pessimist movement may have started with the Y2K "millennium bug" panic. Memorable for many people around the world, Y2K sparked fears of a global meltdown, a destruction of society, and the end of the tech revolution. Though detected years earlier, the Y2K moment arrived at the height of the dotcom boom, an era where people believed the new industries developed through the World Wide Web were going to infinitely grow and profit, where someone could buy a URL like Pets.com and host their marketplace and it would hopefully never reach saturation. By 2000, much of our infrastructure, from shipping to corporate data storage, was also part of the internet industries and a bug like Y2K would have been disastrous. In retrospect, all the panic was unfounded, but excusable as our digital literacies were exceptionally low. Today it seems we are facing crisis after crisis, wondering if the internet has created polarization, conspiracy theories, extremism, and causes young people to become more depressed than ever before in history.

The biggest problem with moral panics is their reliance on pessimism. Where we hope to hear from experts who may assuage our fears, build our resilience, focus on care for the vulnerable, and create strategies for just and equitable futures, we are more likely to hear from people who confirm our worst fear, reminding us we are right to worry. Optimism does not make for good ratings when it comes to moral panics, however, the novel cases of the web's weirdest features, makes it quite difficult to develop a explainer that focuses on the esoteric nature of digital culture, web communities, and the consequences of always being online. What we don't know may scare us and learning it may be too intensive or exhaustive. Therefore, we hope that reporters, producers, directors, and storytellers take on the task of making the difficult to understand more digestible. In the past several years, there have been dozens of awareness media projects that cover internet literacies and digital ephemera, produced to enlighten audiences to the quirks, the horrors, the trends, the careers, and the dynamic of power and control. Nearly all popular projects aim to help the audience feel empowered to make change and increase control of the space beyond the screen.

It is also our responsibility to be somewhat critical of these projects, as they are produced within the structural parameters of their distribution – meaning the producers, directors, and studios hope to return their

160   *Critical Internet Literacies*

investment through views, subscriptions, advertising, and especially growth. When assisting people with understanding critical internet literacies and looking beyond basic use habits, we hope these projects incorporate critiques of their subjects in terms of race, identity, class, access, and vulnerable people. What we hope they do not contain (too much of) are platitudes, prospects of doom, or cherry-picked evidence to support their claims. One issue for making a larger-budget project that provides internet literacies is how much the systems, supported by capitalism, investment, and exclusivity, reshape narratives to fit their models of engagement. A producer interested in educating and informing the public must toe the line between heavy criticism and entertainment, a feat easier conceptualized than produced. Another issue is acknowledging that very often, awareness media must be produced with well-worn story tropes and storytelling that keeps the viewer engaged. Therefore, it is no surprise that most popular piece of internet literacies awareness media is the 2020 Netflix documentary *The Social Dilemma*, directed by Jeff Orlowski.

Orlowski's *The Social Dilemma* is both a documentary and a dramatic recreation of the moral panic in the late 2010s surrounding social media and mobile phones, incorporating the fears that the tech industry is eroding society in some of the most insidious ways possible. The story is told by a who's who of tech insiders, former founders, and academics. Along with the interviews, half the film is a fictionalized recreation of their concerns, focusing on a young white man (played by Skylar Gisondo) who becomes radicalized to the "extreme center" by his social media feeds. The soundtrack throughout the film is moody with affective swells, extremely reminiscent of Trent Reznor and Atticus Ross's immersive soundtrack for David Fincher's 2010 *The Social Network*; the music makes the film feel melodramatic for the entire duration. On the surface, the film provides dozens of trailheads to begin discussing the consequences of social media's never-ending scale and extractive infrastructure as told by some esteemed and recognizable people sharing their insider experiences. On the other hand, nearly the entire film is edited and directed to be as dramatic as possible, using nearly all the techniques the cast warns people to pay attention to when it comes to social media and smart phone use.

The film's main interviewee is Tristan Harris, a Stanford graduate who worked for Google on their Inbox team and as a design ethicist. Harris became somewhat famous for putting together a slide deck at Google titled "A Call to Minimize Distraction & Respect Users' Attention," acting as a sort of Cassandra pointing out the unethical actions that Facebook, Google, and Apple were committing in the name of the attention economy while simultaneously disregarding the fact that nearly everyone uses email. The deck made it all the way to former Google CEO Larry Page, but it gained little traction in the company aside from excitement from

The "Social Dilemma" Dilemma: Critiquing Awareness Media   161

his coworkers. Harris quit Google and founded the Center for Humane Technology (CHT), a non-profit organization hoping to realign technology with humanity's best interests.[4] While Harris isn't the only member of the Center for Humane Technology in the film, he occupies the majority of the screentime in comparison to a dozen or so other interviewees expressing similar concerns. The director, Jeff Orlowski, breaks from his previous documentary subject to produce this project. Before *The Social Dilemma,* Orlowski produced the 2012 *Chasing Ice,* a documentary about nature photographer James Balog who was capturing the melting ice caps and in 2017, Orlowski directed *Chasing Coral,* along similar lines focusing on disappearing coral reefs. Orlowski's previous projects made the *actual* collapse of the environment worth watching and he knows how to tell stories.

While many Americans are not overtly urgent about climate change issues,[5] many find themselves to be far more interested in tackling the issue with our ubiquitous technologies.[6] These concerns are both legitimate and worth interrogating. In no way is the following a call to remove any concern about social media, smart phone usage, and the overall lack of transparency from mega-corporations running digital platforms; this is a call to reconsider how *The Social Dilemma* tells this story and to critique its premise and sensational model of storytelling. By comparison, this chapter will also discuss several other films that aim to make the public more aware of the harms beyond the screen. Nearly all types of awareness media can be analyzed from a variety of critical methods and the films in this chapter, regardless of their quality, still offer space for conversation, workshopping, and further writing. The issue at the forefront here is the seriousness in which people have used *The Social Dilemma* as their primary way of understanding these issues, leaving them unable to move beyond some of the most sensational parts that lean into current moral panics.

The 25–35-Year-Old White Guys in a Room Dilemma

The dilemma of *The Social Dilemma* is that is seems to use all the techniques of the attention economy to tell its story: affective music swells, retention editing, dramatic recreations, sensational platitudes, warnings that seem like clickbait, manipulated bites, lack of critical literacies, pushes for simple solutions, and almost no diversity.[7] At one point, Tristan Harris mentions that a rooms of developers made up of 25–35-year-old white guys should have a "moral responsibility" to understand what they're doing. However, the film is comprised mostly of 25–35-year-old white guys who seem to lack the responsibility to explain their points of view without leaning into tropes and poor metaphors. In a basic reading of the film's aesthetics, storytelling, and affective musical melodrama, it would even be worth comparing the film to Jason Russell's short misguided "white-savior

162 Critical Internet Literacies

industrial complex" documentary *KONY 2012*. Both *The Social Dilemma* and *KONY 2012* attempt to make us aware of issues we have little knowledge of by forcing the viewer into the position of bystander, in no way the problem itself. Better stated by Teju Cole in *The Atlantic* in regard to *KONY 2012*'s model: "There is an expectation that we can talk about sins but no one must be identified as a sinner."[8] The tactics used in these films, both made for web-based distribution, are similar and successful. We are primed to lean into the horrors if we are relieved of being part of the problem ourselves.

On that note, the biggest problem *The Social Dilemma* attempts to tackle is a bit cloudy, seeming to interrogate our role as victim of the digital environments and what control we may have over the hegemony of these systems. There, Orlowski stacks Harris with early VR entrepreneur Jaron Lanier and Professor Shoshanna Zuboff, who all attempt to redefine the phrase: "If you do not pay for it, you are the product." For Lanier, his answer is "It's the gradual, slight, imperceptible change in your own behavior and perception, that is the product" and for Zuboff, who has a pretty good answer in her 2018 book *The Age of Surveillance Capitalism*,[9] says in the film that the tech industry "sells certainty" and "human futures at scale."

This primary concern enables Orlowski to investigate these conditions, however, the film's pace, music, and dramatic recreation-style storytelling give the viewer little or no time to really digest the dozens of points made throughout the film and worse, enables a few interviewees to provide cherry-picked evidence to back their claims without a single amount of pushback from Orlowski. Tristan Harris compares tech manipulation to close-up magic, the type that is done with small distractions and diversions, tricking people into believing magic is real. He also compares the vast infrastructures of social media and mobile phones to a tool, a bicycle in particular, a ridiculous comparison seemingly designed for parents to repeat the next time the discussion emerges around a dinner table. Harris states that trees are worth more dead than alive, seemingly recalling something heard from a philosophy lesson in college and gets close to a critique of capitalism. Unfortunately, Harris comes off as a tech determinist, expressing the notion of doom and pessimism throughout the hour and a half documentary.

As a result, the film seems to be an extended commercial for Tristan Harris and The Center for Humane Technology. It is possible he was using this film as a vehicle to leverage his public appearances or additional invites to congressional hearings where he gets to tell the US Congress that his organization is the only one who may save the future. Orlowski falls into this exciting doom trap and permits most of the men in this film to express their fears as if they're just recently emerging. The film omits any number of original critical views from decades earlier, focusing just on

The "Social Dilemma" Dilemma: Critiquing Awareness Media   163

the voices of the 2010s. This omission is pointed out by media theorist Douglas Rushkoff who has been meticulously critiquing the space since the early 1990s. Rushkoff felt the need to say something when Harris's CHT wanted to start a podcast called "Team Humanity"; Ruskkoff hosts a long-running podcast titled "Team Human." In a YouTube response monologue in 2020, Rushkoff expounds:

> [*The Social Dilemma*] is about tech guys from inside the tech companies who've realized the error of their ways. They've read something by me, or Nicholas Carr, or Sherry Turkle, or Andy Keane, or Howard Rheingold, or Richard Barbrook, or Tim Wu, or even Rafi – the kids' singer! – one of these many books we've been writing about over the last 10–20 years about the ills of social media and how these platforms are being engineered to manipulate people... These technologists are now in this new movie, kinda whistleblowing on the industry. They're quoting us or using our metaphors, but not mentioning our existence.[10]

The omission of foundational concerns is an interesting choice for Orlowski as context would give the audience a far better understanding of the issues. On the other hand, the inclusion of earlier voices may negate the popularity of the film that Netflix was likely attempting to generate. Rushkoff does reframe Orlowski's omission optimistically and expresses that *any* mention of tech critique is something we should consider positive.

In addition, the film seems to undermine itself at every step and weakens its own narrative. At one point, Cathy O'Neil, author of *Weapons of Math Destruction*, smartly points out that algorithms are part of the corporate profit system and should be interrogated as such. O'Neil's excellent point is then questioned by Jeff Seibert, a former Twitter executive (and serial tech entrepreneur),[11] who claims the machines have learned ("that's why it's called machine learning" he says incorrectly) to place the right post in the right order so you spend longer on the site. He then claims that no one knows how they do that. In another scene, co-founder of CHT Aza Raskin tells Orlowski that Renee DiResta of The Stanford Internet Observatory "blew his mind" when she told him about Russia's online tactics during the 2016 election. DiResta explains that Russia would make polarizing Facebook pages on subjects like fracking.

While *The Social Dilemma* brought up many issues with social media that seemed to manifest in the January 6 US Capitol Riot and the leak of The Facebook Papers, the film fails to truly discuss the way radicalization operates over time. Through the thrumming techno beat and overly dramatic recreations, we're consistently told to place the blame directly on the platforms and our access to cell phone media which nudge us to pay attention. However, many critiques pointed out that social media is not the

164 *Critical Internet Literacies*

source of all our ills. *The Verge*'s Adi Robinson points out some issues of blaming platforms:

> Many of the deadliest far-right killers were apparently incubated on small forums: Christchurch mosque killer Brenton Tarrant on 8chan; Oregon mass shooter Chris Harper-Mercer on 4chan; Tree of Life Synagogue killer Robert Bowers on Gab; and Norwegian terrorist Anders Breivik on white supremacist sites including Stormfront, a 23-year-old hate site credited with inspiring scores of murders. These sites aren't primarily driven by algorithms or profit motives. Instead, they twist and exploit the open internet's positive ability to connect like-minded people.[12]

While social media is the space for normalizing hateful rhetoric, the community-based websites and forums are also in need of attention. Robinson notes that people are hungry for "polemics" like *The Social Dilemma* as the black boxes of the web (played as an actor in the film by *Mad Men*'s Vincent Kartheiser) are so well hidden they feel like evil omniscient monsters that rule over society.

Unfortunately, this hunger for polemics like *The Social Dilemma* enables people like social psychologist Jonathan Haidt to launder their marketable versions of a moral panic directly into the mainstream. Haidt uses the film to reinforce the paranoia felt by parents to push his narrow perspective and claims about the horrors of mobile phones in relation to a rise in youth depression. Haidt has even irresponsibly compared internet access to heroin use.[13] He does no differently in the documentary, cherry-picking data to support his claims. To prove his expertise, Haidt often tries to make the internet and digital media seem so esoteric they're only explainable by experts like himself, riding the wave of attention while researchers conclude longitudinal studies that consistently counter his arguments.

In fact, following Jonathan Haidt's recent 2024 book, *The Anxious Generation: How the Great Rewiring of Childhood is Causing an Epidemic of Mental Illness*, the journal *Nature* published a response review by researcher and developmental psychologist, Candice L Odgers who found most of Haidt's claims to be simply untrue. Odgers writes:

> Our efforts have produced a mix of no, small and mixed associations. Most data are correlative. When associations over time are found, they suggest not that social-media use predicts or causes depression, but that young people who already have mental-health problems use such platforms more often or in different ways from their healthy peers.[14]

Haidt, like his peers in the documentary, seem to be pushing for a model of abstinence when it comes to social media and internet use. The problem

The "Social Dilemma" Dilemma: Critiquing Awareness Media   165

with a documentary like *The Social Dilemma* and by extension Jonathan Haidt's work, is that the extreme warnings that persist throughout the film are *intentionally designed* to stoke panic in the audience, leaving us with few options to help the public to manage and negotiate complex issues.

Odgers continues this point in *The Atlantic* and writes:

> Two things can be true: first, that the online spaces where young people spend so much time require massive reform, and second, that social media is not rewiring our children's brains or causing an epidemic of mental illness. Focusing solely on social media may mean that the real causes of mental disorder and distress among our children go unaddressed.[15]

The moral panics, whether they be teen's behaviors at school, our mental health, artificial intelligence taking jobs, or claims of society's immanent collapse, are marketing tools. They normalize extreme positions, reducing our critical functions so we are reliant on people like Tristan Harris and Jonathan Haidt. The film never addresses the critical literacies of the internet that would make us better users and readers, simply blaming us for allowing ourselves to be called "users." The film occasionally feels condescending, negating the more robust use of the web in critical, creative, and optimistic ways. As Adi Robinson notes:

> it's easy to find people thoughtfully engaging with [social media] apps, particularly amid the COVID-19 pandemic, which has turned screens into some of the only safe public spaces. Activists who are deeply critical of Facebook and Google have still built mutual aid networks and organized protests on their networks.[16]

The film would have benefited greatly from an optimistic viewpoint rather than cynical worrying, especially given the fact the film provides no tools to make the system better aside from demanding tech CEOs and legislators incorporate "humane" approaches to the tech – with no explanations of what that means. The film ends with Orlowski asking Harris whether he thinks we'll get there, and his only response is "We have to." Harris is not entirely incorrect, but should have spent more time giving the viewer some agency and ability to persist in spite of social media's hegemony. The film even produces its own plot hole as we watch Skylar Gisondo's Ben in the recreations increase his anxiety due to social events in his life, not social media. And most problematic is that we now find ourselves in situations where those doing their best to illuminate the harms that come from manipulative bad actors hounded by bad actors funded by dark money. In May 2024, Renee DiResta of the Internet Observatory found herself the target of far-right attacks. DiResta's contract was not renewed, and the Internet Observatory was shut down and disbanded following a barrage of

166 *Critical Internet Literacies*

lawsuits by Donald Trump's advisor Stephen Miller's law firm and consistent calls for investigations by Ohio Representative Jim Jordan.

Litigious attacks on researchers, manipulative advertising funded by dark money, and far-right groups like TPUSA sharing propaganda on college campuses are real harms hidden by easy to digest platitudinal worries that affirm moral panics. Parents are worried about their children, young people do have anxiety, systems are inequitable, and we need to hope for changes from the platforms themselves. On the other hand, dark interests with a command of the legal system and influence and power are working to dismantle any safety measures platforms may have in the claim for "free speech" or less restrictive censoring. The Stanford Internet Observatory has uncovered some of the most insidious pieces of propaganda and inorganic mis- and disinformation flows and has directly threatened the dark money interests using the web to their advantage. Who will do this work if we are focusing on unsolvable, but popular, issues like platform regulation or curbing cell phone use? *The Social Dilemma* is a crowded film made more congested by sensational recreations of a singular case study. Its role as a piece of awareness media that seems to be constructed on viral techniques to get views doesn't offer any solutions or any causes for optimistic collective response. Maybe that's the reason their fictional universe in the recreations radicalizes the young man to the "extreme center."

The Awareness Media Syllabus

The interactive, immersive, and overly visual nature of the internet often means that films and media projects are the best vehicle for explaining internet phenomena. However, producing awareness media about the internet for the public is generally a difficult task given the subject's extreme cultural diversity, soft and overt power structures, nuanced references, models of production, and technological underpinnings often coded in jargon. As a mostly visual medium, awareness media about the internet is also exclusionary and inaccessible to a great amount of people. In addition, the nature of the subject matter means that people online will *always* feel as though they know better, or that the project did not fairly represent them or their community. Getting skewered on Elon Musk's X is usually manageable with a thick enough skin, but it will not assuage the funders and studio executives who are often risk-averse to the type of vitriol that pores forth from the digital realms. In any case, we are in a period where the curiosity is high, and the projects are abundant, so we can develop an internet literacies awareness media collection that enables us to watch and rewatch and apply critical internet literacies to their projects.

The following is a sample syllabus containing documentaries and supplemental readings to help us learn about internet content and their creators.

The list contains non-fiction projects that enable conversation and further discussion about the subject matter, especially criticism of their construct, storytelling methods, representation, message, and possibilities for equitable futures. Documentaries on this subject date back to the early 2000s, however, some projects produced before 2017 may contain more disturbing content, terms, and other offensive imagery not acceptable in academic settings. A film like *We Live in Public*, Ondi Timoner's 2008 profile of the eccentric Josh Harris and his "experiments," display on-screen sexual acts and physical abuse. Timoner's story is valuable and profile sheds light on pre-2000 internet culture but should only be shown if properly situated in the discussion; *We Live in Public* is not included in the sample syllabus. On that note, most media about internet subject matter contains adult content, including aggressive imagery, racist language and images, discussions of sex, death, suicide, and cyberbullying. These are issues we'll discuss in the next chapter, but when it comes to curricular placement, these projects are meant for a university-level screening.

A final concern is the director's urge for comprehensive coverage of a subject. As we've read throughout this book, explaining even a benign meme requires an incredible amount of context. Unless Ken Burns was interested in developing a 10-hour-multipart documentary on a cartoon frog, we must be satisfied with Arthur Jones and Giorgio Angelini's 2020 *Feels Good Man*. Telling these stories requires experts who themselves are critically aware of the subject matter, but objective enough to share a more nuanced story without being censored or curtailed by the opinions of the internet audience. Lastly, we must also keep in mind that visual media and non-fiction media about the internet are not always fully accessible, meaning both in terms of comprehension and impairment issues. Unless there is descriptive text or textual supplements, the films will always lack full understanding and will exclude audience members.

Critical Internet Literacies Syllabus

The internet has steadily changed everything around us: who we know; how we meet; how we work; how we date; how we play; who gets famous; whom we trust; what we want; and who we want to *be*.

– Taylor Lorenz, *Extremely Online*, 2023. p. 6.

I want to be politically informed and educated but I also wanna have a good day and be in a good mood. Do you see my problem?

– dreamadove, *Tumblr*, 31 March 2016.[17]

168   *Critical Internet Literacies*

What do we talk about when we talk about the internet? How do we come to know certain terms and its effects? The following documentaries and supplemental readings are designed to encourage deep learning about internet culture, digital phenomena, and societal impacts, including online communities and actual harms. The internet is not neutral by any means as it is a mirror to our systemic and structural realities. As we learn from Joy Buolamwini's "Aspire Mirror" project in *Coded Bias* (2020), systems built by the few do not represent the whole. Meredith Broussard in the same film dismantles the argument made in Jeff Orlowski's *The Social Dilemma* (2020) by explaining that "data is a reflection of our history" and biases in the machine are our own. Both these films teach us important lessons on reading internet media and how we may discuss it with others in a mature and knowledgeable fashion.

Films like Netflix's *The Great Hack* (2019) help us understand the global nature of social media and its most vulnerable parts: the users. Other projects like Hulu's three-part docuseries *Black Twitter: A People's History* (2024) guide us through Twitter's strongest and most creative community, one that continues to hold its space against digital migration as Elon Musk's conversion to X threatens civil discourse. Dan Olsen's *Line Goes Up – The Problem with NFTs* (2022) is a self-produced two-hour-plus documentary on the short-lived NFT craze that dominated the internet; very few people have been able to clearly explain blockchain and digital culture like Olsen. *Feels Good Man* (2020) and *The Anti-Social Network* (2024), two films by Arthur Jones and Giorgio Angelini, bring a flashlight into the darker segments of the web without creating novelty or interest in navel-gazing. More films are provided below in "order" to tell the story of the internet and its criticism.

All films should be viewed more than once as criticism differs from consumption. In addition, nearly all the films on this list are overloaded with details and a second viewing benefits active viewing, note-taking, and contextual mapping. Each film includes supplemental reading or additional viewing to support the material. These are suggestions and can or should be supplemented with more specific readings toward the course of study. Most of the films on this syllabus are rated "TV MA," a rating given by either the platforms or the governing body and nearly all films contain adult content. In each section, particular warnings are provided.

Learning objectives include: 1) The ability to develop a sound understanding of a range of theoretical and methodological approaches to documentary production covering the internet; 2) explore how identity has been socially and visually constructed in term of class, gender, and race; 3) question the very notion of documentary genre, by emphasizing its hybrid and changing nature, which has shifted significantly throughout time and

The "Social Dilemma" Dilemma: Critiquing Awareness Media   169

in different social and cultural contexts; 4) engage with social and historical themes and question their representations; and 5) develop a mature language to discuss and diagnose the societal impact of the internet and detect the issues in calls for regulation, shifts in consumer behavior, and refusal to take part in moral panics.

Media Texts: (in suggested order of screening)

Coded Bias (2020) – dir. Shalini Kantayya – Netflix
The Great Hack (2019) – dirs. Jehane Noujaim, Karim Amer – Netflix
The Social Dilemma (2020) – dir. Jeff Orlowski – Netflix
Frontline: Generation Like (2014) – Frank Koughan and Douglas Rushkoff – PBS
Feels Good Man (2020) – dir. Arthur Jones – Pluto, Tubi, Peacock
Eat the Rich: The GameStop Saga – dir. Theo Love – Netflix (Three Episode Series)
The Anti-Social Network: Memes to Mayhem (2024) – dirs. Arthur Jones and Giorgio Angelini – Netflix
Black Twitter: A People's History (2024) – dir. Prentice Penny – Hulu (Three Episode Series)
Line Goes Up – The Problem with NFTs (2022) – Dan Olsen – Folding Ideas channel, YouTube
Anything For Fame (2023) – dir. Tyler Funk – Paramount+, NFB Canada
Coded Bias (2020) – dir. Shalini Kantayya – Netflix (Rewatch) or *Black Twitter: A People's History* (2024) – dir. Prentice Penny – Hulu (Three Episode Series) (Rewatch)

Supplemental Texts:

Extremely Online: The Untold Story of Fame, Influence, and Power on the Internet (2023), Taylor Lorenz
Distributed Blackness: African American Cybercultures (2020), André Brock Jr.
Race After Technology (2019), Ruha Benjamin
Weapons of Math Destruction: How Big Data Increases Inequality and Threatens Democracy (2016), Cathy O'Neil
More Than a Glitch: Confronting Race, Gender, and Ability Bias in Tech (2024), Meredith Broussard
No Filter: The Inside Story of Instagram (2020), Sarah Frier
Dumb Money: The GameStop Short Squeeze and the Ragtag Group of Amateur Traders That Brought Wall Street to Its Knees (2021), Ben Mezrich

170 *Critical Internet Literacies*

Reading the Internet Critically

1. *CODED BIAS* (2020) – DIR. SHALINI KANTAYYA – NETFLIX

Coded Bias (2020) directed by Shalini Kantayya, the first film in the viewing order, sets the stage for participants to adjust their critical lens for further screenings. Kantayya is best known for her film *Catching the Sun* (2015), a documentary about the solar power industry. In *Coded Bias*, Kantayya follows "code poet" Joy Buolamwini and her work at the MIT Media Lab, specifically the exploration of machine learning bias and infrastructural systemic racism. Buolimwini uses her project the "Aspire Mirror" as her main example as her camera would only detect her when she wore a white face mask; she was nearly invisible in her Black skin. The film, narrated by Buolimwini, discusses the oppressive nature of non-consensual surveillance, racist datasets, gender concerns, and the Black body regarding technologies. The film includes women scholars who are both leaders in their field and passionate researchers who tell a more macro story of the effects of social media and mobile devices. For example, Meredith Broussard states early in the film that we cannot separate the social from the technical and that data reflects history and Buolimwini explains how people can push back against surveillance system and generalized facial scanning technologies Another important note from Virginia Eubanks reminds the audience that the phrase "the future is already here, it's just unevenly distributed" is misread, it's here all at once, society is uneven and often tests of oppressive technology are used on vulnerable communities before the privileged publics. From a critical standpoint, it occasionally feels as though the film extends too much time to algorithms, but at the time, we were not yet thinking of them in this way. *Coded Bias* depicts scenes of protest violence and strong language.

Supplemental:
Race After Technology (2019), Ruha Benjamin
Weapons of Math Destruction: How Big Data Increases Inequality and Threatens Democracy (2016), Cathy O'Neil
More Than a Glitch: Confronting Race, Gender, and Ability Bias in Tech (2024), Meredith Broussard

2. *THE GREAT HACK* (2019) – DIRS. JEHANE NOUJAIM, KARIM AMER – NETFLIX

The Great Hack (2019) directed by Jehane Noujaim and Karim Amer follows the story of Cambridge Analytica, the British consulting firm funded by billionaire Robert Mercer and led in part by Steve Bannon, which was accused of harvesting data and distributing "fake news" to millions of people on Facebook. Noujaim and Amer previously worked on one of

The "Social Dilemma" Dilemma: Critiquing Awareness Media   171

Netflix's earliest documentaries – *The Square* (2013) – about Egypt's role and uprising in the Arab Spring. Most of the film follows the *Guardian's* Carole Cadwaller's reporting and Brittany Kaiser, a Cambridge Analytica whistleblower. Though Alexander Nix, the British founder of the company, refused to cooperate with the directors, his presence haunts the entire documentary like a boogeyman. A critical view may view this film as a likely contributor to the moral panic around fake news and mis- and disinformation. Cambridge Analytica exploited available social media systems using their own tools, but the film seems to want to blame Facebook and Cambridge Analytica for both the election of Donald Trump and Brexit. *The Great Hack* at times seems to be claiming Cambridge Analytica commited intense societal damage, conflating the energy of the two very distinct events. Relying on the fear of the machines that allegedly introduced demagoguery to the US and Britain, the directors lean into the digital tactics blame game. As *Variety* film reviewer Owen Gleiberman points out:

> In presidential politics, these techniques were pioneered, to a notable degree, by the Barack Obama campaign in 2008, and you could make the case that there isn't all that much difference between what Obama did and what Trump did, apart from the difference in the messages being sold.[18]

Though, for comparison to *Coded Bias*, an argument may be made that the manipulative tactics were tested on more vulnerable populations more susceptible to propaganda before the public. A discussion is warranted about fake news, regulation, and "solutions" to an unfixable problem. The film contains graphic imagery and divisive language.

Supplemental:
Bad News: Selling the Story of Disinformation," by Jospeh Bernstein, *Harper's Bazaar*, September 2021.[19]

3.   *THE SOCIAL DILEMMA (2020) – DIR. JEFF ORLOWSKI – NETFLIX*

The Social Dilemma (2020) by Jeff Orlowski is both accessible and problematic. It remains on this list to provide conversation and criticality to the many claims throughout. Aside from the previous concerns extensively explained in this chapter, the film seems to be a long-form commercial for The Center for Humane Technology. The viewer would not be wrong for believing this as several stakeholders in the film have written about their tactics in creating the film. Second, unlike many documentaries of its kind, it includes a dramatic recreation of "everyone's worst fears" as the young white man becomes radicalized to the "extreme center." The film

172   *Critical Internet Literacies*

fortunately does not assume the technology is neutral, but rather places all the blame on the machines rather than society. You may ask why people had become radicalized due to Cambridge Analytica's tactics, but you may miss that society and civil discourse was primed for the tactics. In the case of *The Social Dilemma*, Orlowski seems to want to connect spurious claims of overall increases in mental health directly to social media networks, a claim that has been debunked before and after the film's debut. On the other hand, the success of *The Social Dilemma* likely inspired Netflix to acquire Kantayya's *Coded Bias* a year later. In addition, there is lack of diversity (at a point one may think of "tokenism") in the film and can be compared to other films of its genre. This film has the lowest warning rating of all the films on the list, which may have been intentional on the part of the producers so the film may be included in secondary education. There are many discussions about how to talk about this subject with teenagers and whether *The Social Dilemma* is the proper vehicle for this knowledge.

Supplemental:
What 'The Social Dilemma' Misunderstands about Social Networks"
by Casey Newton, *The Verge*, 2020.[20]

4.   *FRONTLINE: GENERATION LIKE* (2014) – FRANK KOUGHAN AND
        DOUGLAS RUSHKOFF – PBS

Frontline: Generation Like (2014) produced by Frank Koughan and Douglas Rushkoff is now over a decade old but holds up well, especially seeming to present the moment before the internet shifted forever in 2014. *Generation Like* discusses the shift to reward-based interactions on social media platforms. As the young subjects of the documentary learn the internet in real time, they have figured out how the systems are operating, some using it to their advantage. Rushkoff visits the manipulators, so to speak, meeting with Oliver Luckett, the CEO of theAudience, a company that declares itself the "world's first cultural media company" and whose job it is to game online fame through collabs and brand endorsements. The story also weaves the tale of Tyler Oakley's success with that of an amateur influencer Kailee, a *Hunger Games* super fan, to contrast approaches. Rushkoff cogently explains the digital strategy: "What's designed to look like a grassroots wave of excitement is actually a meticulously planned marketing strategy." Did Cambridge Analytica use similar tactics? Part of the film follows Steven Ferndandez who goes by the YouTube name Babyscumbag, a young teen who started producing skateboard and stunt content and switched to prank material for more views. There is a good discussion embedded in the contrast between Kailee and her *Hunger Games* marketing and Steven Fernandez's approach. Kailee sits in a comfortable room of her own, liking posts on Facebook, while the entirety of Fernandez's family

The "Social Dilemma" Dilemma: Critiquing Awareness Media   173

lives in one room in Los Angeles and he hopes his content will raise them out of poverty. While the film ends on a somewhat dire note, the film is informative and framed as a PBS production.

Supplemental:
All Internet Roads Lead Back to 2014" by Steffi Cao, *The Ringer*, 2024.[21]

5.   *FEELS GOOD MAN* (2020) – DIR. ARTHUR JONES – PLUTO, TUBI, PEACOCK

Feels Good Man (2020) is an in-depth and nuanced look at the Pepe the Frog meme, from Matt Furie's creative work to Pepe's co-option by the far right and usage by hate groups to Furie's attempt to regain control of his work. *Feels Good Man* introduces terms and communities not discussed in previous films. Directed by Arthur Jones, a longtime friend of Matt Furie, and produced by Giorgio Angelini, the story is a linear narrative of the Pepe the Frog saga, detailing many of the horrible details with sympathy for Furie. Throughout, we see how much Furie lacked any form of internet literacies and acted as a bystander as his character was perverted into something unmanageable. The film is far too short for all the nuanced details Jones and Angelini attempt to add to this film. While it's well paced, it's overloaded with details that are extremely important to discuss. We are introduced to the subculture of NEETs and their pride in Pepe as well as crypto investors buying NFTs of Pepe the Frog's variations. The most important part of this film is buried in a somewhat boring legal dispute with conspiracist Alex Jones. Jones had used Pepe's likeness in a poster and Furie wins the lawsuit, albeit with a small payout. *Feels Good Man* could be watched through several critical lens, from the way the directors respectfully treat the NEETs to the access to Furie's many unfortunate legal meetings and his attempt to get Pepe off of The ADL's Hate Symbol list. The film benefits from the coda at the end, showing Pepe repurposed once again as a symbol of hope in Hong Kong during the protests – which is discussed in *Coded Bias* as well. *Feels Good Man* is a mature film for mature audiences and contains graphic hate imagery and copious amounts of adult language and internet terms.

Supplemental:
The Joke's On Us" by Helen Lewis, *The Atlantic*, 2020.[22]

6.   *EAT THE RICH: THE GAMESTOP SAGA* – DIR. THEO LOVE – NETFLIX
       (THREE EPISODE SERIES)

Eat the Rich: The GameStop Saga is a Netflix miniseries that details the "GameStop" pump from January 2021. A version of this story is also told in the fictional adaptation of Ben Mezrich's *Dumb Money* (2021).

174   *Critical Internet Literacies*

The docuseries is a calmer version, telling the tale of thousands of young people working collectively on Reddit's subreddit Wall Street Banks (WSB) to "fight back" against Wall Street's short sale of GameStop, a failing video game store. (Note: GameStop is failing because of private equity takeovers, not due to consumer choice.) *Eat the Rich* is designed as a story of both "revenge" and internet culture tactics in the actual stock market. The series feels entirely too narrow, which often happens when trying to summarize internet phenomena in the form of awareness media, but in this case, *Eat the Rich* does a disserve to the "meme stock" traders who invested their life savings, some losing it all, while the educated investors reaped millions in other investments suggested by WSB. *Eat the Rich* is not a financial film, and as reviewer John McDermott writes in an *Esquire* review:

> [That] the filmmakers felt they had to dumb down the particularities of the GameStop saga reflects another depressing truth about the public's relation to the world of high finance: most Americans are financially illiterate, and most of them don't give a shit to learn.[23]

In other words, we get to see the attempt, but not the success when small, viral moments dominate mainstream news but fail to make any change in the in-built inequities of financial systems. This is a mature series that deals with emotions, but is coded as accessible awareness media, and in that way, does more harm than good.

Supplemental:
Revenge Tactic:' GameStop's Massive Stock Surge Isn't Only About Making Money" by Peter Clark, *Time*, 2021.[24]

7.   *THE ANTI-SOCIAL NETWORK: MEMES TO MAYHEM* (2024) – DIRS. ARTHUR JONES AND GIORGIO ANGELINI – NETFLIX

The Anti-Social Network: Memes to Mayhem (2024) is the follow-up project for Jones and Angelini, this time attempting to summarize the "4chanification" of the entire web. As discussed thoroughly in this book, 4chanification is the slow widening of the Overton window as culture lilts to the right and becomes normalized as culture and code. This film is remarkably valuable, as this story has very little ability to be told in a condensed sitting, but on the other hand, the events are difficult to consume and digest in the rapid pace of the film. We move from one point to the next, one event to the next, one troll to the next, without having time to truly understand *why* the 4chanification of the web is enabled by both users and platforms. To viewers with low internet literacies, *The Anti-Social Network* is likely skipped when users come across the thumbnail on

The "Social Dilemma" Dilemma: Critiquing Awareness Media   175

Netflix, leaving just those interested to consume its content. The shocking and controversial content is surprisingly toned down considering the role 4chan has played in civil society. Jones and Angelini point to the optimism that is usually disregarded by reporters and mainstream news, explaining we are witnessing a sort of collective action – which is possible! – but motivated by reasons that technically are not explainable. *The Anti-Social Network* must be presented responsibly, as many of the terms and events are designed as rabbit hole entry points, luring people to "learn more" and "do their own research." In viewing this film, a study guide is useful and a **strong** warning not to visit 4chan's /b/ board after seeing the film. A reminder that you cannot unsee things is necessary. *The Anti-Social Network: Memes to Mayhem* is filled with many inappropriate images, racist language, adult content, and meta-violence and content warnings are advised.

Supplemental:
The 4chan-ification of the web" by Ryan Broderick, *Garbage Day*, 2024.[25]

8.   *BLACK TWITTER: A PEOPLE'S HISTORY* (2024) – DIR. PRENTICE
        PENNY – HULU (THREE EPISODE SERIES)

Black Twitter: A People's History (2024) by Prentice Penny is based on Jason Parham's multipart *Wired Magazine* piece and documents a multi-perspective history of how Black culture uses social media to change culture at large as well as the expression of Black joy. Through dozens of interviews, Penny's three-part docuseries is the most comprehensive look at the fundamental way Black Twitter changed society and how communities may remain resilient in the era of overt white supremacy, in the forms of overt racism and corporate greed. Prentice Penny, who had worked on *Scrubs* and Issa Rae's *Insecure*, produced this docuseries non-traditionally, using the vernacular and visual gifs that supplement Black Twitter's influence. The documentary features Dr. André Brock Jr., Baratunde Thurston, Jemele Hill, and insiders like TJ Adeshola, the former head of Global Content Partnerships at Twitter. The documentary provides an opportunity to explain the expression of diaspora in digital spaces and the ongoing threats against Black citizens. This series is the most robust coverage of the evolution of Black Twitter as Penny takes the viewer from the first days and early influence of the community through Covid and the subsequent social justice movements of 2020 and Elon Musk's takeover. The series uses extremely blunt and honest language to describe the power of the space, including the justice that emerges when communities voice concern in the collective. Black Twitter remains resilient, even under Elon Musk's

176 *Critical Internet Literacies*

X – Black Twitter recognized and amplified Musk's actual far-right ideologies long before the rest of the public became aware. The documentary is well paced and aside from the strong language, is one of the best cultural documentaries ever made about tech.

Supplemental reading:
For Black Folks, Digital Migration Is Nothing New" by Chris Gilliard, *Wired Magazine*, 2022.[26]

9.   *LINE GOES UP – THE PROBLEM WITH NFTS* (2022) – DAN OLSEN – FOLDING IDEAS CHANNEL, YOUTUBE

Line Goes Up – The Problem with NFTs is Dan Olsen's long-form YouTube story and video essay/documentary about the hype cycle that surrounded NFTs. For Olsen, it's not just about a crypto investment, but rather an exploration of culture, economics, grifting, and scams. During the pandemic, many people shifted their time spent online to investing, especially in wildly speculative markets like crypto currency. To make the digital investment seem "worth something," the concept of the Non-Fungible Token was invented, basically allowing anyone to "mint" a digital item onto the Blockchain, thereby allowing it to have some sort of "value" when bought and sold on digital marketplaces. In Olsen's two-hour dismantling of the Web3 technology, he not only explains why the concept is problematic (people were buying links to digital objects, not the digital objects themselves), but how it works on the Blockchain. It is one of the most entertaining educational videos about a niche subject that exists. *Line Goes Up* has nearly 15 million views, an exceptional success considering the subject matter. This film is filled with details and minutiae and requires active viewing to understand the nuance. While the NFT craze has subsided, the current hype around generative AI is a similar construct, one where you may look at Nvidia's (the company that makes the most powerful graphic unit (GPU)) stock price. *Line Goes Up* is highly accessible, contains a full transcript, and explains internet culture in a very easy to view manner.

Supplemental:
The (Edited) Latecomer's Guide to Crypto," annotated by Molly White and dozens more, *mollywhite.net*, 2022.[27]

10.   *ANYTHING FOR FAME* (2023) – DIR. TYLER FUNK – PARAMOUNT+, NFB CANADA

Anything For Fame (2023), directed by Tyler Funk, is a documentary that discusses the creator economy, from small-time influencers to OnlyFans

The "Social Dilemma" Dilemma: Critiquing Awareness Media   177

creators. (Full disclosure: I am a featured expert in this film.) Funk's film follows several "influencers" as they attempt to achieve "clout" and stardom – and what happens when they achieve it. Very few influencers are recognizable, and Funk intentionally cast creators willing to be honest about the process, especially the pains, the struggles, and the earnings. Aside from *Generation Like*, *Anything for Fame* is one of the few pieces of awareness media that features the parents of the creators to share their opinions, many of which help provide emotional color to the narrative. The film primarily focuses on three primary characters: Ava Louise, a TikTok star who became famous for licking an airplane toilet bowl; Jake Hillhouse, who does "Jackass" stunts for views; and Jumanne Clary, who goes by Jumanne Struggles. Representation in *Anything For Fame* is uneven and Jumanne is the only Black person and he's also the least successful. Between Ava's cynicism for the mainstream media complex (at one point she claims that if the media sees you as an object, why not "objectify" yourself) and Jumanne's deep disdain for labor, there is an incredible space for discussions on class, culture, and platform capitalism. These discussions are not included in the film aside from several of the scholars explaining the extreme precarity these influencers must endure for their dreams. The film is aggressive, mostly due to the Jackass-style stunts that may turn viewers off and the frank discussions of pornography and OnlyFans content. A content warning is necessary as Jumanne expresses ideations of suicide and another character's story is told after they died by suicide. Adding this toward the end of the film series helps a discussion that is made stronger by watching all the previous films.

Supplemental:
Millions work as content creators. In official records, they barely exist," by Drew Harwell and Taylor Lorenz, *Washington Post*, 2023.[28]

11.   *CODED BIAS* (2020) – DIR. SHALINI KANTAYYA – NETFLIX (REWATCH)
        OR *BLACK TWITTER: A PEOPLE'S HISTORY* (2024) – DIR. PRENTICE
        PENNY – HULU (THREE EPISODE SERIES) (REWATCH)

In a seminar setting, it is worth rewatching either *Coded Bias* or *Black Twitter* after discussing awareness media in depth. Not only are these two films more outspoken, but both offer the critique necessary to properly read and discuss internet media. Awareness media helps us become *aware*, but typically relieves us from action, however, both these documentaries feature perspectives typically elided by mainstream discourse. If we are to combat the structural white supremacy built into both the code and the culture, we must encourage deepening discussion and reframe our use of

178 *Critical Internet Literacies*

the internet in more equitable terms, focusing on the radical expression that is possible, though under constant threat of surveillance, co-option, and commodification.

Notes

1 Gould, Jack. "Lack of Responsibility Is Shown by TV in Exploiting Teen-Agers." *New York Times*, September 16, 1956. https://archive.nytimes.com/www.nytimes.com/partners/aol/special/elvis/early-elvis3.html.
2 Bella, Timothy. "Politicians Suggest Video Games Are to Blame for the El Paso Shooting. It's an Old Claim That's Not Backed by Research." *Washington Post*, August 5, 2019. https://www.washingtonpost.com/nation/2019/08/05/kevin-mccarthy-dan-patrick-video-games-el-paso-shooting/.
3 Crossman. "Understanding How Moral Panic Threatens Freedom." *ThoughtCo*, July 14, 2019. https://www.thoughtco.com/moral-panic-3026420.
4 The process of realigning technology with humanity's best interest is not explained in the film.
5 Pasquini, Giancarlo, Alison Spencer, Alec Tyson, and Cary Funk. "Why Some Americans Do Not See Urgency on Climate Change." *Pew Research Center* (blog), August 9, 2023. https://www.pewresearch.org/science/2023/08/09/why-some-americans-do-not-see-urgency-on-climate-change/.
6 Auxier, Brooke. "64% of Americans Say Social Media Have a Mostly Negative Effect on the Way Things Are Going in the U.S. Today." *Pew Research Center* (blog), October 15, 2020. https://www.pewresearch.org/short-reads/2020/10/15/64-of-americans-say-social-media-have-a-mostly-negative-effect-on-the-way-things-are-going-in-the-u-s-today/.
7 *The Social Dilemma* was nominated for seven Emmy Awards and won best writing and best editing in 2021.
8 Cole, Teju. "The White-Savior Industrial Complex." *The Atlantic* (blog), March 21, 2012. https://www.theatlantic.com/international/archive/2012/03/the-white-savior-industrial-complex/254843/.
9 "We are the sources of surveillance capitalism's crucial surplus: the objects of a technologically advanced and increasingly inescapable raw-material-extraction operation. Surveillance capitalism's actual customers are the enterprises that trade in its markets for future behavior." (pp.10–11).
10 *They've Joined Team Human! On Netflix's The Social Dilemma | Douglas Rushkoff Monologues*, 2020. https://www.youtube.com/watch?v=JT8HI_Tru_s.
11 Jeff Seibert founded an AI company called Digits and Jeff Orlowski is one of the angel investors in the project. Seibert takes credit for developing *The Social Dilemma* along with Tristan Harris and Jeff Orlowski. Seibert, Jeff. "The Mechanics and Psychology Behind the Social Dilemma." *The Startup* (blog), September 14, 2020. https://medium.com/swlh/the-mechanics-and-psychology-behind-the-social-dilemma-719d618aa8ce.
12 Robinson, Adi. "Telling People to Delete Facebook Won't Fix the Internet." *The Verge*, September 4, 2020. https://www.theverge.com/2020/9/4/21419993/the-social-dilemma-jeff-orlowski-netflix-movie-review-social-media-algorithms.
13 *Jonathan Haidt on Smartphones and Children | Interview*, 2024. https://www.youtube.com/watch?v=Z-nBEX1FgBk.

The "Social Dilemma" Dilemma: Critiquing Awareness Media 179

14 Odgers, Candice L. "The Great Rewiring: Is Social Media Really behind an Epidemic of Teenage Mental Illness?" *Nature* 628, no. 8006 (March 29, 2024): 29–30. https://doi.org/10.1038/d41586-024-00902-2.

15 Odgers, Candice L. "The Panic Over Smartphones Doesn't Help Teens." *The Atlantic* (blog), May 21, 2024. https://www.theatlantic.com/technology/archive/2024/05/candice-odgers-teens-smartphones/678433/.

16 Robinson, Adi. "Telling People to Delete Facebook Won't Fix the Internet." *The Verge*, September 4, 2020. https://www.theverge.com/2020/9/4/21419993/the-social-dilemma-jeff-orlowski-netflix-movie-review-social-media-algorithms.

17 dreamadove. "DreamaDove's Blog." *Tumblr*, March 31, 2016. https://dreamadove.tumblr.com/post/141996229170/i-want-to-be-politically-informed-and-educated-but.

18 Gleiberman, Owen. "Film Review: 'The Great Hack.'" *Variety*, July 24, 2019. https://variety.com/2019/film/reviews/the-great-hack-review-cambridge-analytica-1203277059/.

19 Bernstein, Joseph. "Bad News: Selling the Story of Disinformation." *Harper's Bazaar*, September 2021. https://harpers.org/archive/2021/09/bad-news-selling-the-story-of-disinformation/.

20 Newton, Casey. "What 'The Social Dilemma' Misunderstands about Social Networks." *The Verge*, September 16, 2020. https://www.theverge.com/interface/2020/9/16/21437942/social-dilemma-netflix-review-orlowski-sarah-zhang-memo-facebook-buzzfeed.

21 Cao, Steffi. "How 2014 Changed the Internet Forever." *The Ringer*, May 1, 2024. https://www.theringer.com/tech/2024/5/1/24144418/modern-internet-2014-anniversary.

22 Lewis, Helen. "The Joke's on Us." *The Atlantic* (blog), September 30, 2020. https://www.theatlantic.com/international/archive/2020/09/how-memes-lulz-and-ironic-bigotry-won-internet/616427/.

23 McDermott, John. "'Eat the Rich: The GameStop Saga' Fails Its Heroes – And Villains." *Esquire*, September 28, 2022. https://www.esquire.com/entertainment/tv/a41408398/eat-the-rich-the-gamestop-saga-review/.

24 Clark, Peter Allen. "'Revenge Tactic:' GameStop's Massive Stock Surge Isn't Only About Making Money." *Time*, January 28, 2021. https://time.com/5933931/gamestop-stock-market-reddit-money/. (Disclosure: I am interviewed in this piece.)

25 Broderick, Ryan. "The 4chan-Ification of the Web." *Garbage Day*, May 3, 2024. https://www.garbageday.email/p/4chanification-web.

26 Gilliard, Chris. "For Black Folks, Digital Migration Is Nothing New." *Wired*. https://www.wired.com/story/black-twitter-social-media/.

27 "The (Edited) Latecomer's Guide to Crypto." *Mollywhite.net*, March 25, 2022. https://www.mollywhite.net/annotations/latecomers-guide-to-crypto.

28 Harwell, Drew, and Taylor Lorenz. "Millions Work as Content Creators. In Official Records, They Barely Exist." *Washington Post*, October 26, 2023. https://www.washingtonpost.com/technology/2023/10/26/creator-economy-influencers-youtubers-social-media/.

7 The Moderated Internet
Reconsidering Safety Online

The Human Cost of a Better Experience

We use an internet both moderated and filtered for our experience. Have you stopped for moment to consider what this means? How this impacts your everyday life? Have you considered the costs of this moderation through economics, labor, and infrastructure? There are things uploaded online that you will *never* see, things that are not OK, things that are so utterly unspeakable you may not have the vocabulary to imagine them. This is not because humans are inherently averse to posting horrific content, but rather because humans like *you* have *seen* these things and they have removed them for *you* to make your experience better. These moderators do a thankless job, damaging their mental health for the sake of user experience. Many of these people come from the Global South, outsourced by companies like Meta or Alphabet, sitting in dark rooms with hoods around their computer monitors, watching content filled with horror, eliminating some, flagging others, striking user accounts, and outright banning some others. Occasionally, people like Julie Mora-Blanco, see something *far worse* than they've ever seen in their lives.

"Oh god," Mora-Blanco said aloud when she saw it. It was 2006 and she was a new "content policy strategist" for YouTube. Mora-Blanco didn't describe what she saw, but told Catherine Buni and Soraya Chemaly in their 2016 long-form piece for the *The Verge*, "The Secret Rules of the Internet," that it was related to child sexual abuse material, called CSAM. Mora-Blanco said her teammate helped her with the next steps: hitting "strike" followed by forwarding the information to the National Center for Missing and Exploited Children's (NCMEC) CyberTipline. As soon as she did this, the next piece of horror appeared on her screen.[1] We take for granted the strength and resolve people like Julia Mora-Blanco have when doing this unadmirable job. Soon after witnessing the horror, Mora-Blanco required a walk and some time off the screen, but there's no way to unsee something. She explained to the authors that a goal is to find some sort

DOI: 10.4324/9781003483885-7

The Moderated Internet: Reconsidering Safety Online   181

of humor in life, or this job would destroy you. Mora-Blanco was in her twenties when this incident occurred, and she worked alongside about 60 people of the same age; some were college graduates like herself.

In 2007, YouTube viewers were consuming more than 100 million videos per day, a growth that was only matched by the sheer volume being uploaded. Humans are the intermediary between the uploaders and the safety of the community, but how do they fare against the extreme amount of content uploaded online? That year, following the slew of inherited copyright lawsuits from before the Google acquisition, YouTube began its installation of the Content Verification Program, also known as ContentID, the algorithmic detection software that screens uploads for copyrighted material, down to the pixel level and audio waves. However, training a software to detect malicious content is harder than detecting material already available in a database – humans were still required at a massive scale to train the machines.

The most common solution for most platforms is to create rules. Nearly all platforms have rules laid out in the terms of service. Even 4chan has real rules (aside from their user-generated "rules" they've compiled) and they're usually dictated at the highest levels where the site servers are hosted or from the URL distribution company.[2] On mainstream sites, rules are implemented to reduce the in-flow of the harmful content at the door. In *The Verge* piece, Mora-Blanco explains she was part of YouTube's earliest team called the SQUAD, short for Safety, Quality, and User Advocacy Department. Aside from their human morals and their heuristic "can I show this to my family?" they knew they had to develop strong guardrails. The SQUAD team was responsible for the foundations of the rules along with YouTube's legal team. "They barred depictions of pornography, criminal acts, gratuitous violence, threats, spam, and hate speech. But significant gaps in the guidelines remained – gaps that would challenge users as well as the moderators." (YouTube never responded to Buni and Chemaly for clarification when they wrote their piece.)

Sites like YouTube, Facebook, and Twitter are considered "town squares," spaces where people can share information and discuss it with one another, moving thoughts off-platform and into their homes and offices. How the large sites moderate content sets the standard for what the social media industries consider "harm" and user safety versus the free-for-all possibilities of a site like 4chan. To ensure a community feels safe, it's important to censor material that may negatively affect people. Something like pornography contains a very wide latitude of content and its range of material varies in acceptability based on culture, geography, and the public. However, pornography has many sites for its dedicated distribution and when it leaks into mainstream social media it could result in trauma for people, especially younger users. All people are different with

182   *Critical Internet Literacies*

unique proclivities of their own, but the main spaces are shared. So how does a site create a bar of entry? In the case of YouTube and Meta, they've banned pornography outright. But how do you know if it's pornography aside from the common "you know it when you see it" response?

These questions are what safety teams analyze on a consistent basis alongside questions about criminal acts ("Is it newsworthy?") to violence ("Is it documentary footage?") to hate speech ("Is this covered by the First Amendment in the US or freedom of expression in other countries?") and these debates are in constant fluctuation as time changes. For example, early rules of YouTube changed in 2009 when 26-year-old Neda Agha-Soltan was shot and killed on camera in the middle of Iran's Green Movement in a protest against the election of President Mahmoud Ahmadinejad.[3] Agha-Soltan died on camera and blood poured out her eyes and from the hole in her chest. This was violence and gore, but after much debate, the SQUAD decided to keep the video online with a warning button (invented for this video) warning viewers of graphic material. The video then became a political symbol, showing the violence that counter-protestors (those for the newly elected president) could cause. YouTube shifted its rules to make the site a stronger space for information gathering and pro-democracy content. The video and coverage of Agha-Soltan's death are still online. Today, over five weeks of content are uploaded to YouTube every minute and thousands of people all over the world watch the horrors for us.

The Borderlands of Harm

What is considered "harmful" and how do we know where the borders of that term apply to content? What is the difference between risqué media and softcore pornography? What type of language causes someone to act versus language meant for engagement and clicks? What visual media could cause a viewer to feel trauma? Content moderation is a sticky subject for nearly every platform. There are usually multiple safety teams under the departments of trust and safety, legal, policy, or moderation and they play incredibly important roles in our user experience, most attempting to maintain a collective reality where we can coexist online. Trust and safety teams are typically at odds with the executives of many platforms as they are costly divisions that require resources to operate well and could cost the company money by removing content. In addition, tech executives who operate within the Silicon Valley mantra of "scale at all costs," often see trust and safety as the police of the platform, withholding expression. On the other hand, good content moderation makes platforms stronger and more welcoming, enabling communities feel safe to express themselves on the sites.

The Moderated Internet: Reconsidering Safety Online   183

For example, when you use social media, you hope that you can safely share something with friends and followers and receive likes or comments that provide a modicum of positive responses. This in turn increases your likelihood of returning to the site. What if next time you posted an image of the beach on your Instagram channel, your comments were filled with angry notes, yelling at you and cursing, with slurs and threats? You'd likely decide this platform was no longer fun to use and you'd migrate away from it, even if you previously enjoyed it. Your safety is part of the enjoyment. But what is safety and how do we know it? There are some obvious examples that you may imagine or unfortunately have seen, like terrorist acts or violent events in unedited war footage or dash camera road accidents, but what about pre-teen girls buying retinol from Sephora? What about high school boys practicing jawbone techniques and refusing to answer questions in class? These are off-platform issues caused by non-obvious harms which require context and mitigation to manage as they spread to civic spaces. What *we* consider harm may not be what *others* consider harm.

In March 2019, Simon van Zuylen-Wood of *Vanity Fair Magazine* delved into Facebook's speech moderation team. In his piece "'Men Are Scum:' Inside Facebook's War on Hate Speech," he writes of his experience while embedded within Facebook's content moderation team. The story begins with a woman named Marcia Belsky who was kicked off the platform for 30 days because she posted "Men are scum."[4] Van Zuylen-Wood was invited to sit on the meetings to discuss how to deal with the issue, especially considering the discussion was happening within the context of the #MeToo movement – one that pointed out some of the ways men had behaved poorly over many years. At the time, Facebook was still reeling from accusations that it had hosted damaging disinformation that affected the 2016 US election and hate speech toward Muslims was at an all-time high.

Van Zuylen-Wood explained that while Mark Zuckerberg is usually seen as the definitive decision maker of the platform's rules, policy questions like this are Content Moderation team leader Monika Bickert's responsibility:

> At 42, Bickert is currently one of only a handful of people, along with her counterparts at Google, with real power to dictate free-speech norms for the entire world. In "Oh, Semantics," [the policy meeting room] she sits at the head of a long table, joined by several dozen deputies in their 30s and 40s. Among them are engineers, lawyers, and P.R. people. But mostly they are policymakers, the people who write Facebook's laws. Like Bickert, a number are veterans of the public sector, Obama-administration refugees eager to maintain some semblance of the pragmatism that has lost favor in Washington.[5]

184   *Critical Internet Literacies*

The day of Van Zuylen-Woods's visit, the team was there to discuss "terrorism, non-sexual adult nudity, editing disturbing content on the pages of dead people, and, finally, 'men are scum.'" The moderation issue at hand for "men are scum" was based on Facebook's limitation of "gender-based attacks." The moderators felt loosening these rules may backfire and lead to more misogynistic posting on the platform.

There is a 40-page rule book that helps moderation teams at Facebook understand what material isn't allowed on the site and in the "men are scum" case, it follows a rule that prevents attacks against "protected characteristics" like gender, sexuality, race, or religion. While it may at this point be fair to consider that genders are treated differently online (they are), from a policy standpoint it requires sets of rules to share with their 15,000 plus humans who actually do the content moderation off-site. The moderation teams at Facebook had to consider what it means to make this balance work: can women be scum? If they cannot be called scum, neither should men. Note here as well there is no etymological debate around the term "scum," just rather that the slur may be applied to one gender or another. Van Zuylen-Wood writes:

> If you take a step back, it's kind of an idealistic way to think about the world. It's also a classically Western, liberal way to think about the world. Give everyone an equal shot at free expression, and democracy and liberty will naturally flourish. Unfortunately, the more Facebook grows, the less democracy and liberty seem to be flourishing.

One thing to keep in mind is that the borders of what we may consider harm shift based on social climate. The *Vanity Fair* story was taking place following Facebook's public failures in the mid-2010s and now there was far more attention to these types of issues. They looked at how hate speech operates on the platform. Hate speech is extremely difficult to manage on any social media site because of the room for interpretation and intent. As we discussed in Chapter 5, the idea of satire or irony discharges many of the claims of what we would consider hate speech. If it technically has no immediate reaction of the intention to cause actual harm, is it covered by the freedoms of speech granted by the US constitution? One policy the Facebook team looked at was the word "dyke," removed as a slur. However, when used between friends, it may have a casual intent and it was reinstated.

The restrictions on the First Amendment are not enough to cover the variations of speech on the internet. We know we are restricted from incitement and "clear and present danger," based on the 1919 Supreme Court case *Schenk vs. United States* and later narrowed in 1969 in *Brandenburg vs. Ohio* barring the acts of "imminent lawless action." Another important

The Moderated Internet: Reconsidering Safety Online 185

limitation is incitement to suicide, upheld by the Massachusetts Supreme Court in 2017. In addition, there are limitations on citizens' ability to defame another person, and both libel and slander are considered limited, and perpetrators are not protected from consequences of committing either. The First Amendment also does not cover false advertising or copyright violations. This leaves platforms to decide everything else, making decisions between "free expression" versus "free speech" versus platform safety.

On the other hand, First Amendment restrictions are limited to the United States, and while the tech companies are US based, their content is restricted by the internet systems of each respective country. The European Union has numerous additional regulations on speech. Content moderation isn't just about US ideals and appropriate use of language, it's about making the experience work for users where they live. For example, until 2018, women were not allowed to drive cars in Saudi Arabia and images and videos of that nature would be filtered for that country. Moderation requires global perspectives and people with direct knowledge of the local environment. While we may not consider seeing a woman driving "harmful," before 2018, that type of imagery could be flagged as intentionally harmful to the woman driving the car as she may have been punished for doing so. As laws change, so do the content moderation standards.

The Moderation Game

To manage the deluge of content uploaded online every minute to Facebook and YouTube, companies hire tens of thousands of people to moderate their users' content, but these moderators are not employees. Silicon Valley companies typically hire third-party companies to moderate their sites, often using low-cost labor, much of it coming from the Philippines. In the 2018 documentary *The Cleaners*, directors Hans Block and Moritz Riesewieck interview some of these workers and inquire into their mental health levels.[6] Many moderators screen about 25,000 images a day, absorbing horror at an unimaginable scale. The "cleaners" in the film feel proud of their work because they make the internet a better place, but do so at great cost – the suicide rate is quite high among the workers. Block and Riesewieck estimate there are at least 20,000 people in the Philippines that do this type of work for US social media companies and tech companies.[7]

Like the industry of fast fashion, many people do not realize the amount of invisible labor that goes into our consumer behavior. Until the late 2010s, almost all content moderation services were done outside the United States on low-cost labor, but as Meta has scaled, there are new offices in California, Arizona, Texas, and Florida. In 2019, journalist Casey

186 *Critical Internet Literacies*

Newton investigated the "secret lives of American Facebook moderators in America," in a piece he called "The Trauma Floor," for *The Verge*. In the article, Newton investigates some of the people who work at Cognizant, a vendor for Facebook, and Newton documented a day in the life of "Chloe" as she moderates Facebook content. Her training consisted of watching a man get murdered followed by learning the rules of the platform. According to Newton, she was visibly shaken, unable to sit without tearing up – she had to leave, but no one followed her; this was her job.[8] Newton interviewed dozens of "process executives" who filter content, most all of them were barred from sharing specific details due to strong non-disclosure agreements forced upon them by Facebook.

Unlike the bright lights and free food at the Facebook offices, these operators were in tight cubicles with black filtered screens. Newton writes:

> Collectively, the employees described a workplace that is perpetually teetering on the brink of chaos. It is an environment where workers cope by telling dark jokes about committing suicide, then smoke weed during breaks to numb their emotions. It's a place where employees can be fired for making just a few errors a week – and where those who remain live in fear of the former colleagues who return seeking vengeance.

Many of the employees, inundated by the horrors of the material, start leaning into fringe beliefs like flat earth theory or Holocaust denial or 9/11 conspiracies. It's possible our minds are not designed to engage with this much horrid material, and it seems Facebook has little care for supplying assistance to these workers.

In other environments like Reddit or Discord, moderation is distributed on the platform with free labor. In Robert Peck's 2019 *Wired* article, "The Punishing Ecstasy of Being a Reddit Moderator," Peck explains his role as the moderator of the subreddit r/aww, one of the largest subreddits on the site with over 35 million subscribers. Robert Peck's full-time job is a professor of rhetoric at the University of Iowa, but enjoys his role at Reddit, making r/aww a happy place to visit. Peck explains that the rules of the subreddit are easy to follow: users should post material of "adorable positivity" and must be original content (called "OC") and they should avoid any images or comments that show harm to humans or animals.[9] But Peck, along with the army of thousands of other volunteer Reddit moderators, are up against a litany of bad actors, abusers, and worst of all, bots.

Bots aren't just machines, they could be users from troll farms, meaning spaces not unlike the content moderation offices of Meta, but in this case working to sow discord on websites. More likely than "harms," bots are more interested in running scams, posing as real users, baiting people with

The Moderated Internet: Reconsidering Safety Online 187

phishing tactics like bogus links or trails to other accounts where they get snared in a trolling game. Sometimes, long unused accounts get hacked and start posting again; Peck and other moderators call these accounts "zombies." Moderators like Robert Peck are highly aware of these tactics. Peck writes:

> From dawn to dusk, scammers – be they bots, trolls, or propagandists – scour the internet searching for pictures or memes that have gone viral in the past: comfort foods, videos of things falling over, puppies. Often puppies. By sharing puppies, they hope that you will appreciate them, upvote them, and share them, and in so doing lend the zombie account the further appearance of credibility. It's hard to go wrong with dogs hugging over a fence. It's tough to accuse someone of being a foreign agent for showing you a pic of a six-week-old Labradoodle.

Some zombie accounts are malicious, some post spam, some gibberish, but if they come across a moderator, they're likely going to get banned.

The conditions that bring a person to become a content moderator differ; moderators like Robert Peck do the work as a benefit for the community and the health of Reddit because he belongs to the community and wants the environment to succeed. On the other hand, people like Julie Mora-Blanco are more likely to be the person who screens the content you'll never see. Recent college graduates are often recruited by companies like TikTok, Meta, or Alphabet with the alluring job opportunity of working "for" a tech company, though most are completely unaware of the mental health costs of the job. The jobs are paid reasonably, enough for a recent graduate to succeed, but they are also somewhat naïve to what harms people may be doing online, as this is rarely taught in schools. There's also levels of nuance, context, and intent that must be learned over time and it could take months of brain-destructing time before a moderator becomes good at managing the policies of a site.

How do you think you would fare as a content moderator? Would you know what to do? In 2023, Mike Masnick of TechDirt developed a web version of a card game that he used to teach policy and moderation to tech industry folk. Masnick developed "Moderator Mayhem" using Engine, a non-profit firm that helps advocacy startups.[10] Cory Doctorow explains the game:

> You play a mod who has to evaluate content moderation flags from users while a timer ticks down. As you race to evaluate users' posts for policy compliance, you're continuously interrupted. Sometimes, it's "helpful" suggestions from the company's AI that wants you to look at the posts it flagged. Sometimes, it's your boss who wants you to do a

188 *Critical Internet Literacies*

trendy "visioning" exercise or warning you about a "sensitivity." Often, it's angry ref – working from users who want you to re-consider your calls.[11]

Doctorow believes the game is so well built that people shouldn't even engage in conversations about moderation policy *without* playing the game – though this book disagrees, it should be in conversation as much as possible. Masnick's interest in developing the game followed the trendy discussions that developed following Elon Musk's takeover of Twitter. Musk notoriously dislikes moderation and sees trust and safety as people who are out to restrict expression and free speech. (Though Musk considers himself a "free speech absolutist," he is extremely far from this, personally banning accounts or posts he finds threatening to his worldview.)

Masnick was interested in converting the card game into an online version as many trust and safety teams and moderators hire people with little experience in the field. There are pressures from a variety of angles that cause stressors on the job and Masnick felt his game could provide insight into how policy operates. Masnick writes:

A friend of mine in the trust & safety world once suggested that these conversations would be a lot more useful if everyone had to spend a few days moderating an actual community, and could learn how content moderation is not about "suppressing viewpoints," but almost always about understanding really complex scenarios in which you have to make decisions in a very limited period of time, with limited information, and where there may not be any "right" answer. Enter: Moderator Mayhem. It's a browser-based mobile game, and you will learn that you have to make your moderation decisions by swiping left (take down) or right (keep up), and try to align content with the policies of the company (a fictional review site called TrustHive).[12]

Playing the game starts with a warning advising users that this game is meant for ages 18 and up and while the game doesn't explicitly show disturbing content, it makes references throughout. The fictional TrustHive warns that people are allowed to review "anything" and it's all fair game. You may interact with content flagged as "spam," "violence," "illegal" – all while being timed. You may get cards that asks you to review an image of something like cocaine flagged as illegal and your job is to take it down. Sometimes, you may keep posts up if the context requires it, something like an empty syringe may be flagged as "illegal," but does not show anything illegal.

These are the borderlines of harm. The "boss" in the game explains that occasionally, there is no answer, and you need to move on, especially

The Moderated Internet: Reconsidering Safety Online 189

because you are scored based on time, and as you review, new cards are stacked for you to deal with. The boss states, "Your job requires that you make good decisions at a fast pace. TrustHive is counting on you." Letting you know that if you do a good job, you may get promoted. You must use the "look closer" function quite often, as context helps play the game. There are no usual simple "leave up" or "take down" options, every flag is nuanced. Hate messages may be OK when the topic is about a politician, but not OK when about a consumer at a restaurant. It takes time to learn how to play the game, but the most important trick is to stay calm. Occasionally your manager will stop the game play so you may play with puppies for a bit!

Moderator Mayhem is a good simulator, and it is highly recommended that you play this game before teaching this subject or applying critical internet literacies in regard to moderation or trust and safety. There is much nuance in safety and harms and in the following, we'll discuss concretely what harms require additional critical approaches. In an era where people like Elon Musk demand "transparency" for these actions of platform safety and health, we need to expand the conversation beyond the idea of "suppression of speech" and "limits on expression" to enhanced user experience and a desire to create equitable environments for all users. Trust and safety is more than just platform engagement, it requires us to think about the consequences off-platform as well, as our role in our communities is intertwined with our digital lives.

Reconsidering Slow Harms

In his 2013 book, *Slow Violence and the Environmentalism of the Poor*, author Rob Nixon argues that the systemic issues of imperialism, colonialism, and capitalism contribute to global harms in ecology and environmental damage. Unseen by these major issues are the harms to the most vulnerable populations, especially the poor and destitute. While activists may focus on the most visible of harms, they are often blind to the issues affecting poor people and their livelihoods. In our digital world, we have become reliant on new economies, new systems of information delivery, and new spaces for consumerism, but we too fail to consider how the most vulnerable are affected. As we've discussed in earlier chapters, it's extremely easy to simply place blame social media, the behemoth that connects us all, but in doing so, we manage to completely ignore the systemic issues that drive harms.

Young women's mental health is often the most controversial concern on social media. Though social media is *supposed* to be used by people aged 13 and up, we can be confident that this is not upheld strongly. Both young men and women do not stop developing until they are in their twenties,

190   *Critical Internet Literacies*

but they interact with social media content in their most formative years. Along with that, the societal pressures, long part of the teenage experience, are now combined with the comparative realities of a life broadcast online. Following the leak of the Facebook Papers, we collectively found out that Facebook was well aware of the fact that Instagram users blamed the platform for "increases in the rate of anxiety and depression," setting off a wave of handwringing and calls for regulation from the public.[13] In Facebook's competitive nature, especially against TikTok, it shifted some of its algorithm to court young users, especially the lucrative teen girl market.

A young woman named Anastasia Vlasova was profiled in a *Wall Street Journal* piece about the Facebook Papers and she admits to having to see a therapist in her teenage years. Vlasova explained that she developed an eating disorder because of her time on Instagram, especially after being exposed to fitness influencers on the app. In their internal papers, Facebook found that 32 percent of teen girls said they felt bad about their bodies – a number that unfortunately hasn't changed all that much from before social media.[14] But Vlasova wasn't wrong to put the blame on Instagram, they could be doing far more to keep young women safe from these harms, but it seems Instagram would rather focus on growth and profit. Women's bodies have been a contentious part of modern life, often dictated by norms of patriarchal society and media trends and fashion. Noting this, what happens when these ideals are misunderstood by young women or girls?

In early 2024, Sephora makeup and product stores complained that pre-teens and younger girls, some as young as eight years old, were crowding the store, many looking to buy products like the anti-aging cream retinol. Young Gen Alpha girls, those born between 2010 and 2024, are heavy consumers of TikTok media, and according to *Mashable*'s Elizabeth de Luna, most girls enjoy Get Ready With Me videos by influencers like Isa Escu or Katie Fang, both of whom popularized certain types of skin products.[15] The question of harm arises on whether or not this trend causes young girls to "rush into adulthood," mimicking their favorite influencers, and attempting to appear like older girls. Second, should influencers like 18-year-old Katie Fang, who is still learning how to be an adult, be responsible for her audiences' habits? Technically, there is no overt harm for tweens to use retinol aside from the damage to their (or their parents') wallets, but over-washing skin could cause issues. Retinol is used for both anti-aging and acne, so young influencers may use it for different reasons, but is nearly useless for pre-teen girls.

These harms are not social media based, rather situated in the quiet patriarchal messages embedded in advertising and marketing that insist women should present themselves as younger-looking. This is also an example of the insidious nature of brand packaging designed to lure consumers to products they may not need through aesthetics and consumer

The Moderated Internet: Reconsidering Safety Online 191

culture trends. Makeup brands like Drunk Elephant or Glow Recipe sell products packaged with minimal design and bold colors, designed to be an aesthetic for influencers to show off on screen. Whereas makeup products once resided behind a mirror, these products are designed to be on a counter to enable women to display their ownership of those products and in some ways, their affinity for a certain influencer over another. In other words, this slow harm, that of teaching young girls to do adult things and wear adult products and potentially sexualize themselves when they are too young, is a borderline issue. Depending on your perspective, this could be harmful to young girls in the long term, as they attempt to keep up with makeup trends invented by the brands since they're marketed by influencers who uncritically share their makeup tutorials with their new products. This could also provide an opportunity for parents (who supply the money to buy the makeup) to open conversations about consumer culture and influencer messaging or to encourage stores like Sephora to develop age-appropriate sections or workshops.

Other harms are more obvious. In the early 2010s, young women migrated to Tumblr to share their interests. According to danah body and Alice Marwick, users often believed Tumblr to be more of a private space for expression than sites like Twitter or Facebook and expressed themselves differently.[16] There was a rise in concerning hashtags on Tumblr that resulted in generally celebratory blogs about eating disorders, where young women were using hashtags like "pro-ana" (for pro-anorexia) and "thinspiration" to show off their weight loss. These hashtags would produce a feed of images of extremely thin women, aiming to show off unhealthy goals like having a "thigh gap" or flat stomachs. Under the conditions of social expectations, these young women were stressed into conforming to these perceived beauty standards.

Figure 7.1 An example of brand packaging by Drunk Elephant that is marketed directly to younger girls and influencers.

192 *Critical Internet Literacies*

Many of these hashtags include text that inspires self-harm. Pro-ana seems like an important hashtag to remove, but in 2012, platforms were still learning about harms. Tumblr's policy team responded by removing any hashtags that glorified self-harm such as material that encourages eating disorders, cutting, anorexia, bulimia, or suggestions of suicide on a case-by-case review.[17] As you may imagine, pro-eating disorder posts were confusing to the most vulnerable crowds, slowly harming them through an influx of imagery and eating disorder messaging. However, Tumblr could not remove the hashtag outright as the #proana hashtag was also being hijacked by pro-recovery information, an activist tactic to help disrupt the flow of harmful messaging. Here we have an example of self-moderating, in which the platform team required more knowledge of each post rather than outright bans of any subject. In a study published in 2017, researchers found that the existence of pro-ana tags were in the minority compared to pro-recovery tags, and that "It is important therefore that we truly understand the nature of online communities before introducing interventions."[18]

This is the importance of our interest in internet literacies when it comes to these harms – there is no simple solution and understanding online behavior means to spend extra time reading the internet and its messaging. You may see how moral panics may lean into these extreme stories, enabling grifters to take advantage of people with low internet literacies to simply blame the platforms. After the Facebook Papers, people like Jonathan Haidt were able tell his readers that we must act immediately to hold platforms accountable, as we cannot wait until researchers can show without a reasonable doubt that it's the platforms fault. (Unfortunately, we'll have to wait forever because that will never be definitive.) Time after time, studies have shown it's more complicated than blaming the platforms. In a well-cited response by Jessica Grose for the *New York Times*, Grose notes that even studies are inconclusive: "these studies cannot tease out whether girls who are inclined toward eating issues, for a variety of reasons, spend more time on social media, or whether the social media causes the issues."[19] Grose remembers watching MTV as a child – watching people with "chiseled abs" and "oversexualized women" – and recommends that there can be a way of finding a solution through interventions, discussions, and the introduction of internet and social media literacies at a young age.

When Harms Are Systemic

Slow harm is hard to detect for some time as mental health disorders may take years to develop. On the surface, women are typically targeted far more often with overt sexist and misogynistic and inappropriate sexual advances online. For example, 29-year-old scientist Katie Bouman led a

The Moderated Internet: Reconsidering Safety Online   193

team of astrophysicists to write an algorithm that produced the first-ever image of a black hole. In 2019, the image was posted online, along with a tweet from MIT celebrating Bouman's work: "Here's the Moment When the First Black Hole Image Was Processed, from the Eyes of Researcher Katie Bouman."[20] The tweet contained an image of an overjoyed Bouman, clasping her hands over her mouth in sheer joy. What followed, unfortunately, is what Mary Beth Griggs of *The Verge* called a "sexist scavenger hunt," with sexist trolls attempting to find out how much work she contributed to the project.[21] Griggs continues:

> This isn't just an online trend. Women in science are cited less than their male colleagues. They have a harder time getting work published in notable journals, including the flagships Science and Nature. They are likely paid less than their peers (a 2013 study found that women working in physics and astronomy were paid 40 percent less than men). And they are more likely to face workplace harassment.

As a systemic issue, it's exacerbated online by trolls and misogynists. Ben Collins wrote for NBC News:

> On YouTube, the first video result for users who search for "Katie Bouman" returns a video titled "Woman Does 6% of the Work but Gets 100% of the Credit: Black Hole Photo." The video is riddled with inaccuracies, and largely draws from a falsehood created on Reddit and pushed heavily by a "men's rights" community.[22]

Since #Gamergate, the normalization of misogyny has become a burden for social media sites, search engines, and the internet at large. Disaffected young men who engage in this behavior are boons to platforms as they increase time spent. Also, as previously noted, the way content moderators and policymakers apply their rules tends to forgive men even though the systemic issues continue.

In 2013, multiple celebrity women's nude photographs were hacked from their iCloud accounts and posted to 4chan, Reddit, Tumblr, and Twitter. Celebrities like Kate Upton, Kirsten Dunst, and Jennifer Lawrence became victims of a crime now known as non-consensual pornography, previously called "revenge porn." Lawrence told Sam Kashner at *Vanity Fair* that her first instinct was to make a public statement, or an apology for the images that she had only intended to share with her boyfriend intimately. She was incensed and angered, especially at grifting bloggers like Perez Hilton. However, Lawrence reframed the discussion, telling Kasher, "It is not a scandal. It is a sex crime. It is a sexual violation. It's disgusting. The law needs to be changed, and we need to change."[23] By looking at the

194   *Critical Internet Literacies*

images, you are "perpetuating a sexual offense." This reframing helped change the laws by moving away from the systemic propensity to blame the victim.

Even women who use social media casually are often victims of sexist remarks when men sexualize them. As young people desire a career as an influencer, they may not have the recognition that someone like Jennifer Lawrence does, but this does not stop the harms from reaching them. In June 2024, the *Wall Street Journal* did a profile on a young teen influencer and her family's concerns about her following. The story follows the tribulations of a mother who created an Instagram channel for her teen daughter during the pandemic as a way of bonding with her child. Her intentions were well meant; the mother is a former marketing manager, and the young girl is a local dancer. Within a month, the young girl became quite popular on Instagram and brands began to reach out and offer her endorsements, however, along with the fame arrived an unruly audience. Katherine Blunt writes:

> The mom also began to notice a disturbing trend in the data that showed up on the account dashboard: Most of the girl's followers were adult men. Men left public comments on photos of the daughter with fire and heart emojis, telling her how gorgeous she was. Those were the tamer ones. Some men sent direct messages proclaiming their obsessions with the girl. Others sent pictures of male genitalia and links to porn sites.[24]

The mother found that 92 percent of her young teen's followers were adult men and accepted a "grim reality" that her daughter was followed by men who take interest in young girls.

Blunt points out that while she reported the article for *WSJ*, the young girl's account was shut down twice as Meta believed there was harm to minors. While the mom and girl hadn't broken any policies, the platform was concerned with the deluge of comments. Both times the mom petitioned successfully for the account to be reinstated. This type of issue does not just happen to influencers either. In a TikTok video by @anniej4 recorded in late June 2024, Annie tells a story about a time when she was at the Men's College World Series game with her friend and the camera stopped on them eating ice cream for about 20 seconds. She said, "we all knew what was going to happen with that video clip, and lo and behold, the creeps of TikTok got a hold of it."[25] Annie talks about the fact that people in the comments section were absolutely disgusting, stating that it is evident that women are not welcome in the sports world, and seen as sexual objects just for eating ice cream.

Annie further explains that she was self-conscious about eating a hot dog, hoping that no one would catch her on camera. This non-consensual

The Moderated Internet: Reconsidering Safety Online   195

harassment is all too common for women, and as much as we believe that the standardized misogyny and sexism of the past was left behind, it is always prevalent. Clarissa-Jan Lim calls this situation "Panopticontent," or the act of becoming viral without your consent.

> Our appetite to document and post – whether it's ethical or not – is reinforced by the seduction of social media fame. There are whole genres of online content in which people are being recorded or photographed without their knowledge or consent – on the subway, at a shopping center, in a car, on the sidewalk, at a restaurant, at a bar. Many of these videos present strangers as NPCs, or nonplayer characters, an internet term referring to people who aren't seen as fully realized individuals and are simply part of the backdrop. These strangers are displayed as a spectacle to gawk at and be judged by an audience of millions around the world: People experiencing homelessness are objects of pity and disgust. A couple making out in public are objects of ridicule.

How are online platforms responsible for this? What can we do to manage these harms? Are young women aware of these issues? The internet is not bound by its digital code, it is everywhere all at once. No amount of blame on a platform will help these young women, in fact, it does quite the opposite – it lets the platform make the rules.

Users like Annie and the young Instagram influencer do have ways of protecting themselves using the tools of the platform. On both Instagram and TikTok, users can filter out specific words, block users, or manage hashtags. They can auto-block users crossing those lines, but in no way does it stop another user from saving the video and reposting it on their own account. Users can petition for removal, but what if they are unaware of the content being repurposed? These harms are tangible and dangerous, and we need to increase our conversations about these issues with our children immediately and discuss them with our family and neighbors. Critical internet literacies should not be confined to tech-focused classes, but rather any time the discussion of online personalities emerges.

Toxic Masculinity

There is an ongoing epidemic of disaffected young men who feel "marginalized" by society. These young men occasionally feel lost and turn to masculinity influencers like Andrew Tate or Jordan Peterson for advice. Tate, boosted by Elon Musk's X, is quite possibly the most dangerous of these influencers, consistently spewing horrific advice, repackaged in hustle culture posts. Tate, a former professional kickboxer, has been banned from TikTok, YouTube, and Facebook due to his aggressive hatred of women

196 *Critical Internet Literacies*

and alleged criminal acts involving sex trafficking. However, Tate disguises his content as business advice and manages to continue to attract young men to his content. At one point, Tate was charging $49.99 a month to join his "Hustlers University," an online program to create "skill development," but it was shut down as it really taught young men how to run scams and dropshipping marketplaces.

Before he was banned, Tate had nearly 5 million fans on Instagram and nearly a million on TikTok. Before he could be removed, his misogyny had infected the platform, causing young men to lash out in classrooms and direct anger toward young women they knew. In a personal essay about his young cousin who is a fan of Tate's, Sasha Mistlin of *The Guardian* writes:

> Imagine you are a young man and your first time encountering Tate is not in a newspaper article like this, but rather a YouTube video titled "FIX YOUR MIND – Motivational Speech." In the video, Tate dishes out harsh truths about money, success and endeavor. It is easy to see how it could inspire someone feeling powerless or confused about their place in the world: "You've got to play the cards you're dealt," he says. "If you're 5ft 2in you need to become strong, and rich, and charismatic. If you're 6ft 4in, you need to become rich, strong, well-connected. It's the same game." It is this messaging – the subtler, motivational stuff – that has given him such a following. If Tateism has a message, it's about male emancipation. [26]

Young men need to learn about their masculinity and their roles in society. Mistlin notes that while social media has amplified people like Tate, it is a systemic issue that needs to be addressed. Mistlin continues, "Reprehensible it may be, but Tate's baseless misogyny and 'me-first, get-yours' narcissism is alluring to young men at a time when mainstream culture is telling them to check their privilege for reasons they don't fully understand."

The pendulum that empowered the #MeToo movement is the same pendulum that empowers young boys to act out in ways they truly do not understand. Tate is a grifter, possibly one of the worst – and most successful – out there. His words infect men of all ages who feel confused and find an allure to the simple "success" messaging Tate espouses. Mistlin argues that new frameworks for online safety are required to manage these messages and he, like many men, did not get a proper sexual education as a young person and the internet is full of answers – even when they may be pointedly incorrect. Tate represents a genre of content that overlaps directly with the Christian Nationalist revival of traditional living and "values"-based lifestyles. These harms sit quietly in the back of a young man's mind, waiting until someone like Katie Bouman becomes famous for her achievement. Rather than enjoying her achievement, she is deemed

The Moderated Internet: Reconsidering Safety Online   197

a sign that men are lacking pathways to success. It's all disguised in a catachresis of "white male marginalization," a term that does not exist, but does so in a grifter's spirit.

Public Misogyny: Mewing and Acting Out

If you haven't heard the term "mewing," it's because it's made up. Unfortunately, it was invented by two orthodontists who have spread a heterodox pseudo-scientific approach to jaw strengthening. Dr. Mew believes that by you can force your jawline into a stronger shape "by placing the tongue on the roof of the mouth as opposed to the bottom of the mouth, where most people usually rest their tongue when their mouth is closed." According to *Vogue*, the mewing term has over 10 billion views on TikTok alone.[27] Young men believe a strong jaw is a way of both attracting women and showing they have strong features, a dominate sign of masculinity.

According to Gabby Cullen, writing for *TinyBeans* about the trend:

> Kids will put a finger to their lips like they're shushing someone, then run their finger along their jawline, which, according to [TikTok teacher, Mr.] Lindsay,[28] is a sign the kid doesn't want to answer your question. "I'm mewing; I'm working on my jawline. I'm doing my jawline exercises." Lovely. This might also be followed by a good amount of laughter, as students (especially boys) take pleasure in confusing any and all clueless adults.[29]

Like the online to mainstream pipeline, mewing is encoded with additional layers of misogyny and sexism and further encoded within in-group messaging. As Gen Alpha learns these tactics, we must be considerate of how much this is tied directly to harmful parts of the web.

In a research study conducted in 2023 in Australia, researchers found that "manfluencers" like Andrew Tate have inspired young men to act out in classrooms in their country. The authors of the paper interviewed 30 Australian women teachers and found "widespread experience of sexual harassment, sexism, and misogyny perpetrated by boys towards women teachers, and the ominous presence of Andrew Tate shaping their behaviors."[30] The researchers found that young men, attracted to manosphere spaces, expressed several forms of "male supremacy" in classrooms, from sexist remarks to teachers to harassment of female fellow classmates. In their acknowledgement of the hegemonic traits of toxic masculinity, they found that Tate's omnipresence and popularity seem to make these actions more acceptable because he's a famous influencer. The researchers point to the wildly under-researched domain of the manosphere as a cause for alarm.

198 *Critical Internet Literacies*

Perhaps there's no better resource for this subject than Laura Bates who elucidates the depths of this issue in her 2020 book *Men Who Hate Women*. Bates, who spent time undercover in the manosphere and incel forums, discovered the issues that underly much of this overt toxic masculinity. Here, it is worth quoting Bates in full:

> Superficial analyses of incel communities have sought to imply that class is the biggest factor driving new recruits to the cause: that this is about poor, white boys being left behind. Others have suggested it is a specific response to shifting labor markets, as manual jobs become increasingly scarce and women are employed in ever greater numbers in more powerful roles. But in the time I have spent immersed in these conversations and message boards, it has become apparent that the socioeconomic background of members is too diverse to wholly confirm any one of those theories. The membership of these groups spans from blue-collar workers, angry about immigrants "displacing" them at work and in the bedroom, to highly privileged private school graduates, furious that their "rightful" place at the top of the political food chain is being challenged. What they do seem to have in common is a craving to belong, and this need is met in spades by a *community that excels at conveying a tribal sense of cohesion.*[31] [Italics added.]

Mewing is a surface-level tactic, likely brushed aside by its seeming ridiculousness: clenching teeth and positioning your tongue may help for a photograph, but it will not reshape your jaw. Male confidence does not come from putting down women and no matter how much these online spaces provide cohesive feelings of "tribal" belonging, they are superficial.

But how can you blame these young men when the content is so accessible and successful entrepreneurs and billionaires like Elon Musk perpetuate these ideologies? In other words, a critical approach to this topic happens by having discussions about what is online, what is off-platform, and where the spaces of expression overlap. We are amid a cultural shift and this book is written as an analysis of the current position of the reactionary pendulum, but it will swing back. Our only ability to understand what results from the next swing is gaining our literacies about its current position.

Fighting the Robots: Algospeak

There is no silver bullet to solve a policy issue. No one solution may offer a "fix" for moderation, especially when the need to scale is part of the Silicon Valley techno-imperialistic approach. As social media sites scale, new large language models must be trained to manage harm and attempt active

The Moderated Internet: Reconsidering Safety Online   199

approaches to harm mitigation. However, we must keep in mind, lacking a surveillance superstructure, proactivity is not possible at scale, and the only way to manage harms ahead of their occurrence is to approach the issues from a systemic vantage point. On the other hand, surveillance capitalism is increasing exponentially, making our targeted advertising more precise, we are faced with the complications of moderation at scale, acting more strictly as time goes on. In the earlier examples about #proana and words like dyke being repurposed, platforms cannot easily grasp the positive use cases exhibited by people as they build communities and interact with one another.

On TikTok, where the algorithm is "content aware," the moderation is far stricter than most other platforms. TikTok's algorithm *is* TikTok, and it makes up the system that helps create the "For You Page" feed, watching videos and analyzing them, including the overlayed text that users add to their videos for both accessibility and enhanced viewing. TikTok is aware of its very young user base and will automatically filter out negative connotations like the middle finger or any types of nudity. In reading the screen, it also filters out words on screen that it considers harmful – whether spoken aloud or in text. Words like "suicide" or "kill" are obvious, but what happens when the platform overreaches? Are words like "nipples" or "lesbian" harmful? On Instagram, there is a community guideline that enforces the standards for photos and videos that should be "appropriate for a diverse audience" which includes limitations on "female nipples" aside from in context of breastfeeding or health-related situations.[32] In other words, harm is reconsidered as "appropriate" for "diverse" audiences, meaning that *some* people may be offended, and therefore limitations are placed. TikTok follows the same measure, but in a bit more of an authoritarian way as the site's machine algorithm runs most of its filtering.

In response to this moderation tactic, users have come up with a novel reaction to this alleged censorship: "algospeak." Algospeak, coined by Taylor Lorenz, is code speak designed to turn words or phrases into "brand-safe lexicon" that helps users "avoid getting their posts removed or down-ranked by content moderation systems." Lorenz explains, "For instance, in many online videos, it's common to say 'unalive' rather than 'dead,' 'SA' instead of 'sexual assault,' or 'spicy eggplant' instead of 'vibrator.'"[33] These memetic workarounds then become part of the language itself but are not banned because users must have in-group knowledge of the language to decode the algospeak. Algospeak is a reactionary tactic against the machines, but it did not start online. Lorenz writes:

> Tailoring language to avoid scrutiny predates the Internet. Many religions have avoided uttering the devil's name lest they summon him, while people living in repressive regimes developed code words to discuss taboo topics. Early Internet users used alternate spelling or "leetspeak"

to bypass word filters in chat rooms, image boards, online games and forums. But algorithmic content moderation systems are more pervasive on the modern Internet, and often end up silencing marginalized communities and important discussions.

Here we return to the issue of blaming platforms. Lorenz notes that the authoritarian approach to content moderation is an issue when it comes to actual marginalized communities. Many vulnerable communities do not have the privilege of open discussion in their off-platform lives and rely on their digital communities and digital culture as support systems or environments of resilience. Banning terms like lesbian makes little sense to most people, but TikTok is concerned with the vocal minority upset by LGBTQ+ issues. This becomes more apparent when we talk about trans rights and support for trans folk online. Already vulnerable, trans folk use the web as a space *for* safety, rather than one of escape. Moderation that leans into censorship and filtering means that it is siding with more bigoted users and risk-averse brands over the few that really need the support.

Figure 7.2 TikToker Adam Aleksic, who goes by the name @etymologynerd on TikTok and Instagram, explains how emojis are workarounds to content moderation.

The Moderated Internet: Reconsidering Safety Online   201

On the other hand, the code-switching of the language, shifting from "lesbian" to the on-screen writing "le$bian," is a workaround. When the AI reader sees the text "le$bian," it reads it out loud as "le-dollar-bean," unable to parse the dollar symbol as an "S." Le-dollar-bean then becomes the new term that is used by the community. This is the fight against the machines that dictate speech and doubles as in-group communication, one that becomes supportive by its coded reality. "Nipples" become "nip-nops," "LGBTQ" becomes "leg booty," and so on. Lorenz explains it goes even further with symbology:

> Black and trans users, and those from other marginalized communities, often use algospeak to discuss the oppression they face, swapping out words for "white" or "racist." Some are too nervous to utter the word "white" at all and simply hold their palm toward the camera to signify White people.

This shift in language could result in the collapsing of language or, if adopted widely enough, could result in the algorithms learning how workarounds operate, leading to a never-ending evasive system. More problematic, it means that terms of social justice or equality are equated with actual harmful terms used by racists, misogynists, and bigots who already code their language to avoid content moderation. These are not two sides of the same coin and culturally, we need to confront these systems as they're being built, acknowledging what harm really means. In our polarized, hypermediated present, we need internet literacies to not only learn how these systems are operating, but to extend care to those truly vulnerable, pushing away from the false equivalent of white male marginalization and to fight for the rights for trans folk and people of color. As a matter of making the internet more functional and usable, that is what it means to reconsider safety.

Notes

1 Buni, Catherine, and Soraya Chemaly. "The Secret Rules of the Internet." *The Verge*, April 13, 2016. https://www.theverge.com/2016/4/13/11387934/internet-moderator-history-youtube-facebook-reddit-censorship-free-speech.
2 Servers like Cloudflare or Amazon's CloudFront establish rules at the top level, disallowing extreme harms from being hosted on their servers. Sites like 8chan were forced to leave their server after an immense amount of harmful content inspired terrorist attacks. 8chan was banned from Cloudflare, renamed as 8kun and hosted on VanwaTech, but soon was banned again and is now hosted on DDoS-Guard, a more forgiving server that also hosts neo-Nazi sites like the Daily Stormer.
3 Tait, Robert, and Matthew Weaver. "How Neda Agha-Soltan Became the Face of Iran's Struggle." *The Guardian*, June 22, 2009, sec. World news. https://www.theguardian.com/world/2009/jun/22/neda-soltani-death-iran.

202 *Critical Internet Literacies*

4 Zuylen-Wood, Simon van. "'Men Are Scum': Inside Facebook's War on Hate Speech." *Vanity Fair*, February 26, 2019. https://www.vanityfair.com/news/2019/02/men-are-scum-inside-facebook-war-on-hate-speech.

5 Zuylen-Wood, Simon van. "'Men Are Scum': Inside Facebook's War on Hate Speech." *Vanity Fair*, February 26, 2019. https://www.vanityfair.com/news/2019/02/men-are-scum-inside-facebook-war-on-hate-speech.

6 *Im Schatten Der Netzwelt*. Documentary. Gebrueder Beetz Filmproduktion, Grifa Filmes, Westdeutscher Rundfunk (WDR), 2018. This film is no longer available for streaming online. Block and Riesewieck offered Facebook a view of the final cut and there was no response.

7 *"The Cleaners" Who Scrub Social Media*, 2018. https://www.youtube.com/watch?v=FwbwxStnI3M.

8 Newton, Casey. "The Secret Lives of Facebook Moderators in America." *The Verge*, February 25, 2019. https://www.theverge.com/2019/2/25/18229714/cognizant-facebook-content-moderator-interviews-trauma-working-conditions-arizona.

9 Peck, Robert. "The Punishing Ecstasy of Being a Reddit Moderator." *Wired*, March 21, 2019. https://www.wired.com/story/the-punishing-ecstasy-of-being-a-reddit-moderator/.

10 https://moderatormayhem.engine.is/.

11 Doctorow. "Pluralistic: Revenge of the Linkdumps." *Pluralistic* (blog), May 13, 2023. https://pluralistic.net/2023/05/13/four-bar-linkage/.

12 Masnick, Mike. "Moderator Mayhem: A Mobile Game To See How Well YOU Can Handle Content Moderation." *Techdirt*, May 11, 2023. https://www.techdirt.com/2023/05/11/moderator-mayhem-a-mobile-game-to-see-how-well-you-can-handle-content-moderation/.

13 Wells, Georgia, Jeff Horwitz, and Deepa Seetharaman. "Facebook Knows Instagram Is Toxic for Teen Girls, Company Documents Show." *Wall Street Journal*, September 14, 2021. https://www.wsj.com/articles/facebook-knows-instagram-is-toxic-for-teen-girls-company-documents-show-11631620739.

14 Grose, Jessica. "The Messy Truth About Teen Girls and Instagram." *New York Times*, October 13, 2021, sec. Parenting. https://www.nytimes.com/2021/10/13/parenting/instagram-teen-girls-body-image.html.

15 Luna, Elizabeth de. "TikTok, Tweens, and Sephora: Everything You Need to Know, According to the Tweens Themselves." *Mashable*, January 21, 2024. https://mashable.com/article/sephora-tweens-teens-drunk-elephant.

16 Marwick, Alice E., and Danah Boyd. "I Tweet Honestly, I Tweet Passionately: Twitter Users, Context Collapse, and the Imagined Audience." *New Media & Society* 13, no. 1 (February 2011): 114–33. https://doi.org/10.1177/1461444810365313.

17 https://www.tumblr.com/staff/18563255291/follow-up-tumblrs-new-policy-against.

18 Branley, Dawn B., and Judith Covey. "Pro-Ana versus Pro-Recovery: A Content Analytic Comparison of Social Media Users' Communication about Eating Disorders on Twitter and Tumblr." *Frontiers in Psychology* 8 (August 11, 2017): 1356. https://doi.org/10.3389/fpsyg.2017.01356.

19 Grose, Jessica. "The Messy Truth About Teen Girls and Instagram." *New York Times*, October 13, 2021, sec. Parenting. https://www.nytimes.com/2021/10/13/parenting/instagram-teen-girls-body-image.html.

20 MIT CSAIL [@MIT_CSAIL]. "Here's the Moment When the First Black Hole Image Was Processed, from the Eyes of Researcher Katie Bouman. #EHTBlackHole #BlackHoleDay #BlackHole (v/@dfbarajas) Https://T.Co/

The Moderated Internet: Reconsidering Safety Online   203

n0ZnIoeG1d." Tweet. *Twitter*, April 10, 2019. https://twitter.com/MIT_CSAIL/status/1116020858282180609.

21 Griggs, Mary Beth. "Online Trolls Are Harassing a Scientist Who Helped Take the First Picture of a Black Hole." *The Verge*, April 13, 2019. https://www.theverge.com/2019/4/13/18308652/katie-bouman-black-hole-science-internet.

22 Collins, Ben. "The First Picture of a Black Hole Made Katie Bouman an Overnight Celebrity. Then Internet Trolls Descended." *NBC News*, April 13, 2019. https://www.nbcnews.com/tech/tech-news/first-picture-black-hole-made-katie-bouman-overnight-celebrity-then-n994081.

23 Kashner, Sam. "Both Huntress and Prey." *Vanity Fair*, November 2014. https://archive.vanityfair.com/article/2014/11/both-huntress-and-prey.

24 Blunt, Katherine. "The Influencer Is a Young Teenage Girl. The Audience Is 92% Adult Men." *WSJ*, June 16, 2024. https://www.wsj.com/tech/young-influencers-instagram-meta-safety-risks-6d27497e.

25 "Annie on TikTok." *TikTok*, 25 June 2024. https://www.tiktok.com/@.anniej4/video/7384547695400193323?_t=8nZxsZ2kuOV&_r=1.

26 Mistlin, Sasha. "Why Too Many Young Men Love Andrew Tate – and Why We Need to Understand That, Not Dismiss It." *The Guardian*, March 9, 2023, sec. Opinion. https://www.theguardian.com/commentisfree/2023/mar/09/andrew-tate-young-men-social-media-motivational-sexism.

27 Pérez, Christina. "What in the World Is Mewing? And Will It Actually Sculpt Your Jawline? Here's the Truth." *Vogue*, March 15, 2024. https://www.vogue.com/article/how-to-mew.

28 https://www.tiktok.com/@mr_lindsay_sped.

29 Cullen, Gabby. "Why Are Kids 'Mewing' in Class?" *Tinybeans* (blog), May 1, 2024. https://tinybeans.com/what-does-mewing-mean/.

30 Wescott, Stephanie, Steven Roberts, and Xuenan Zhao. "The Problem of Anti-Feminist 'Manfluencer' Andrew Tate in Australian Schools: Women Teachers' Experiences of Resurgent Male Supremacy." *Gender and Education* 36, no. 2 (February 17, 2024): 167–82. https://doi.org/10.1080/09540253.2023.2292622.

31 Bates, Laura. *Men Who Hate Women: The Extremism Nobody Is Talking About*. London New York Sydney Toronto New Delhi: Simon & Schuster, 2021.

32 https://help.instagram.com/477434105621119.

33 Lorenz, Taylor. "'Algospeak' Is Changing Our Language in Real Time." *Washington Post*, April 8, 2022. https://www.washingtonpost.com/technology/2022/04/08/algospeak-tiktok-le-dollar-bean/.

8 Creating Content with Accessibility

Making the Internet Usable for All

According to the Center for Disease Control in the United States, up to 27 percent of US citizens have some type of disability, and the most common disability is regarding cognition (12.8%).[1] Globally, over 15 percent of the world's population, or around 1 billion people, live with disabilities and assuming similar statistics to the US, likely higher. The internet, a space of visual ephemera, coded messages, memes, and videos, is an overwhelmingly inaccessible space for many people. In fact, only about 3 percent of the entire internet is considered accessible, meaning over 95 percent of all sites do not have proper visual contrast settings or proper alt-text for images or have broken links and non-operational buttons.[2] Unfortunately, many aspects of digital accessibility are not often at the forefront of internet development and due to the polarization of progressive projects, digital accessibility is under attack as it is occasionally part of corporate environmental, social, and governance (ESG) departments.[3] Accessibility should be at the forefront of our future internet developments and we should acknowledge, that like safety, an increase in accessibility makes the internet experience better for everyone.

When discussing ability, we need to put aside our inherent privilege, meaning if you use the internet without thinking about it, you have a privilege that many users do not. As a primarily visual medium, the internet privileges those who can interact with its elements, from websites to social media. If you are seeing impaired, the most common tool for accessing the internet is a screen reader. Screen readers like Apple Voice Over or NVDA are options for text-to-speech (TTS) conversion, and some other readers also convert text to braille for communication.[4] According to the National Federation of the Blind, there are over 7 million people in the US alone that have a seeing impairment ranging from "low vision" to "visually impaired" and of those, over 85 percent use some sort of screen reader to access the internet.[5] In this chapter, rather than a focus on technology,

DOI: 10.4324/9781003483885-8

there is a focus on the content and the way that creators engage with accessibility tools as well as why we must put accessibility at the forefront of our creative endeavors. Accessibility is also a starting point to explain the internet to young people, especially children, helping them make sense of ever-changing digital environments as they reach the ages to engage with content and creativity. Through accessibility, we may have a better way of using internet literacies to approach the analysis of content and media online.

We may assume that most users are unaware of the ways to make content accessible to those who may be using screen readers. For example, a screen reader translates the website into voice, reading the text top-to-bottom, letting the listener know when a link is available. When the screen reader reaches an image, the screen reader accesses the alt-text, which is typically user-generated descriptions of the image, and if an image doesn't contain alt-text, the reader is left without context of the image on the site. Emojis, which are typically read as emotional shortcuts, are read by their Unicode descriptor with a screen reader. Emojis are code, and while most see them as small images on the computer or phones, they are written in Unicode and a screen reader reads them from their definition. For example, the reader may read the classic smiling emoji by its Unicode definition: "Slightly smiling face" rather than simply "smiling face" read by the code U+1F642. You already may imagine how difficult it may be for visually impaired users to get the full context of an emoji in a post or a website. (You can find the entire database of emojis, their Unicode, and their variations on the Emojipedia website, emojipedia.org.)

For example, if you post a peach emoji, you're likely referring to a "butt" rather than the fruit, since internet parlance overwrites the original meaning with the codification of new terminology. Likely, most screen reader users have no issue figuring out something like "peach" in context, but something like the "skull" emoji may need internet literacies to truly read because Gen Z users use the skull emoji to express laughter rather than the crying with tears emoji. In Gen Z slang, they may say "dead" rather than "lol," shorthand for "dead from laughing" and use the skull over the face emoji.[6] While this is fairly baseline, imagine it from the perspective of someone using a screen reader and having it read the word skull, not the verbalization of dead. The same goes for emojis like the eggplant (male genitalia), billed cap hat (meaning "lie" for Gen Alpha users), or the electric plug emoji (meaning drug dealer or someone who hooks you up with something). Hootsuite put together an ongoing database to help users understand these variations, as they continue to shift as culture shifts, but contextual emoji use is helpful.[7] So does this mean that every website and social media site needs accessibility for those who may need it? In theory,

206   *Critical Internet Literacies*

yes. It could be the difference between someone finding the right information or simply lacking that information.

As the web evolves to graphical representation and visual languages, keeping up with accessibility is an increasing concern. Hopefully accessibility is a division or service at a company, but accessible websites continue to be a problem on sites for higher education or compliance in healthcare sites where the necessary information may be buried several pages deep. If you are interested in the guidelines, they are available at w3.org (w3 is shorthand for World Wide Web) under the Web Content Accessibility Guideline (WCAG).[8] The compliance is broken into access categories of Perceivable (containing guides on text, color, descriptive audio, and shapes), Operable (keyboard use, seizure warnings, navigation, and mouse use), Understandable (reading level, language, errors), and Conformance (processing). When you visit a professional website, you may scroll to the bottom of the site and see if the word "accessibility" is shown, if so, there may be an alternate, more accessible site, or an explanation on how the site operates.

Global Access and Digital Literacies

Other forms of access extend beyond the screen. While we may hear the term "access" and think of material presented on the screen, it is also simply about literally *accessing* the web. This means places like public libraries, schools, and internet cafes play a large role in giving people access to information that most people don't even think about. These access points not only work as "third spaces," allowing community members to connect with one another, they are also civic tools that help people remain engaged with their world around them. On the other hand, many of these public access points do not inherently come with "instructions" and internet literacies are taken for granted. For example, in 2007, when new wireless internet networks were supplied to rural towns in Peru, documentarian Audubon Dougherty found that the country was given subsidies to supply the internet and a small amount to train villagers to be local leaders to teach internet use.[9]

In Dougherty's 2009 film *On the Line: Internet in Rural Peru*, she documents how the company Rural Telecom installed over 2,000 access points to the internet from the Amazon Rainforest to the most rural plains in the country. In each village, local leaders were taught how to access the internet, write blogs, write emails, and provide opportunities to learn more about farming and education and guided on how to share these digital literacies with their communities. At first, the internet was a boon to the rural villages, helping young people get access to education outside their needs, like chemistry and mathematics, and became especially helpful

Creating Content with Accessibility 207

during a large outbreak of the flu. Unfortunately, the subsidies did not include upkeep. The machines, often older computers with boxy CRT monitors, broke quite often and the local leaders were not technologists, they were cultural leaders aiding with internet literacies. Some users became accustomed to the connection and began to rely on it, but then after losing the connection, fell into tough times when they were unable to connect. A further issue was the reliance on the internet as the access point to information, so when it failed, there were no analog sites of information – some rural towns have no library at all.

There were two resulting outcomes from this experiment. One, the loss of educated students to towns with higher connection, an issue known as "brain drain," where the "haves" and the "have-nots" are delineated by geography and access. For children, this was problematic because they'd have to travel to different towns, often a dangerous act in forested areas. Dougherty also found that the biggest issue was the lack of internet literacies for use. When young men accessed the machines, many used them to download games and play without a connection. Internet access was not (and still isn't) cheap, and in towns which barely had access to plumbing, the internet was not the priority. Everyone wanted training for the internet and Dougherty found that in towns without training, men would gain just enough access to go online, but not use it productively – some users went online to gamble or download pornography. Internet literacies require upkeep and updating and access is not just putting a computer in a *cabina* internet café for users to sit behind, they are community products.

Fortunately, Dougherty found positive use cases after some citizens realized the power of sharing. In one small village, an old colonial bridge was falling apart, and the community used the internet to raise awareness and solicit funds. They received enough to make a difference and rebuild the bridge. Underlying the documentary is also a story about mobile telephone use and its growth, especially as mobile use was becoming more prevalent. In Peru, nearly everyone had a mobile phone even when they may not have had landlines or internet. While government subsidies were supplying towns with internet, Mexican entrepreneur Carlos Slim connected most of Latin America and northern South America with his telecommunications company América Móvil. Slim, now worth over $100 billion, saw the opportunity to capitalize on connection, a trend repeated by Facebook in the following years, known as "Free Basics."

Free Access Is Never Free

Unlike Carolos Slim's early, nearly monopolistic hold on Latin America's cellphone connections, Facebook developed its own version of an access point using a phone application. In 2013, Mark Zuckerberg published a

208   *Critical Internet Literacies*

white paper titled "Is Connectivity a Human Right?" where he laid out his plan to connect 5 billion people to the internet.[10] Facebook's Free Basics program claimed to "bridge the digital divide by creating an 'on ramp' to the Internet through a closed, mobile platform that gives users free access to a handful of online services, such as AccuWeather, BBC News and Wikipedia."[11] Free Basics is an app that does not require a paid service connection to the internet, but users must own their own cellphone. It uses available 2G or 3G signal to connect and, according to Facebook, gives users access to "news, maternal health, travel, local jobs, sports, communication, and local government information."[12]

Free Basics is not full access to the internet and preys on the most vulnerable, connecting them through Facebook's portal of information. In a study by The Office of Intellectual Freedom, part of the American Library Association, researchers found that Free Basics is a concern for educators, social studies teachers, and librarians in rural regions of the world. Joyce Johnston wrote in 2016:

> right now, trending topics are identified and posted not by editors or news staff, but by an algorithm that can't tell the difference between real news and spoofs, satires or opinion pieces. While the situation may provide some hilarious teachable moments for high schoolers, reliable information should be expected from Free Basics' claim to provide it.[13]

While Mark Zuckerberg sees Free Basics as a way for his company to scale and connect people, Free Basics has some glaring issues, for example, because subsidized internet places limitations on language and information. In larger markets like the Philippines, the main language on Facebook is Tagalog, but it does not have versions for rural regions and lacks over 100 other dialects that connect Philippines communities. What this does to access is quite problematic. As Benedict Anderson argued in *Imagined Communities*, the limitation of printed language develops a loss of culture, changing the concepts of nationalism, as dominant language becomes the de facto standard for a region. On a long enough timeline, secondary and rural dialects are lost, along with their histories and culture, slowly flattening the diasporic connections to their homelands. This does not seem to be a concern for Zuckerberg. In addition to these concerns, Facebook is not connecting users to the internet as an act of "social good," but rather to track Free Basics users' data. "All user activities within the app are channeled through Facebook's servers. This means Facebook can tell which third-party sites users are looking at, when and for how long," Olivia Solon writes for *The Guardian*.[14]

Following outcry in India in 2016, one of the largest internet markets in the world, Free Basics was banned when the telecommunications regulators ruled the service infringed on net neutrality. Explained by *The Verge*, "by subsidizing content, companies like Facebook get to pick and choose winners, creating incentives for customers to use certain services because they don't eat into their data. This in turn makes it harder for smaller players to compete and quashes innovation."[15] Toussaint Nothias argues in their article "Access Granted: Facebook's Free Basics in Africa" that the banning of Free Basics in India did not stop Facebook from expanding its program into 32 countries in Africa. By 2019, Free Basics was offered in 65 countries, including the 32 African countries. Nothias explains Zuckerberg's extended plans:

> By offering access to basic online services free of data charge, users would get a taste of the Internet and ultimately want to pay to access the whole Internet. The "free" services would be entirely text-based, such that shouldering the connectivity costs would be reasonable for telecom operators, and that ultimately, they would gain customers and increase their sales.[16]

On the other hand, Nothias notes that India's pushback was an outlier, and nearly all other adoptees of the program have been quiet about its existence but follows Olivia Solon's point that Zuckerberg's program "fits within two broader and interrelated trends in the digital industry, digital experiments on marginalized populations and data extraction."

Coated in a veneer of accessibility, Free Basics continued to be advertised as an important way to connect to the world, however, the larger issues of access remain, like owning a smart phone or even access to electricity. Free Basics is a form of digital colonialism and Silicon Valley's extension into vulnerable regions, offering a version of "access" they deem appropriate. The access to Free Basics lacked something even more important that at least the subsidized internet of rural Peru provided: digital literacies. Free Basics not only gave a limited portal to the internet, but it also gave free use of WhatsApp, Meta's international encrypted chat software. Over 2.5 billion people use WhatsApp and those on Free Basics get access over the air. For many, WhatsApp is simply a chat app, but around the world, news and local information is shared via WhatsApp through forwarding, link sharing, and bulk messaging. WhatsApp, like other messaging apps (and social media), avoids the responsibility of editorial filtering by claiming they're not a publisher, but rather a place for sharing and sometimes, the lack of digital literacies results in extreme issues, only determined by their unfortunate results.

In 2018, the United Nations issued a report that Facebook and its messaging apps played a significant role in spreading hate and contributed to the 2017 Rohingya genocide in Myanmar's Rakhine state.[17] The Carnegie

210 *Critical Internet Literacies*

Endowment for International Peace also followed up with implications that Facebook also played a role in "fueling the normalization of extreme violence" in Ethiopia. The article, "Facebook, Telegram, and the Ongoing Struggle Against Online Hate Speech," claims Facebook bears responsibility for this due to Free Basics. Caroline Crystal, the article's author, writes:

> In 2018, the UN's fact-finding mission in Myanmar reported that the role of social media in Tatmadaw violence was significant and that Facebook specifically was a "useful instrument" for spreading hate speech "in a context where... Facebook is the Internet," largely because of the platform's Free Basics service, through which the app was preloaded onto virtually every smartphone sold in the country from 2013 to 2017 and incurred no data charges. In this way, Facebook became a widely available and free way to communicate and access the internet in a country undergoing a rapid digital transition.[18]

The internet access point, pre-loaded by Facebook, was just *there*. No instructions given. Mark Zuckerberg's goal of connecting people did not include any digital literacies. Two decades on from the "Eternal September" – where the user's main complaint was the lack of literacies –Mark Zuckerberg wanted billions of people to jump online without giving any guidance. There is no clear correlation between Zuckerberg's goal of connecting people to the internet *and* advancing human rights through these tools of expression. The abject lack of digital literacies provided by Facebook tell us that Meta is far more interested in surveillance and profit from vulnerable communities than making the world a more beautiful and connected place.

Digital Literacies and Making Creative Work Accessible

Digital literacy builds upon both media literacy and skill-building for using the internet or digital tools. There are a variety of specific approaches that many other texts have already covered, but here we can focus on the five pillars of digital literacy: information and data literacy, communication and collaboration, digital content creation, safety, and problem-solving.[19] These pillars undergird much of this book and work as basic frameworks for considering accessibility and constructive creativity online. Wherever there is access to the internet, some form of education to teach users these basic structures should be included, first considering critical thinking followed by managing identity and safety. A holistic approach is recommended; however, teaching digital literacy is resource intensive, requiring problem-based learning and current examples to teach (a chore when each Google search is precarious). As content and creation are constantly

Creating Content with Accessibility 211

evolving, it requires educators to truly feel part of the digital systems online, making sure that their comfort level reaches some level of internet fluency, before applying pedagogical approaches to the digital literacy education.

Reconsidering digital literacy within the framework of critical internet literacies allows us to reframe the skills within the context of accessibility beyond connection, directly engaging with the content itself, whether they be static images, text on screen, streaming audio, or moving video. One of the larger issues of applying digital literacy techniques to media on the modern internet is the propensity for internet media to be so layered, referential, and nuanced it makes reading it quite difficult. By applying critical thinking to some internet media, you may inadvertently create a rabbit hole, gamed by bad actors aware of the resources necessary to educate users on all the layers of the content itself. For example, in her controversial 2018 SXSW keynote "What Hath We Wrought," danah boyd explained that some of the skills of media literacy and digital literacies play into the game the conspiracists developed online. One concerning issue, especially for those who use Free Basics access, is that users may access alternative perspectives on critical subjects like history, culture, and policy.

When we apply media literacy, boyd explains, we are usually applying skepticism and doubt, seeking for a more comprehensive example:

> But the hole that opens up, that invites people to look for new explanations… that hole can be filled in deeply problematic ways. When we ask students to challenge their sacred cows but don't give them a new framework through which to make sense of the world, others are often there to do it for us.[20]

boyd argues that we need to recalibrate our approaches to media literacy training, not away from critical thinking (as boyd doesn't want to see a world full of "sheeple") but to understand that we now live in a world of networks. "We need to understand how those networks are intertwined and how information that spreads through dyadic – even if asymmetric – encounters is understood and experienced differently than that which is produced and disseminated through mass media." On the other hand, there is absolutely no reason that we should encourage people to avoid teaching media literacy because of the internet's difficulty, rather we should teach more of it, and it should be engaged with in every classroom, not just media-related courses.

One of the most fundamental ways any educator may engage with critical media literacies is through accessibility. Framing discussions around "who is left out" enables a unique way of interrogating the internet media that may be coded in partisan views or layered with multi-meaning references.

212   *Critical Internet Literacies*

In addition, we can use these skills to take a step back and consider *how* internet media is read, meaning quite literally, how does someone *see or hear* internet content. If irony and meta-media can be weaponized by literally anyone online, we should have a way of slowing down and explaining their layers and connections, seeking ways of knowing what's true. As Cory Doctorow explains a piece for Boing Boing in 2017, "we're not living through a crisis about what is true, we're living through a crisis about how we know whether something is true. We're not disagreeing about facts, we're disagreeing about *epistemology*."[21] (Emphasis Doctorow's.) The work of seeking what is true is an ongoing act of knowledge-building and sense-making and empowers every active reader of the internet better at learning. But we also must be aware that as the internet shifts to more prominent use of video and images, it creates an ever-growing issue with access to that knowledge.

Accessibility for Creative Work

How may we do a better job at increasing out digital literacies while also making the web a better place? Consider that the internet is infrastructure, and its content is both cumulative and reactionary. We consume internet media through applications, but browsers are the primary tool to access media on the World Wide Web and often lack automated accessible tools. In other words, it's up to the users to consider accessibility for others. Since the beginning of hypertext markup language, code has offered the ability to include accessibility. Both Tim Berners Lee and Ted Nelson, who both developed versions of hypertext (the World Wide Web and Xanadu respectively), included accessibility tags in their code. However, when they were developing their code, the web browser we know today did not exist, but any good technologist was aware that eventually, the web would be filled with visuals. We tend to forget that visual media online *is* code. This means when you see an image, you are experiencing a file on a hard drive being called onto the browser via a line of code. The image itself is made of code, one that allows it to be perceived as visual media. When websites or social media present an embedded video – which is common through embedding code or link sharing – you're technically viewing a window that looks through to the source content. Lacking any description leaves the viewer unaware of what is appearing on screen.

Alt-text is one of the most important ways to share descriptive information with a screen reader, low-speed connection skeletal websites, or through text-based internet. Alt-text is nearly exactly what it sounds like, alternative text, meaning a description of the file. If you are visually

Creating Content with Accessibility   213

impaired, the reader scrolls down the page and reads the alt-text rather than the image filename. Meg Miller and Ilaria Parogoni write for the *New York Times*:

> Many social media platforms have features that enable people to add alt-text to their posts manually. On sites that permit a longer word count on posts, like Instagram, people may even include the description of the image they are sharing in the caption accompanying it. Despite the presence of these options, the practice remains little known and mystifying to many.[22]

The authors cite two studies that do not bode well: the non-profit Web-AIM found in 2021 that over 60 percent of images online lack alt-text and a Carnegie Melon study in 2019 looked at over a million tweets and found that far less than 1 percent of all tweets included alt-text.

What can alt-text look like? And example of a line of HTML code may look like this:

```
<img src="girl_at_the_park.jpg" alt="a girl in a coat at the park" width="500" height="600">
```

This example shows a modest attempt at describing the image and it is possible that within the context of the website, it may make sense. On the other hand, alt-text does not have a character limit in html and is only limited by the platform's alt-text guidelines, and therefore, a responsible user should be as descriptive as possible. Considering most social media allow either unlimited or up to 1,000 characters, there should be a reasonably robust description. For example:

```
<img src="girl_at_the_park.jpg" alt="a photograph of a young woman with light hair in a brown, full length coat posing near a fence in a park in the fall season. The young woman is framed on the right side of the image and is looking leftward wistfully. The leaves are turning colors and are out of focus." width="500" height="600">
```

The file name and image size remain the same, but now a screen reader may be able to better describe the details for the person reading the content. We should reconsider the act of adding descriptions to our creative work as an extension of the storytelling. Not only does alt-text increase the accessibility for users but it also enhances our creative abilities. To describe our media, especially supplemental supportive content like images, gifs, or memes in our work, we learn new storytelling skills.

214   *Critical Internet Literacies*

Critical Issues with Alt-Text

Due to the overall lack of knowledge or advocacy for alt-text, many may not realize that alt-text is also the system in which large language models are trained for generative AI. In 2024, the main "solution" for adding alt-text to images on websites and social media has been to consider how generative AI may assist in accessible tools by "reading" images and creating descriptive text for alt-text. However, generative AI models also require robust descriptive alt-text for their datasets to train their large language models (LLM). Consider this: AI cannot technically see images; AI is made up of processing units and computers and require input of immense amounts of text-based samples. AI training uses a technique known as "scraping," which scours the web and downloads data into a training set. If someone were to request a prompt to generate a cat, the LLM would gather as many descriptions of cats as possible, generating a synthetic version of the cat based on a text-to-image generation. This of course, is reliant on enough data of the appearance of cats to create a description, later modified by teams of people at an AI company, which later results in a cat that is realistic as possible. On the other hand, when we consider how descriptions of human subjects are created, we are faced with the biases that exist on much of the internet. In 2021, several researchers were given access to the LAION-400M dataset, the system that generates images for Stable Diffusion and MidJourney generative AI systems and they discovered "misogyny, pornography, and malignant stereotypes" in the source data.

Researchers Abeba Birhane, Vinay Uday Prabhu, and Emmanuel Kahembwe found that in the rush to bring generative AI to the market, AI companies used irresponsible approaches to build datasets like "crawl over curate" and "scale over noise," believing that immense amounts of data will override any need for curatorial approaches to training models with resource-intensive humans.[23] To keep models generating more realistic outputs requires immense amounts of input data. On the other hand, the internet is filled with problematic origin data, and a more curatorial approach may have been far safer. Since alt-text is both inconsistent and mostly missing, the alt-text that *does* exist often contains systemic issues. The researchers used a reverse search of the dataset to connect to the original content and found that much of the descriptive text was filled with not safe for work (NSFW) inputs. The researchers write:

> Upon querying the search portal (the version available on September 12th, 2021) with non-NSFW queries, we encountered a significantly high ratio of NSFW results that contained vivid depictions of sexual violence and other troubling imagery. Even the weakest link to womanhood or some aspect of what is traditionally conceived as feminine

Creating Content with Accessibility 215

returned pornographic imagery... These images were not just prototypically "NSFW" from a parochial nudity perspective but also included explicit rape scene imagery as well as photo-shopped images of female celebrities.

The researchers found that the crawl over curate approach was sourcing its data from wherever it could find it, using porn sites and malicious descriptions in its original scrape. Alt-text is also somewhat problematic in *who* writes alt-text and *why* they may do so.

When the researchers searched for the origin content of banal terms like "school girl" and "school boy" they found that much of the extant data perpetuated "historical, social, and cultural stereotypes and political biases." They write:

> The sample images reveal how the specific semantic search engine version meant to fetch images from LAION-400M, not only risked amplifying hyper-sexualized and misogynist representation of women, but also presented results that were reminiscent of Anglo-centric, Euro-centric, and potentially, White-supremacist ideologies.

In other words, the hegemony of both patriarchy and systemic racism results in overwhelming bias that is then transferred *into* the datasets. Generative AI companies claim they are working on fixing biases, but at the current moment, it reproduces the current systems in the worst ways possible. For example, if you prompt a visual generative AI like MidJourney to produce an image of an "attractive" person, nearly all outputs generate white people, requiring qualifiers like "black," "brown," "Asian" to produce races aside from the biased "default."[24] Even worse, these qualifiers like "Asian" result in hypersexualized or fetishized images due to the endemic racism on the web.[25]

There are other issues about alt-text misuse as well, including regulations on how alt-text is managed on social media sites. Nearly all social media sites now provide accessibility tools for image posting but unfortunately most users either don't know how to use them, or worse, they intentionally misuse them. Before Elon Musk's takeover of Twitter, there was a large push to teach users how to manage the accessibility tools, but even then, success was mediocre. Katie Deighton of the *Wall Street Journal* explains that some users – and corporate Twitter accounts – have used the alt-text tool to add hyperlinks, caption photo credits, and source citations. "Others have used alt-text as a place to hide jokes, supplementary information, or alternative captions from the main post. On one occasion, an account used the alt-text field to publish the address of a politician, a trolling tactic known as doxing."[26] On the other hand, through her interviews, Deighton

216   *Critical Internet Literacies*

found that most people aren't intentionally bad users of accessibility tools, they just don't know they exist.

Making Internet Media Accessible

Let's say you post a meme on Twitter or Facebook, how would you describe it? With its embedded references and layered innuendos, could you share the true meaning of the image though its textual description? Not only is it important to attempt this tactic, but this provides an opportunity to discuss meme meanings and internet language with children and people just learning to use the web. As we try to make the web more inclusive and accessible, there is an impetus to increase these digital literacies, especially for those who may not have the privilege to access the media easily. Knowing what we know now, content like memes, reactionary content, and media filled with algospeak provides us with challenges previously unheard of in traditional media spaces.

Memes have an intense diversity and their reactionary frameworks make explaining a meme difficult. In addition, many images that we consider memes are just simply screenshots of viral tweets, meant to convey referential subtext to an in-group. To post these without any alt-text is not only irresponsible, but sadly leaves many people out of the conversation. Thankfully, many online tools, including accessibility tools by Google and Apple, have the power to read text in screenshots and display it on the device, but they lack the internet literacies to properly explain the images to the user. Some memes may require hundreds of characters to explain. Fortunately, those with some level of internet fluency may help with their descriptions. In an article for Medium on the subject, I interviewed Arianna Collura, a visually impaired woman who was born with aniridia, a rare condition where she was born without her irises.

As a result of her disability, she does not use social media all too often, but when she does, Arianna says that alt-text "allows those with visual impairments to have access to the world of images through imagination. We're able to hear what someone tells us and if it's descriptive enough we can try and see it." The downside, she admits, is that if someone was born completely blind, "alt-text can't describe something they've never seen before and expect the person to grasp that image."[27] When it comes to memes, Arianna believes that visually impaired people should have as much access as possible to the digital content because the visually impaired should be able to "engage in the conversations that memes stimulate." Without access to memes, "the visually impaired would miss out on a big part of what's happening within society. This is why alt-text should be included in memes, but it should be as descriptive as possible. Besides, having an extra tool in the toolbox never hurt."

Creating Content with Accessibility   217

Fortunately, there are spaces that specifically focus on accessibility to memes like the Facebook group "Memes and Jokes for Blind Folks" which posts a variety of memes along with their descriptive text.[28] This easily searchable page has over 11,000 members and dozens of contributors, each adhering to the cause of making memes "accessible for everyone." One example, shared by Jessica Prescott Johnson on July 7, 2024, is a meme that uses a screengrab from the children's show Bluey with the embedded caption, "I don't want a valuable life lesson, I just want ice cream." Johnson's alt-text follows:

> Surrounding text says, "I don't want a valuable life lesson. I just want an ice cream." The image is a still from the Australian kids' TV show Bluey, which features a family of anthropomorphic dogs. Bluey is blue and about 6 years old. Her sister Bingo is orange and about 4 years old. They are outside on a sidewalk at a city park. Bluey is sitting and frowning while reaching towards an empty ice cream cone. Bingo is on the ground in the fetal position howling with disappointment.[29]

In this case, the meme is easy to interpret and describe, but in many cases, the references may add additional characters which are often limited by the platform. While Twitter/X may have a 1,000-character limit, the blogging site Medium (which tells writers to include images in their posts) ironically only has a 500-character limit for photographs. If an internet culture writer were to use Medium as their platform, more intense memes would lack the space to properly describe their images. A more nuanced meme example may run up against character limits on a platform.

If you were to describe an image from the Instagram account @northwest_mcm_wholesale, you'd have to be aware of the niche in which the account sits, as well as the context of the trend being displayed in the meme. For a short period in July 2023, the account was making fun of people who were posting "liminal spaces" and calling them a "vibe." What this really means, from a literal standpoint, is that there was a short-term trend in Portland, Oregon, where some people were performatively photographing abandoned malls or empty hallways and calling them "liminal." This trend is downstream from a strange, esoteric meme online known as "the backrooms," which feeds off our innate curiosity with the uncanny while it mixes with memory and nostalgia. The performative act of photographing these spaces and bragging about them is a form of privilege, one which the account sought to point out with a meme focusing on the plight of the janitor who must maintain and clean these spaces.[30]

218   *Critical Internet Literacies*

Here is an example of the description of the meme using alt-text, including references:

> A two-sided meme with five sections. On the left side of the image are two variations of Wojak known as the "soyjack" and he is wearing glasses and a Carhartt beanie surrounded by a Sony Alpha camera, signaling wealth, and a cup of takeaway coffee. Underneath is a pink haired feminine Wojak variant, known as "daddy's girl," with dyed pink hair and a side braid; her hands are up at her sides waving excitedly and she is surrounded by a Sony Alpha camera, a cup of takeaway coffee, and the TikTok logo, meaning she is likely making content for that platform. The caption next to the masculine figure at the top is "Liminal space – Such a vibe" and the text next to the pink haired doomer girl is "Rare aesthetic!" On the right side of the meme are three boxes, the top and bottom images are two different photographs of an empty mall hallways. The middle is a graphic of another Wojak variation, facing left, known as the "Wojak stage 2.5 doomer" as he has red eyes, a scraggly beard, and unruly black hair. To the doomer's left is a janitorial mop and rolling bucket.

Not only is the audience expected to be aware of the variety of Wojaks used in the meme (see Chapter 4) but they are also supposed to understand the nuanced references to performative acts of photography and privilege in contrast to the labor of the working class meant to support their hobby. This alt-text, written from the perspective of internet fluency, is over 1,000 characters, and therefore, limited by several platforms.

A meme like this, containing the simple caption "Monday Mall posting," excludes nearly every user who uses accessibility tools. On the other hand, describing these memes can be an act of internet literacies that we have not yet used in many educational settings. Scrolling through Herman Wakefield's @northwest_mcm_wholesale Instagram meme page there are potentially thousands of pages of descriptions. Technically, it would be the responsibility of the meme administrator to add these captions, but lacking that, we can use these esoteric niche memes as examples of how to translate a meme into text, thereby opening the possibility of better machine training that is curatorial and intentional, focused on meaning and humor, over scale and profit. Returning to my interview with Arianna, she concludes: "education (for both the able bodied and disabled) and monitoring is key." She believes that the people who abuse alt-text are harmful because anyone, not just the visually impaired, may click on a link inside of alt-text because they are too trusting of the person who wrote the text. We need to be considerate and intentional when we use the web as a tool for everyone. "Alt-text can be an amazing tool," Arianna says, "we

Creating Content with Accessibility   219

simply need to integrate it with care and consideration so that the visually impaired can also laugh at Michael Scott and Pepe the Frog."

Making Multimedia Accessible

For several years in the early 2010s, dozens of creators, academics, technologists, and policymakers would meet at the Open Video Conference to discuss ways to make web video more accessible, from acquisition to distribution. The conference, hosted by the non-profit Open Video Alliance, aimed to make video more "open," meaning video could be searchable, exchangeable, and web accessible.[31] Their goal through these conferences was to help video makers understand the platforms they use as well as the ways video online was restrictive and closed source. In the early days of streaming media and shifts to higher quality codecs, the Open Video Alliance had the rare opportunity to persuade platforms to adopt new models and codecs that would aid education and accessibility. Codecs like MPEG-4 could be universalized and along with an additional open-source skin for playing video, the code developed by Mozilla, could be captioned by anyone, removing the burden from the creator and making video content not only subtitled more accurately, but in multiple languages and in native dialects.

By the mid-2010s, the initiative was no longer. YouTube, seeking its dominance against its new streaming competitors like Netflix, Hulu, and other social media like Facebook (with their short-lived "Facebook Watch" "pivot-to-video" projects), leaned into proprietary codecs and onboard tools. According to Cisco, over 80 percent of all traffic on the internet is video consumption.[32] Unfortunately, when accessibility tools become platform specific (due in part of the competitive edge each platform sought to express over one another) it results in harm to users of all kinds, as accessibility locked behind walled gardens is like no accessibility whatsoever. These platforms also developed their own accessibility tools for video, like automated captioning and live captioning, that were mediocre to say the least. For its part, YouTube did temporarily enable a tool that the Open Video Alliance championed that enabled the community to add subtitles, but as you can imagine, this tool was abused in many inappropriate ways. The initiative was scrapped in 2020, but viewers encouraged creators to make their own captions, and by 2021, captioning had surprisingly increased.[33]

Captioning and subtitles are also not just to assist those who may need an increase in accessibility, they assist in viewing habits of younger viewers. In 2019, Verizon and Publicis conducted a study and found that nearly 70 percent of viewers watched video content online with the sound off, especially in public places, and most importantly, 80 percent of the viewers

220 *Critical Internet Literacies*

were *more likely* to watch an entire video if captions were visible.[34] Young people in particular enjoy watching videos silently (sometimes during their education courses) and in a 2023 YouGov survey, they found that 63 percent of adults under 30 prefer watching television with subtitles, even if they are fluent in the language being spoken.[35] Reading video is part of the video consuming experience now, and young people seem to enjoy captioning and subtitles. In fact, without captioning, algospeak would not exist.

Captioning tools today are far more advanced than they were years ago. Aside from YouTube's automated captioning, there are tools like Descript, Otter.ai, and Rev.com that transcribe video data into text and create timestamped SubRip Subtitle (SRT) files that can be uploaded directly to YouTube. When language cannot be read by an AI software, sites like Rev.com offer human transcription that occasionally takes some time (hours to days) but offers clarity and accuracy. Increasing digital literacies is not just about making the video accessible through its readability, but our way of comprehending the material. Captions and subtitles are the easiest method to help bring new viewers into a creator's space. On TikTok, captions can be directly printed onto the screen in a variety of fonts, enabling the creator more control over the visuals. TikTok's algorithmic system often misspells words or mishears them, so it is still up to the creator to fix the errors. On the other hand, as we discussed in the last chapter, sometimes it is worth keeping the misspelling or algospeak to avoid a content moderation issue if the creator is speaking about a sensitive topic.

Another video accessibility option is known as audio description. Audio description is an art. The FCC describes audio description as "a narration describing the important visual details in a video that cannot be understood from the soundtrack alone."[36] Audio descriptions are like alt-text, spoken in-between voice expressions on video. The descriptions are there to help people who may have a visual impairment or auditory issues or even to help those on the autism spectrum. Descriptive video is the most robust of accessibility tools and the FCC mandates a minimum of 87.5 hours of audio must be descriptive every quarter per broadcast channel. According to The Audio Descriptive Project, streaming services like Netflix and Hulu have been sued because they have failed to provide enough audio descriptions on their videos; as of 2022, Netflix provided descriptive video on 549 titles.[37]

Finally, podcasts and audio tools can benefit from accessibility tools in the form of transcriptions and supplied resources that help listeners gain more information on the recording. These transcripts may also act as archival material, aiding researchers and scholars working with a variety of source material. The archive of text is important as we progress through internet literacies and teach young people about the internet, providing a living and growing textbook for learning from. Podcasts work within

Creating Content with Accessibility 221

a niche, and often several podcasts will interview the same subject from a different angle. The archive of responses provides more robust and holistic coverage of a given topic, especially when it comes to cultural or political subjects.

New Users, New Opportunities for Internet Literacies

We are the internet. We are consumers, creators, and privileged to be part of a growing infrastructure that will remain part of our lives for likely as long as we live. When everyone came online all at once, we learned digital and internet literacies in real time, across all generations. For the elderly, it was especially difficult to gain proper skills to use the internet and many struggled to adapt to changing technologies. Those with disabilities were often not considered as part of the development of the visual web and many accessibility tools have been built in reaction to this issue. Now, young people are coming of age and logging onto the internet, and we have at least two decades of knowledge to share with them. Not helping young people learn how to make the web more accessible is a choice, not the other way around.

Internet literacies require us to know that access should be the basic introduction to the internet's ephemera. Responsible use is easily encouraged if we spend a nominal amount of time sharing what we know about accessibility projects like alt-text, captioning, and ability privilege. These are not hot button topics though some have been converted into cultural issues by reactionary figures online. To combat their shallow outlook, we need to reconsider access as creativity, not just equitable use. Young people who feel empowered to make the internet their own can then be more creative as they put the tools behind them and focus on the ways to make their work better and more consumable by their friends and their possible audiences and communities.

Notes

1 "Disability Impacts All of Us Infographic." *Centers for Disease Control and Prevention*, May 15, 2023. https://www.cdc.gov/ncbddd/disabilityandhealth/infographic-disability-impacts-all.html.
2 "WebAIM: The WebAIM Million – The 2024 Report on the Accessibility of the Top 1,000,000 Home Pages." https://webaim.org/projects/million/.
3 Elbein, Saul. "5 Things to Know about the Growing Fight over ESG." *The Hill*, July 13, 2023. https://thehill.com/policy/equilibrium-sustainability/4095977-5-things-to-know-about-the-growing-fight-over-esg/.
4 Visser, Cassandra, and Danny Trichter. "Everything You Need To Know About Screen Readers | A.Checker." *Accessibility Checker*. https://www.accessibilitychecker.org/blog/screen-readers/.
5 "Blindness Statistics." *National Federation of the Blind*. https://nfb.org/resources/blindness-statistics.

222 *Critical Internet Literacies*

6 "Skull Emoji 💀." *Know Your Meme*, December 9, 2021. https://knowyourmeme.com/memes/skull-emoji-💀.

7 https://blog.hootsuite.com/emoji-meanings/.

8 https://www.w3.org/TR/WCAG21/.

9 Dougherty, Audubon. "On the Line: Internet in Rural Peru (Full Version)." *YouTube*, 2009. https://www.youtube.com/watch?v=d8GhGH4dqi0.

10 Zuckerberg, Mark. "Is Connectivity a Human Right?" *Facebook*, 2013. https://www.facebook.com/isconnectivityahumanright.

11 Advox. "Can Facebook Connect the Next Billion?" *Global Voices Advox*, July 27, 2017. https://advox.globalvoices.org/2017/07/27/can-facebook-connect-the-next-billion/.

12 https://developers.facebook.com/docs/internet-org.

13 Johnston, Joyce. "Is Free Basics' Internet Access Really Worth It?" *Intellectual Freedom Blog*, October 17, 2016. https://www.oif.ala.org/free-basics-internet-access-really-worth/.

14 Solon, Olivia. "'It's Digital Colonialism': How Facebook's Free Internet Service Has Failed Its Users | Facebook." *The Guardian*, July 27, 2017. https://www.theguardian.com/technology/2017/jul/27/facebook-free-basics-developing-markets.

15 Vincent, James. "Facebook's Free Basics Service Has Been Banned in India." *The Verge*, February 8, 2016. https://www.theverge.com/2016/2/8/10913398/free-basics-india-regulator-ruling.

16 Nothias, Toussaint. "Access Granted: Facebook's Free Basics in Africa." *Media, Culture & Society* 42, no. 3 (April 2020): 329–48. https://doi.org/10.1177/0163443719890530.

17 "Report of the Independent International Fact-Finding Mission on Myanmar*." *Human Rights Council*, September 12, 2018. https://www.ohchr.org/sites/default/files/Documents/HRBodies/HRCouncil/FFM-Myanmar/A_HRC_39_64.pdf.

18 Crystal, Caroline. "Facebook, Telegram, and the Ongoing Struggle Against Online Hate Speech." *Carnegie Endowment for International Peace*, September 7, 2023. https://carnegieendowment.org/research/2023/09/facebook-telegram-and-the-ongoing-struggle-against-online-hate-speech?lang=en.

19 "What Is Digital Literacy? A Complete Guide for Educators." *University of San Diego – Professional & Continuing Education*, December 19, 2022. https://pce.sandiego.edu/digital-literacy/.

20 boyd, danah. "You Think You Want Media Literacy… Do You? | Apophenia." *Zephoria.Org* (blog), March 9, 2018. https://www.zephoria.org/thoughts/archives/2018/03/09/you-think-you-want-media-literacy-do-you.html.

21 Doctorow, Cory. "Three Kinds of Propaganda, and What to Do about Them." *Boing Boing*, February 25, 2017. https://boingboing.net/2017/02/25/counternarratives-not-fact-che.html.

22 Miller, Meg, and Ilaria Parogni. "The Hidden Image Descriptions Making the Internet Accessible." *New York Times*, February 18, 2022, sec. Arts. https://www.nytimes.com/interactive/2022/02/18/arts/alt-text-images-descriptions.html.

23 Birhane, Abeba, Vinay Uday Prabhu, and Emmanuel Kahembwe. "Multimodal Datasets: Misogyny, Pornography, and Malignant Stereotypes." *arXiv*, 2021. https://doi.org/10.48550/ARXIV.2110.01963.

24 Tiku, Nitasha, Kevin Schaul, and Szu Yu Chen. "These Fake Images Reveal How AI Amplifies Our Worst Stereotypes." *Washington Post*. Accessed July 9, 2024. https://www.washingtonpost.com/technology/interactive/2023/ai-generated-images-bias-racism-sexism-stereotypes/.

Creating Content with Accessibility 223

25 See: Heikkilä, Melissa. "The Viral AI Avatar App Lensa Undressed Me – without My Consent." *MIT Technology Review*, December 12, 2022. https://www.technologyreview.com/2022/12/12/1064751/the-viral-ai-avatar-app-lensa-undressed-me-without-my-consent/.

26 Deighton, Katie. "Misuse of Twitter's Alt Text Feature Draws Criticism From Accessibility Advocates." *The Wall Street Journal*, July 15, 2022. https://www.wsj.com/articles/misuse-of-twitters-alt-text-feature-draws-criticism-from-accessibility-advocates-11657879200.

27 Cohen, Jamie. "Why We Need to Make Memes More Accessible." *Creators Hub* (blog), July 20, 2022. https://medium.com/creators-hub/why-we-need-to-make-memes-more-accessible-39cc6d6162a9.

28 https://www.facebook.com/share/VEJmvebUtJugxskC.

29 https://www.facebook.com/share/p/3Bhs1H12WUL678DD/.

30 https://www.instagram.com/p/CuztdvaJmNZ/?img_index=2.

31 Lovink, Geert. "The Open Video Alliance for an 'Open' Video Ecosystem on the Web." *Institute of Network Cultures*, November 14, 2010. https://networkcultures.org/blog/2010/11/14/the-open-video-alliance-for-an-open-video-ecosystem-on-the-web/.

32 https://www.cisco.com/c/dam/m/en_us/solutions/service-provider/vni-forecast-highlights/pdf/Global_Device_Growth_Traffic_Profiles.pdf.

33 O'Dell, Liam. "YouTube Pulled Its Community Captions Feature, So Now More Creators Are Making Their Own." *The Verge*, May 21, 2021. https://www.theverge.com/2021/5/21/22443577/youtube-captions-increased-deaf-campaigners.

34 McCue, T. J. "Verizon Media Says 69 Percent Of Consumers Watching Video With Sound Off." *Forbes*. Accessed July 9, 2024. https://www.forbes.com/sites/tjmccue/2019/07/31/verizon-media-says-69-percent-of-consumers-watching-video-with-sound-off/.

35 Ballard, Jamie. "Most American Adults under 30 Prefer Watching TV with Subtitles – Even When They Know the Language." *YouGov*, August 11, 2023. https://today.yougov.com/entertainment/articles/45987-american-adults-under-30-watching-tv-subtitles.

36 https://www.fcc.gov/document/fcc-expands-video-description-rules-0.

37 https://adp.acb.org/.

9 Building Resilient Online Communities

Creators Make Content and Build Communities

"Online creators don't just produce content; they define the norms and dynamics of their medium," writes Taylor Lorenz in the conclusion of her important book *Extremely Online*.[1] Here, the sentiment is echoed in this conclusion as well. The internet we use and the content we consume are made by the creators that develop it and nearly all are not compensated appropriately for their labor. On the other hand, bad actors, grifters, and scammers have figured out ways to manipulate these spaces, enriching themselves over the benefit of the whole. While some may claim "the internet was a bad idea" or find themselves in a perpetual feeling of "doomscrolling" in an age of overwhelming media, the internet is not going away. It is our obligation and responsibility to treat it seriously even when it resists categorization and easy models of interpretation. Unlike traditional and legacy media, the norms and dynamics of the medium are constantly in flux; some days you wake up and the "discourse" is following a single issue, some days it's so chaotic it feels "off," but every day, billions access the internet and try their best to belong.

In this book, we've focused on the ways to reconsider content, creativity, and safety online, often maintaining a focus on those who misuse the platforms or inspire off-platform harm. On the other hand, the internet can be a space of joy, freedom, expression, and beauty if you know where to look for it. Platforms profit from engagement, and nothing sells like anger, but what if we didn't engage? What if we know how these systems work, and we withhold our inclination to join in the chaos? What if we decide for a day to use what we see online as a learnable moment, a moment to press pause in the infinite scroll? There are creators and media online that prove resilience is possible and persist beyond the constraints of commodification at scale. BlackPlanet did so in the early aughts, never buying into the "move fast and break things" mentality of Facebook or the "scale at all costs" model of Silicon Valley. The community was vibrant and passionate and resilient.

DOI: 10.4324/9781003483885-9

Building Resilient Online Communities 225

We've read of missed opportunities that were misguided by systemic issues as well. Operation Chanology, though coded in its lulz, shows that online shitposters have managed to organize in collective action. The mainstream media enjoys the novelty, pointing at their quirky behavior, silly white masks and their slogans – often questioning their harms, but rarely focusing on their *reasons* for organizing. The systemic issues that encourage young men to follow Andrew Tate or join dark forums are still here decades later, and we need to address them. Teenage years are fraught with tough times, awkward moments, and being "weird" and we should express compassion to those learning their identities in the age of hypermedia; the internet is also a place for sharing these feelings in a positive way. Not all teens find themselves in rabbit holes and most teens have positive thoughts about their online communities. If we talk to young people about the internet maturely, we may guide them, like a coach, to better prepare themselves for the changes in the next decades, especially when a third to half of all young people want to be creators.

We should remind ourselves that when the multichannel networks formed on YouTube, we saw how thousands of people came together in a "union" to argue for equality and wealth distribution. However, because they existed *within* the structure of YouTube, they did not have the tools to bargain, but they did exhibit collectivity at scale. The creator economy is precarious and there is no union for creators or established safety nets and there most definitely is not a steady paycheck. But being a creator in the "creator economy" means forging a path, defining a niche, persistence in production, catering to your fans, developing new media, and a willingness to develop a performance identity that serves the platform. Sometimes, it can get to be too much. In 2022, YouTuber Emma Chamberlain explained on her podcast *Anything Goes*:

> Sometimes I feel like a zoo animal with everyone looking at me… But there is a place to run: You can quit! But you don't want to quit, because it's your dream and there are so many beautiful and amazing things about it. I love this and I wouldn't want to do anything else, but fuck it's hard.[2]

Once part of the creator economy, it is hard to extricate yourself, especially when your brand extends to your creator media. But reconsider the process in terms of marking your point in the archive. You were there to help make the internet better by sharing your ideas with your community. In the deluge of media uploaded with the simultaneity of its "rot" and "enshittification," we still hold a place of power against the machines. Our content becomes memory in the archive, and we may make space for joy and belonging, experimentation and art, compassion and sharing. By

226 *Critical Internet Literacies*

growing our influence, even a little, we may use our critical approaches to develop "ecosystems of support," helping teachers, parents, local politicians, mutual aid groups, and even law enforcers to create spaces for curiosity and change, where we can help people increase their literacies, reduce panic, and open conversations. Tech can only do so much. It is the people that make the internet the medium as it exists.

Resilient Creators

In conclusion, it is worth pointing out some creators that have been extremely helpful in the development of this project. Creators and accounts that resist overt commodification and grift and place sharing as a higher priority than profit. Creators like Blair Imani (@blairimani on Instagram), who produces a segment called "Smarter in Seconds" helping viewers learn more about terms and language used in progressive spaces, explaining deep issues in an accessible manner.[3] If you are interested in keeping up with Gen Z and Gen Alpha slang, Philip Lindsay's TikTok channel (@mr_lindsay_sped on TikTok) is easily the best resource for up-to-date

Figure 9.1 Influencer Blair Imani produces a segment called "Smarter in Seconds" where she helps viewers learn new vocabulary and progressive terms.

Building Resilient Online Communities 227

shifts in vernacular and attitude, bringing a humorous approach to kids in school.[4] Speaking of language, linguist Adam Aleksic's @etymologynerd Instagram page covers the esoteric nature of language, especially how it operates in dynamic spaces like the internet.[5] These creators are helping us understand our present.

There are other creators like Teddy Siegel, who runs @Got2GoNYC – an important resource channel, especially for women and the less abled community, to find accessible bathrooms in New York City.[6] Siegel explains that in her process of discovering safe and clean bathrooms, overt systemic issues like racism and ableism persist, but hopes her channel (with almost 200,000 followers) can persuade politicians to make change.[7] Other positive channels include Andy Min and Thomas Sullivan's @__we_love_you_, which is a page that explains why it's OK to be vulnerable and find optimism in the chaos.[8] And it goes without saying at this point, but people should follow Taylor Lorenz's accounts as she provides internet literacies.[9] Perhaps evidence of the most resilient channel on Instagram at this moment is that of Palestinian filmmaker Bisan Owda.[10] Bisan uses both her channel and her broadcast channel to share on-the-ground information from Gaza during its strife. Bisan's work is a clear display of why calls to "ban" social media or cellphones are the incorrect response. Beyond the memes, advertising, odd content, Instagram is a site of awareness, strength, resilience, and community engagement. Without it, some may never know about stories unfolding around us all the time.

Finally, there are many podcasts and newsletters that help us read the internet more critically. Ryan Broderick's *Garbage Day* is the most esoteric, but the most in-depth, speaking to the public from an internet fluent standpoint.[11] Kate Lindsay's *Embedded* is similar, providing in-depth interviews with creators.[12] Kyle Fitzpatrick's *The Trend Report* is also valuable for up-to-date emerging trends and important links.[13] QAA's podcast, formerly called "Qanon Anonymous," provides humor when explaining – in great detail – internet culture that burbles up from the extremes[14] and Paris Marx's "Tech Won't Save Us" podcast provides a leftist critical perspective on the tech industries.[15] Matt Soeth's "Safety is Sexy" explains how Trust and Safety works from an accessible standpoint, helping listeners make sense of the invisible structures behind the systems.[16] Idil Galip and Erinne Paisley's "Net Nonsense" is academic humor mixed with critical internet literacies and the two experts explain the esoteric extremely well.[17] WBUR's "Endless Thread" podcast, especially the early episodes, explain the stories behind the most famous memes and internet personalities we know.[18]

Lastly, there are three series that are recommended to learn more about internet culture through a critical lens. First, NBC News's Brandy Zadrozny's "Tiffany Dover is Dead*" podcast explains how Covid

228 *Critical Internet Literacies*

conspiracies operate and how one young women ended up at the center of the issue.[19] And although we may be critical of Kevin Roose's approach to internet media, his "Rabbit Hole" podcast for the *New York Times* is an insightful and unique approach to his long-form article "The Making of a YouTube Radical."[20] Finally, Josh Chapdelaine's "Everyone Knows That: The Search for Ulterior Motives" is an exploration of the "lost media" communities on Reddit and delves deep into the work that Reddit moderators must do to keep their communities thriving.[21] These projects help us go deeper into the conventionally difficult-to-explain nuance of internet culture, media, and criticism. Hopefully, these accounts, creators, and communities inspire you to make your own project and help people reconsider content, creativity, and safety online.

Notes

1　Lorenz, Taylor. *Extremely Online: The Untold Story of Fame, Influence, and Power on the Internet*. New York: Simon & Schuster, 2023.
2　Chamberlain, Emma. *The Truth about YouTube*, 2022. https://open.spotify.com/episode/0aBOcPKuUirp5sIt9d0VAv.
3　https://www.instagram.com/blairimani/.
4　https://www.tiktok.com/@mr_lindsay_sped.
5　https://www.instagram.com/etymologynerd/.
6　https://www.tiktok.com/@got2gonyc.
7　Ricciulli, Valeria. "This TikToker Is on a Mission to Make Public Bathrooms Accessible." *Teen Vogue*, April 29, 2022. https://www.teenvogue.com/story/teddy-siegel-tiktok-bathrooms.
8　https://www.instagram.com/__we_love_you_/.
9　https://www.instagram.com/taylorlorenz/.
10　https://www.instagram.com/wizard_bisan1/.
11　https://www.garbageday.email/.
12　https://embedded.substack.com/.
13　https://1234kyle5678.substack.com/.
14　https://soundcloud.com/qanonanonymous.
15　https://techwontsave.us/.
16　https://www.matthewsoeth.com/safety-is-sexy-podcast.
17　https://linktr.ee/netnonsense.
18　https://www.wbur.org/podcasts/endlessthread.
19　https://www.nbcnews.com/podcast/truthers/needle-tiffany-dover-dead-episode-1-n1294465.
20　https://www.nytimes.com/column/rabbit-hole.
21　https://shows.acast.com/everyone-knows-that-the-search-for-ulterior-motives.

Index

adpocalypse 76, 78
Age of Surveillance Capitalism 14, 162
Agha-Soltan, Neda 182
Aleksic, Adam 200, 227
algospeak 84, 106, 198–201, 216, 220
alt-text 102, 204, 212–18
Anonymous (online collective) 33–4
anonymous (users) 30, 33, 44, 113–4
apophenia 103, 144
Arab Spring 37, 171
Armstrong, Heather 35
artificial intelligence 5, 10, 27, 58, 76, 83–4, 165, 201, 214, 220
astroturfing 46
attention economy 1, 144, 160–1
audio description 220

bad faith: acting in 48, 54, 80, 89, 153–4; actors 9, 36, 87; definition of 80
Balenciaga 139–40
Ballinger, Colleen 71
Barlow, John Perry 25–6, 45
Bates, Laura 15, 198
Baxter, Raven 88
Beran, Dale 30–1
Biden, Joseph 123–5
Bishop, Sophie 88
black box 5, 17, 81, 164
Black Lives Matter 43, 109, 136
BlackPlanet 29–30, 37, 224
Black Software: The Internet and Racial Justice, from AfroNet to Black Lives Matter 28, 62
Black Twitter 15, 29–30, 39, 43–5, 48, 62, 175
Boogaloo (militia) 109–10, 112
Bouman, Katie 192–3, 196
boyd, danah 37, 211

Brock, André 15, 29–30, 44, 111, 175
Broderick, Ryan 47–8, 49, 55, 80, 115, 227
Brownlee, Marques 58
bulletin board services (BBS) 24, 101
Buolamwini, Joy 168, 170
ByteDance 5, 83

CapCut 83
Carlson, Tucker 43, 121, 145, 146, 153
Center for Humane Technology 161–3, 171
Chamberlain, Emma 225
Christian, Aymar "AJ" 15, 70
Christian Nationalism 118, 120, 125, 132, 141, 196
CHT *see* Center for Human Technology
citizen journalism 37
Coded Bias (film) 168–70, 172, 173, 177
Collins, Ben 42, 45–7, 193
core(s) 85–6, 98; cottagecore 86, 141
cyberpunk(s) 24–6, 30
cyberspace 23, 25–7

D'Amelio, Charlie 83, 85
Dark Brandon 124
Dark MAGA 124–5
Declaration of the Independence of Cyberspace 26
devious licks 3–5, 7
Dibbell, Julian 45–6
digital dualism 11–14, 27–8
DiResta, Renee 163, 165
Distributed Blackness: African American Cybercultures 15, 29–30, 169

230 Index

Doctorow, Cory 10, 187–8, 212
Doge 103, 104–7, 111–13
DogeCoin 104, 105
Donaldson, Jimmy 45, 52–8, 74, 147
doomer *see* Wojak
Douyin 5, 10
"Do What You Can't" (commercial) 74–5
Dr. Horrible's Sing–a–Long Blog (webseries) 70
Duncan, Mike 97–8

EFF *see* Electronic Frontier Foundation
Electronic Frontier Foundation 26
enshittification 10, 225
Eternal September 24, 210
Everyday Life (content) 85–7, 125; *see also* Get Ready With Me
Extremely Online (book) 16, 35, 167, 169, 224
extremely online (term) 3, 120, 153
extremism 9, 42, 76, 141, 159

Facebook Papers 16, 120, 163, 190, 192
fashwave 120–1, 124
fast fashion 57, 86, 185
fear of missing out 1, 3, 17, 86
Feels Good Man (film) 113–14, 167–8, 173
feels good man (phrase) 113–15
FOMO *see* fear of missing out
For You Page 5, 199
4chanification 34, 43, 117, 131, 136, 174
4channers 33, 138, 143
Free Basics 207–10, 211
fringe 9, 33, 144–5, 148, 155, 186
Fuentes, Nicholas 48, 78, 119, 121
Furie, Matt 107, 113–14, 119, 173

Galip, Idil 126–7, 227
Gamergate 193
gatekeeping/gatekeepers 13, 53, 56, 69, 147
generative AI 176, 214
GeoCities 25
Get Ready With Me 71, 86–7, 89, 99, 190
Gibson, William 23
Goldman Sachs 56

grammar: aesthetic 59; cultural 141; meme 107; platform 3, 41, 79, 85–6; textual 103; video 57, 64, 83–4, 90; visual 9, 12–3
grift 10, 36, 42, 64, 132, 226; grifter(s) 43, 78, 158, 192, 196–7, 224; grifting 36, 131, 176, 193
groomer 141, 145, 146
groyper 48, 119, 141, 150–2
GRWM *see* Get Ready with Me
Guy Fawkes mask 31–4

Haidt, Jonathan 164–5, 192
Harris, Josh 61–2, 167
Harris, Tristan 81, 160–3, 165
Hobbs, Renee 12
Homestar Runner (webseries) 105–6
hyper–niche 14, 85–6, 117, 125, 127–8, 141

Imani, Blair 226
incel 36, 103, 123, 144, 198
influencer creep 17, 87–8
involuntary celibate *see* incel
irl memes 3, 112

January 6, 2021 (event) 14, 46, 103, 113, 123, 147, 163
Jennings, Rebecca 47, 86
Jurgenson, Nathan 28

Kabosu 104, 106–7
Karen (meme) 111–12
Kellner, Douglas 13
Khare, Michelle 56–7
Kimmel, Jimmy 133–4, 150, 151
kindness content 52, 53, 54
Kjellberg, Felix 59, 72–3, 76–7
KnowYourMeme 3
Kolman, Morry 114, 115
Kontras, Adam 65
KONY 2012 161

large language models 76, 198, 214
Lawrence, Jennifer 72, 193–4
LibsofTikTok *see* Chaya Raichik
Lindsay, Phillip 197, 226
LinkTree 57
LLM *see* large language models
lobotomy (meme) 96–100
lolcats 106

Index

Lorenz, Taylor 16, 35, 45, 47–8, 88, 118, 127, 145–6, 152, 167, 199–201, 224, 227
Louise, Ava 134, 177
lulz 33, 143, 225

machine learning 76, 163, 170
Maker Studios 73, 77
makeup artistry 71–2, 86, 99
Masnick, Mike 187–8
The Matrix 24, 42
McCulloch, Gretchen 106–7
McIlwain, Charlton 15, 28, 62
MCN *see* multichannel network
Memes and Jokes for Blind Folks 217
#MeToo 43, 99, 183, 196
mewing 154, 197–8
Moderator Mayhem (game) 187–9
moot *see* Christopher Poole
moral panic(s) 1, 4, 6, 16, 27, 48, 158–61, 164–6, 171
Mota, Bethany 72–3
MrBeast *see* Donaldson, Jimmy
Mr Lindsay *see* Phillip Lindsay
MUA *see* makeup artistry
mukbang 89–90
multichannel network(s) 72–3, 77, 225
Musk, Elon 10, 14, 43–4, 45, 47, 82, 87, 105, 131, 168, 175, 188–9, 198
MySpace 30, 37, 40, 113

NEET(s) 32, 114, 123, 173
Neistat, Casey 74–5
NetNoir 29–30, 62
NFT 168, 173, 176
nostalgia 16, 120, 135, 141, 217
NPC (meme) 116–17

Oakley, Tyler 65–7, 71–2, 172
Odgers, Candace L. 164–5
OnlyFans 57, 58, 176–7
OOTD *see* Outfit of the Day
Open Video Alliance 219
Orlowski, Jeff 160–3, 165, 168, 171–2
Outfit of the Day 86, 99
Overton window 9, 34, 142, 174
Owda, Bisan 227

parasocial: relationships 71, 79; tactics 70, 71, 77
pareidolia 101–2

Parham, Jason 43–8, 175
Paul, Logan 76–7
Pepe the Frog 14, 32, 107, 113–17, 119, 123, 173, 219
Peterson, Jordan 78, 81, 195
PewDiePie *see* Kjellberg, Felix
pickup artist(ry) 35, 82, 114
Platform Capitalism (book) 13
platform capitalism (term) 59, 177
platform colonization 8, 13
Podray, Brad 54
Poole, Christopher 31, 34, 43
populism 64, 78, 115, 122
Proud Boys 98
PUA *see* pickup artist

QAA Podcast 43, 227
Qanon 118, 119, 132, 136, 138–41

Rae, Issa 70, 175
Raichik, Chaya 48, 140–1, 145–7, 148
Ramsey, Franchesca 65–7
recommendation system(s) 5, 76, 81
red pill 42
Reeve, Elle 40–1
#Resistance 118, 122, 123
retention editing 14, 53, 69, 161
Rogan, Joe 118, 146–50, 152
Rohingya genocide 16, 209
Roman Empire (meme) 96–9
Roose, Kevin 14, 81, 116–17, 228
Rufo, Christopher 131, 141, 152–4
Rumble 60, 82, 151
Rushkoff, Douglas 26, 163, 172
Russell, Legacy 15, 28

Sephora 86, 132, 154, 183, 190–1
Share, Jeff 13
Shifman, Limor 101, 126, 128
shitpost/shitposter 116, 122, 127, 225
slap a teacher (challenge/hoax) 2, 6–7, 16–7, 148
Something Awful 30–1
Southern, Lauren 79–81
spectacle 1, 31, 195
Srnicek, Nick 13, 59
Sung, Morgan 46, 48, 49
surveillance 23, 28, 39, 170, 178, 199, 210
surveillance capitalism (term) 14, 199

232 Index

Targeted Victory 7, 16–7
Tate, Andrew 36, 81, 140, 195–7, 225
tradwife 36, 99, 125, 132, 135–7, 140, 142
Trump, Donald 14–15, 78–9, 109, 113, 115, 117–19, 122–5, 142–3, 153, 166, 171
Turkle, Sherry 27–8, 30

very online *see* extremely online
vibe 125, 217–8
vibe shift 3
Vine 5, 77, 86, 109

Wayfair 138–40
We Live in Public (film) 61, 167
We Need Girlfriend (webseries) 69
white flight 37
Williams, Estee 132, 135–7, 142
Wojak 32, 115–17, 121, 218

X (Elon Musk's) 53, 82, 88, 146, 148, 150, 166, 195

Zadrozny, Brandy 153–4, 227
Zakarin, Scott 61–2
Zuckerberg, Mark 37, 126, 183, 207–8, 210

Printed in the United States
by Baker & Taylor Publisher Services